T0256566

Swarm Intelligence

Scrivener Publishing
100 Cummings Center, Suite 541J
Beverly, MA 01915-6106

Concise Introductions to AI and Data Science

Series Editor: Dr. Prasenjit Chatterjee, MCKV Institute of Engineering, West Bengal, India; Dr. Loveleen Gaur, Amity International Business School (AIBS), India; and Dr. Morteza Yazdani, ESIC Business & Marketing School, Madrid, Spain

Scope: Reflecting the interdisciplinary and thematic nature of the series, Concise Introductions to (AI) and Data Science presents cutting-edge research and practical applications in the area of Artificial Intelligence and data science. The series aims to share new approaches and innovative perspectives in AI and data analysis from diverse engineering domains to find pragmatic and futuristic solutions for society at large. It publishes peer-reviewed and authoritative scholarly works on theoretical foundations, algorithms, models, applications and case studies on specific issues. The monographs and edited volumes will be no more than 75,000 words.

Please send proposals to one of the 3 editors:
dr.prasenjitchatterjee6@gmail.com; gaurloveleen@yahoo.com; morteza_yazdani21@yahoo.com

Publishers at Scrivener
Martin Scrivener (martin@scrivenerpublishing.com)
Phillip Carmical (pcarmical@scrivenerpublishing.com)

Swarm Intelligence

An Approach from Natural to Artificial

Kuldeep Singh Kaswan

School of Computing Science & Engineering, Galgotias University, Greater Noida, Uttar Pradesh, India

Jagjit Singh Dhatterwal

Department of Artificial Intelligence & Data Science, Koneru Lakshmaiah Education Foundation, Vaddeswaram, AP, India

and

Avadhesh Kumar

Pro Vice-Chancellor, Galgotias University, Greater Noida, Uttar Pradesh, India

Scrivener
Publishing

This edition first published 2023 by John Wiley & Sons, Inc., 111 River Street, Hoboken, NJ 07030, USA
and Scrivener Publishing LLC, 100 Cummings Center, Suite 541J, Beverly, MA 01915, USA
© 2023 Scrivener Publishing LLC
For more information about Scrivener publications please visit www.scrivenerpublishing.com.

Wiley Global Headquarters
111 River Street, Hoboken, NJ 07030, USA

For details of our global editorial offices, customer services, and more information about Wiley products visit us at www.wiley.com.

Limit of Liability/Disclaimer of Warranty
While the publisher and authors have used their best efforts in preparing this work, they make no representations or warranties with respect to the accuracy or completeness of the contents of this work and specifically disclaim all warranties, including without limitation any implied warranties of merchantability or fitness for a particular purpose. No warranty may be created or extended by sales representatives, written sales materials, or promotional statements for this work. The fact that an organization, website, or product is referred to in this work as a citation and/or potential source of further information does not mean that the publisher and authors endorse the information or services the organization, website, or product may provide or recommendations it may make. This work is sold with the understanding that the publisher is not engaged in rendering professional services. The advice and strategies contained herein may not be suitable for your situation. You should consult with a specialist where appropriate. Neither the publisher nor authors shall be liable for any loss of profit or any other commercial damages, including but not limited to special, incidental, consequential, or other damages. Further, readers should be aware that websites listed in this work may have changed or disappeared between when this work was written and when it is read.

Library of Congress Cataloging-in-Publication Data

ISBN 978-1-119-86506-3

Cover image: Pixabay.Com
Cover design by Russell Richardson

Set in size of 11pt and Minion Pro by Manila Typesetting Company, Makati, Philippines

Printed in the USA

10 9 8 7 6 5 4 3 2 1

Contents

Preface

In the era of globalization, the emerging technologies are governing engineering industries towards a multifaceted state. The escalating complexity brought about by these new technologies has led to a new set of problems; therefore, there has been a demand for researchers to find possible ways to address any new issues that arise. This has motivated researchers to appropriate ideas from nature to implant in the engineering sciences. This way of thinking has led to the emergence of many biologically inspired algorithms, such as genetic algorithm (GA), ant colony optimization (ACO), and particle swarm optimization (PSO), that have proven to be efficient in handling computationally complex problems with competence.

Motivated by the capability of the biologically inspired algorithms, this book on Swarm Intelligence (SI) presents recent developments and applications concerning optimization with SI techniques based on ant, cat, crow, elephant, grasshopper, water wave, whale, swarm cyborg and particle swarm optimization. Particle swarm optimization, commonly known as PSO, mimics the behavior of a swarm of insects or a school of fish. If one of the particles discovers a good path to food the rest of the swarm will be able to follow instantly even if they are far away from the swarm. Swarm behavior is modeled by particles in multidimensional space that has two characteristics: a position and a velocity. These particles wander around the hyperspace and remember the best position that they have discovered. They communicate good positions to each other and adjust their own position and velocity based on these good positions. Ant colony optimization, commonly known as ACO, is a probabilistic technique for solving hard computational problems which can be reduced to finding optimal paths. For example, PSO is inspired by the behavior of ants in finding short paths from the colony nest to the food source. Ants have small brains and bad vision, yet they use a great search strategy. Initially, real ants wander randomly to find food. While returning to their colony they lay down pheromone trails. If other ants find such a path, they are likely to follow the trail and deposit more pheromones if they eventually find food. Instead of designing complex and centralized systems, nowadays designers rather prefer to work with many small and autonomous agents. Each agent may prescribe to a global strategy. An agent acts on the simplest of rules. The many agents co-operating within the system can solve very complex problems with minimal design effort. In general, multi-agent systems that use some swarm intelligence are said to be swarm intelligent systems. They are mostly used as search engines and optimization tools.

The goal of this book is to offer a wide spectrum of sample works developed in leading research throughout the world about innovative methodologies of swarm intelligence and foundations of engineering swarm intelligent systems; as well as applications and interesting experiences using particle swarm optimization, which is at the heart of computational intelligence. The book should be useful both for beginners and experienced researchers in the field of computational intelligence.

Kuldeep Singh Kaswan
School of Computing Science & Engineering, Galgotias University
Greater Noida, India
November 2022

Introduction of Swarm Intelligence

Abstract

Because biology is swarming intelligence, for millions of years, many biological processes have addressed complex issues through information exchange with groups. By thoroughly examining the behavioral factors aspects of individuals and integrating compartmental observations with mathematical or simulated modeling, the processes of the collective conduct in biological systems are now understood. We use insect-world examples to demonstrate how structures are developed, collective choices are taken, and how enormous groups of insects may move as one. This first chapter encourages computer programmers to look more carefully at the biomedical domain.

Keywords: Swarm behavior, collective behavior, particle swarm optimization (PSO), swarm agents, optimization method, global behavior, fish schooling

1.1 Introduction to Swarm Behavior

- A swarm may be described as an organized grouping of organizations that interact (or agents).
- In a swarm, individuals cooperate to achieve a global goal more efficiently than a single person could.
- Although an individual's conduct is straightforward, group activities can become very difficult.
- Computer scientists use birds (for flocks), ants, poultry (for schools), bees, and wasps in swarm intellectual ability studies [1].

1.1.1 Individual vs. Collective Behaviors

- Swarming and individual behaviors are closely interconnected.
- Individuals form and determine the behaviors of the swarm. On the other hand, the swarm's behavior affects the

Kuldeep Singh Kaswan, Jagjit Singh Dhatterwal and Avadhesh Kumar. *Swarm Intelligence: An Approach from Natural to Artificial*, (1–36) © 2023 Scrivener Publishing LLC

environment under which a person acts. Individuals specialize in one specific duty in a colony of ants. Taken together,
activities and behaviors of ants guarantee the construction
of optimum nesting systems, the protection of the queen and
larva, the purification of nests, the search for the optimum
sources of food, the improvement of assault methods, etc.
Global behavior arises non-linearly from the activity and
interconnections of members in the swarm [2].

The connection between refining aid interactions between people boosts
experienced environmental knowledge and optimizes swarm development.

- The collaboration between people is determined genetically
  or through social interaction.
- Social relationships may be direct or indirect.
- Visual, auditory, or chemical contacts are immediate interactions [3].
- Indirect relationships happen when some people alter the
  environment, and others react to a different world.
- Social networking provides lines of communication to communicate knowledge.

1.2   Concepts of Swarm Intelligence

Swarm intelligence (SI) is a system that produces globally integrated functioning patterns due to the combined conduct of (unsupported) agents
communicating locally with their environments [4].

- On the basis of SI, communal (or spread) issue solving may
  be explored without central authority or global modeling for
  function improvement, optimization of paths, timings, optimization of structures, design, and processing, and video
  analysis, productive implementations; and
- PSO (particle swarm optimization) and ACO (ant colony
  optimization).

1.3   Particle Swarm Optimization (PSO)

- The intent of the design is to visually recreate the beautiful
  and unexpected dance of a flock of birds.

- The objective of identifying patterns governs birds' capacity to fly simultaneously and alter their course quickly, with an ideal grouping.

This PSO technique has become a convenient and straightforward optimization method [5].

1.3.1   Main Concept of PSO

- PSO is a population-based search technique where people are sorted into a pool, called particles. The possible answer to the optimization problem is every particle in the swarm.
- In the PSO system, each particle is "flown" in a multifunctional search area, adapting its search space to its own and adjacent particles' experience or knowledge.

Therefore, a particle uses its best position and its neighbors' most vital position to the situation itself towards the optimal solution.

- The consequence is that, while still exploring a region surrounding the perfect option, nanoparticles are flying towards the global minimum.
- Every particle's effectiveness is measured based on a specified fitness function linked to the challenge.

1.4   Meaning of Swarm Intelligence

Pattern recognition is the systematic gathering of naturally occurring dispersed, self-organized systems. The idea is used in machine intelligence development. In 1989, it was presented in the methods used in cellular cyborgs by Gerardo Beni and Jing Wang.

Swarm intelligence (SI) systems generally consist of a community of essential agents or boots that interact independently and with each other. Nature, in particular living organisms, frequently inspires. The agents obey elementary principles. While no command and control structure determines how the agents behave, local exchanges lead to the formation of "intelligent" universal behaviors, which are unknown to the agents. Examples of natural SI include organisms, flocking of birds, hawk chasing, herding of animals, and growth of bacteria, fish schooling, and microbiological information.

Swarming concepts are called swarm cyborgs, but swarm intelligence refers to a broader range of algorithms. In the framework of forecasting issues, swarm prediction has been utilized. Similar techniques in synthetic intellectual capacity for genetic engineering to those suggested for swarm cyborgs must be studied [6].

1.5 What Is Swarm Intelligence?

The study of decentralized, self-organized networks is cognitive swarming that can rush in a coordinated way. Swarms exist naturally, and evolutionary habitats, such as ant colonies, flocks of birds, and animal husbandry, have been studied by scientists to discover how distinct bioproducts cooperate with their environments to achieve a shared objective.

In cyborgs, swarm knowledge involves the observation of nature and the use of concepts by scientists in machines. A cyborg swarm, for instance, may consist of small, identical appliances, each with sense. If data is exchanged with the other gadgets in the group acquired by one cyborg agent, it allows the users to act as a unified group. A cyborg swarm is typically straightforward, and agents frequently use sonar, radar, or camera to acquire additional data [7].

1.5.1 Types of Communication Between Swarm Agents

Isolated bots or swarming agents can interact in several ways, including:

- Point to point: Information is transmitted immediately from the agent to warn the swarm of places, impediments, or objectives.
- Broadcasting: One agent in the swarm immediately broadcasts information to the rest of the swarming via sound, light, or wireless media.
- Contextual information exchange: An agent leaves a message inside the swarm that can transmit information to affect the behavior of other members. The way insects leave behind a trail of pheromones to take their equivalents to a particular area is comparable.

1.5.2 Examples of Swarm Intelligence

Pattern recognition has a lot of uses. Small, drone-like cameras for risky search and recovery operations can show optimization techniques.

The cyborgs may execute an extremely light duty in destructed regions, such as looking for survivors if scheduled for working together as a single unit. Pattern recognition is also used to mimic crowds, such as augmented reality games in films and the importance of technology.

"Smart dust" is a term used to characterize a microelectromechanical system (MEMS) that is tiny enough to remain hanging in the air. Researcher think that smart dust should analyze environmental details in distant worlds.

1.6   History of Swarm Intelligence

Independent creatures in naturalistic cloud computing usually have no idea of a high-level purpose but may mimic complicated real-world systems. When satisfied, numerous low-level objectives make this feasible. This enables significant collective activity resulting from these stupid and non-influent single individuals. A reintroduction to the modeling of natural things such as fire, wind, and liquid in computer-based animation tracks back to the early efforts of William "Bill" Reeves in 1983, culminating in the Pixar film *Luca* in 2021. During the development process, agents or "droplets" were created. In the virtual simulation, they undertook modifications, wandered around, and were finally rejected or "died." Reeves found that such a pattern could represent the dynamism and shape of natural surroundings, which had been unfeasible with conventional surface depictions. The Boid model (1986) created basic principles that enhance the independence of particle behaviors and set simple low-level norms that may lead to emerging behavior by boids (bird-oid objects) and particles. Therefore, the sophistication of the Boid model is a direct result of the fundamental interconnections between each component. Craig Reynolds established three different swarming regulations for the following particles: segregation, alignment, and cohesion. While the concept of separating enables molecules to move away from one another to prevent crossover, the harmonization and cohesive ideas need directional upgrades to advance towards the aggregate direction and location of the adjacent troops. The intrinsic intermodulation distortion of books makes the group dynamically chaotic, but the negative criticism produced by the essential low-level rule influence makes the behavior orderly. If each book knows the true identity of each other book, it's computerized by an $O(n^2)$ complexity. Reynolds offered a neighborhood model with an interchange of information between boxes, thereby lowering the complexity to $O(n)$ and accelerating the use of algorithms. In 1995, an expansion of Reynold's work officially established the Support Vector Machine method. In this method, the flock or swarm has unexpectedly converged unanimously, including local information sharing to the closest neighbor speed comparison. Therefore, the velocity of particles has been randomly disturbed, resulting in sufficient fluctuation and consequent lifelike swarm behavior. These characteristics were removed because the flock looked to convergence without attracting them. This scenario concluded with a community of agents that more closely followed a swarming than a flock's dynamics [7].

1.7   Taxonomy of Swarm Intelligence

The evaluation of taxonomy is provided in this part of the PSO algorithm.

- Continuity: The PSO is split into two sections, continuous and discontinuous, from the consistency in the area where these particles are situated. As a change in the locations of the nanoparticles in the same dimension, the travel route of the nanoparticles continues. However, this motion route changes the likelihood of the orientation coordinate's value being zero or one in a discontinuous state.
- Fuzzification: The PSO is examined from two perspectives from a defuzzification point of view. The fuzzy model of the method is evaluated in a few PSO applications, such as multi-target quadratic allocation issues. Accelerating and positional representation in vector form are translated to fuzzy matrices from real vectors.
- Accordance: At times, the swarming development process is almost stopped and stagnant during the PSO. This is sometimes because certain particles are inactive; in other words, they cannot be searched locally and globally; therefore, their current or previous locations don't move much, and their speed is almost nil. One option is to substitute these passive nanoparticles with new elements to retain the present rotation of the nanoparticles based on PSO particles. The accelerated PSO (APSO) technique is used. But this halt is occasionally caused by a swarming propensity to reach a balance condition that prohibits other regions from being searched and caught at a local minimum. An energy dissipation system that introduces negative mobility and causes

chaos among particles is developed to tackle this problem utilizing the dissipative PSO (DPSO) algorithm. By using this method, the above-stated stagnant condition is almost averted. The two techniques described above are used concurrently in this regard. In other words, on the contrary, an adam optimizer is utilized to enhance swarm variety when the algorithm finds equilibriums in the final few runs, and the dissipative algorithm is designed to introduce negative volatility in the PSO. Therefore, an adaptive method for the weight update tricks is devised to maintain domestic and international optimization balance. The dynamically adaptive dissipative PSO (ADPSO) algorithm was used. Both static and dynamic conceptions may be evaluated in the printed images.

- Attraction: There are three techniques, namely attraction, repulsion, and emotional connection, to tackle difficulties such as premature convergence. The additional operator is used in the attracting phase to upgrade the speed equations, while the subtracting operator is used during the repelling phase. The electrons are transported in the attraction stage and in the repelling step they get away. In the attraction/repulsion stage, the swarming development is carried out through attracting and repelling periods.

- Topology: From the standpoint of availability of particle knowledge, the PSO method is split into several topologies. All particles are linked to one another by "guest" particles. Indeed, all the electrons are mutually influenced. But each component is in the list topology attached to neighboring particles, and a network is established. Pyramidal morphology is another type of morphology that is like a three-dimensional triangle that displays the three-dimensional connection of the components. A virtual network in the star network impacts and influences the whole community. Smaller network topology consists of isolated sub-spans and particles, a homogenous example. The up/down and each neighborhood side are placed on a loop in a two-dimensional space in the von Neumann topology. The Vis-best topology proposed in this work for the first time is an averaging state of common lbest and guest topologies. In these topologies, the knowledge may be split between particles in a discreet immediate neighbor and between all particles in a particle monitoring zone. In reality, the particles in each other's observing area are conscious of the excellent spot and can draw a closed condition to the facts.

Many more topologies have been spontaneously developed in addition to the above-stated topologies [8].

- Activity: There are two kinds of activities. Each particle attracts the other swarm in active mode to represent sexual interactions in a whole multitude. But with passive movement, a sociological phenomenon is not displayed in the entire hive, although there is an interest for each component from other nanoparticles.
- Group: There are two types of clustering. 1) The first type is an inactive (passive) agglomeration with a passive swarm and a physical property; e.g., as plankton is filled with liquid, the water flow maintains it. 2) The second type is a grouping that divides itself into two groups; i) A proactive accumulation in which an absorbency source is aggregated. Food or water may be this resource; ii) A gathering separate from the assembly. There are no environmental and physical variables in the absorption source. It is also split into two kinds: a) the passive kind, which gravitates from one molecule to another but does not show a social activity; and b) the social kind in which the particles have social interactions and are severely linked.
- Mobility: The PSO efficiency increases by updating the particle locations to use a clear illustration and dynamic methods occasionally. For example, the DAPSO algorithm was suggested to balance exploitation and exploration within PSO and preserve the various particles. The distance of each particle is computed for the optimal location to modify the particle velocity. However, conventional static methods are used in contrast.
- Divisibility: The PSO is classified into indivisible and non-divisible kinds from particle division. The main swarm is separated into sub-swarms to enhance the efficient algorithm or improve the swarm variation or multi-objectivity.
- Particle types: Particles in PSO sometimes are permitted to follow qualitative behavior rather than Newton's conventional dynamics. In other words, the particles utilize a

qualitative motion rather than a Newtonian one in the solution space. The findings are better than the classical state in high dimensions. In particular, the necessary parameters for setup are reduced.

In IEC standardization, FF is substituted with the concept of the user. That is, the user opines on each particle, considering current criteria, since the transferring of information between the particles of this iteration is not limited to the PSO, unlike EC and IEC. Since it also applies particle information for former repetition, the IPSO and IEC mechanisms are distinct. The IPSO is the same as the PSO since the user and not the FF user identifies the optimal particles.

- Particle trajectory sign: There are two viewpoints when determining the traveling route of the nanoparticles. From a positive point of view, the nanoparticles change positions from their best prior locations to the top international site in the swarming, which is the same as the traditional perspective. In the pessimistic view, the particles adapt to the worst places, i.e., they strive to avoid taking the worst classes.
- Recursivity: The PSO process presents two methods from a repetitive perspective factor. In the first view, information is utilized to adjust the process to prevailing circumstances, and we have a recursive PSO during the process. In the following perspective, however, the process has no control mechanism.
- Hierarchy: The hierarchical method of PSO attempts to position particles in a dynamic hierarchical structure in a way that is equivalent to the quality of the solutions given in a higher degree of hierarchical structure. The particles at higher levels influence the entire swarm more.
- Limitation: From the point of view of restrictions, the PSO is split into restricted and unrestrained kinds. The method is limited to a normal state, the same as the classic algorithm. The speed and position update formulae are the same in both situations. The exception is that in the traditional (constrained) case, there have been up and down limits for the location and speed when the limitations are exceeded. However, there is no such restriction in the UPSO situation [9].

- Synchronicity: This algorithm has been retrieved from the PSPSO algorithm. The distinction between synchronicity and a synchronicity in PSO is in positions and speed update calculations. The PAPSO performs continuously and gains opportunities to update the velocity and location of the particles. To decrease the imbalance, the algorithm dynamically balances the load with a chain-centered approach
- Combinatorial: The PSO variant, dubbed CPSO, is used with continuum and integer parameters to optimize the combining issues. The conventional PSO algorithm is its counterpart; it is just constant.
- Cooperation: Various stars can be utilized jointly to optimize distinct components of the case to enhance the productivity of classical PSO. It's known as CPSO. An unpleasant situation, however, will occur with a distinct swarm.
- Objective: In light of multi-target and single techniques addressing such issues, development models are classified into mobile and non-problem from the perspective of objective numbers. In the multi-target method, many targets with one swarm, but in accordance with the priority of the goals, are to be optimized.
- Another optimal combination: This technique has been coupled with other optimization techniques such as simulated annealing (SA), ant colony optimization (ACO) or genetic algorithm (GA) to enhance performance and resolve issues, such as entrapment in an optimal location, and promote variety to discover improved alternatives to PSO.
- Speed type: The speed parameter is key in the PSO to indicate the direction of the particle's motion. By altering this parameter utilizing several heuristics, numerous instances are shown in the taxonomies; and better results may be achieved.
- Uncertainty: In stochastic cases, information about stochastic models are utilized rather than utilizing guest information from the standpoint of the information source shared across swarms.

1.8   Properties of Swarm Intelligence

The typical swarm intelligence system has the following properties:

- It is composed of many individuals.
- The individuals are relatively homogeneous.
- The interactions among the individuals are based on simple behavioral rules that exploit only local information that the individuals exchange directly or via the environment.
- The system's overall behavior results from individuals' interactions with each other and their environment; that is, the group behavior self-organizes.

1.8.1 Models of Swarm Behavior

Craig Reynolds has created a 1986 artificial life software, Boids, which replicates bird flocking. His papers were published at the ACM SIGGRAPH Conference in 1987 on this topic. An abbreviated form of "bird-oid object" is referred to as "boid," referring to a bird-like item [10].

Boids are an example of emerging behavior, just like with most artificial lifetime simulations; which means the complexity of boids arises because of the interaction between the agents (in this instance, boids) and a series of basic rules. In the primary universe of boids, the following laws apply:

- Separation: steering to avoid crowding local flockmates.
- Alignment: steering towards the local flockmates' average heading.
- Cohesion: steering to move toward the average position of local flockmates.

More complicated rules such as preventing obstacles and searching for objectives can be implemented.

1.8.2 Self-Propelled Particles

In 1995, Vicsek *et al.* developed self-propelled particles (SPP), often known as the Vicsek model, based on a particular boid model previously established by Reynolds in 1986. In SPP, a swarm is modeled by a collection of objects that move at a steady rate but respond to a random disturbance by increasing the average intercultural experience of the other nanoparticles in their local area. The SPP models indicate that independent of the swarm animal species, the swarmed creatures share certain features at the governmental level. Jamming systems produce emergent behaviors, some of which are universal and stable at many different sizes. It has become a problem in theoretical physics to create minimum statistical methods to represent such conduct.

1.9   Design Patterns in Cyborg Swarm

It was demonstrated that the performance of a swarm depends on several environmental and swarm characteristics. Consequently, the relative success of one cyborg control strategy over another control strategy is a function of these characteristics. Cyborg swarm designers should thus decide what cyborg control algorithms to implement based on the available mission facts. To this end, design patterns can provide a valuable set of guidelines.

A single design pattern can be understood as a "template" for a particular part of a cyborg control algorithm. For example, a design pattern might suggest how information about worksites is exchanged between cyborgs. Multiple design patterns can be combined to create a cyborg control algorithm suitable for a given mission, which can be implemented on all or a subgroup of cyborgs in a swarm because they include a description of cyborg behavior and discuss consequences of that behavior on macro-level swarm characteristics and performance; design patterns aid the decision-making of developers by providing solutions that work well in particular missions. In this research study, only design patterns for homogeneous cyborg swarms are considered. Therefore, any description of their consequences on swarm-level behavior is written assuming that all cyborgs execute the same control algorithm. However, in general, design patterns could also be applied in heterogeneous swarms, where only a sub-group of cyborgs would behave according to a particular design pattern.

The following essential mission characteristics that need to be considered when selecting appropriate design patterns have been identified throughout this research study:

- Worksite density, i.e., how probable it is that a worksite can be found by a cyborg, given its current location?
- Worksite volume, i.e., how quickly a worksite gets depleted when cyborgs perform work on it.
- Misplacement of reward from worksites, i.e., whether cyborgs need to travel away from worksites to obtain compensation, for example, to drop off resources in the base during the collection task.

- Dynamics of the environment, i.e., whether the worksite characteristics, such as their location, change over time. In dynamic environments, worksite characteristics are temporary, and reward needs to be extracted from worksites as quickly as possible.

Furthermore, there are four characteristics of a swarm that result from its control strategy:

- Scouting efficiency, related to how quickly the swarm can discover new worksites.
- Information gain rate, related to how quickly information enters into the swarm and spreads within it as a result of scouting and communication between cyborgs.
- Tendency to incur misplacement cost, CM, related to how much time is spent by cyborgs approaching worksites that they have become subscribed to, as well as the number of such cyborgs.
- Tendency to incur opportunity cost, CO, related to how long it takes cyborgs to discover that the worksites that they are subscribed to have disappeared from the environment, as well as the number of such cyborgs.

The first two swarm characteristics describe how cyborgs obtain information and share it. The last two characteristics define how efficiently a swarm can transform knowledge gained. The introduced Information-Cost-Reward (ICR) framework expresses the relationship between the hive, environmental factors, and swarm characteristics. Under this framework, a swarm is understood as a single entity capable of decentralized cognition at the collective level that emerges from individual cyborgs' information processing, actions, and interactions.

When the environment is static and worksites are challenging, control strategies with a high information gain rate are suitable. However, since high information gain rate is usually achieved by communication between cyborgs, it can be associated with an increase in the tendency of swarms to incur misplacement and opportunity costs. Consequently, when worksites are relatively easy to discover, hives a high propensity to perform than swarms with a lower. Furthermore, when the environment is dynamic, i.e., when new information is generated over time, a good scouting efficiency and a common tendency to incur costs are more critical. Finally, prices can be facilitated by the environment. For example, the negative effect of misplacement cost during the collection task is more minor in swarms where cyborgs exchange information where resources need to be dropped off.

In this chapter, general lessons learned from simulation experiments are formalized as design patterns. Each pattern captures a specific aspect of cyborg behavior and describes environmental conditions for a suitable design choice. The methodology for design pattern creation is first introduced, followed by a catalog of seven design patterns. Next, the rules for combining design patterns with control strategies are presented, and examples are given. The chapter ends with a discussion of the relevant aspects of existing swarm cyborg literature. It is shown that the design patterns introduced here can be found in cyborg control algorithms used in a broad range of automated experiments and that the essential characteristics of these design patterns remain the same across different implementations. Finally, it is demonstrated that the methodology for design pattern creation established here can be applied to extend the design patterns catalog. The new design patterns can easily be combined with the existing ones.

In the swarm work cycle within the Information-Cost-Reward framework, worksite distribution in the environment is characterized by the probability, $p(W)$, of a worksite being located at a given point in space. Scouts search for and spread information about worksites. This process is affected by the swarm's scouting and communication strategies and produces the expected reward, R', while reducing the swarm's uncertainty cost, CU. After paying certain misplacement costs, workers turn information into reward, R, CM. They also alter the environment by depleting worksites, decreasing $p(W)$, and potentially increasing opportunity cost, CO, paid by the swarm.

Design methodologies, such as probabilistic finite state machine models and evolutionary algorithms, and relevant future research directions are identified.

1.9.1   Design Pattern Creation

A total of nine cyborg control strategies were explored throughout the primary control strategies; solitary, local broadcaster, and bee were experimented with separately. Two add-on strategies, opportunism and anticipation, were analyzed with the three primary methods to determine whether they improved swarm performance in dynamic environments. To translate these strategies into design patterns, logic modules, each describing a unique aspect of a cyborg control algorithm, need to be identified. Inspired by the object-oriented design pattern principles, it is proposed here that a swarm cyborg design pattern should:

- Describe a particular stand-alone module of a cyborg control algorithm regarding cyborg behaviors, relevant internal and external data structures, and relationships between them. Such a module should satisfy a particular functional requirement, and its description should be independent of other modules that deal with different needs.
- Describe suitable environments and swarm tasks where the pattern is understood to be an appropriate design choice.
- Be possible to combine with other design patterns.
- Be implementation non-specific, i.e., only describe high-level behavior, rather than a particular algorithm or implementation.

The last point is critical. To generate general knowledge from specific experiments, we need to dispose of implementation details, such as particular control algorithms or parameter values, and instead identify available patterns of cyborg behavior and their implications on swarm performance. The Information-Cost-Reward framework is helpful in this endeavor, as it describes cyborg behavior in terms of "information flow" instead of "control code" and the result of the behavior in terms of individual "costs" rather than simply "performance improvement" or "performance degradation." Descriptions of swarm behavior that use the ICR framework are thus not dependent on particular cyborg hardware or software. The behavior results can be understood in detail concerning environmental characteristics.

An essential step in creating a design pattern is identifying what category it should belong to. Categorizing the set of processes that need to be formalized as a design pattern can assist in choosing what cyborg behaviors and data structures are relevant. Based on the performed experiments with the consumption and collection tasks, it is proposed here that a swarm cyborg design pattern should belong to one of three categories, each answering a particular question:

- Transmitter patterns: What entity transmits information?
- Exchange patterns: Where and when is information shared?
- Update patterns: How is information updated?

Each design pattern description should include the following:

- Design pattern name and category;
- A list of suitable applications;
- Description of the cyborg behaviors;
- Dependencies on other behaviors of the cyborg, including recommendations about which other design patterns it works effectively with;
- A list of parameters associated with the cyborg behaviors, as well as, if possible, their impact on swarm performance;
- A list of consequences that the design pattern has on swarm characteristics, expressed in the terminology of the ICR framework. Since it is often not immediately apparent by looking at cyborg behavior descriptions, the design pattern consequences should identify how particular micro-level routines affect the emergence of macro-level outcomes.

The design pattern name, category, suitable applications, behavior description, and consequences are compulsory. On the other hand, some patterns might not have dependencies or parameters.

1.9.2   Design Pattern Primitives and Their Representation

An essential part of a design pattern is an explicit description of the cyborg behaviors that the mark represents. A visual description, i.e., a diagram, is often handy when a design pattern needs to be understood quickly. A textual description that follows a well-specified syntax is more suitable when a design pattern needs to be translated into program code.

A visual and a textual description require a well-specified modeling language with unambiguous syntax and semantics to clearly express relevant entities and processes. Various modeling languages for object-oriented design patterns exist, for example, UML. While these languages are helpful in traditional software development, their utility for modeling multi-agent embodied systems, such as cyborg swarms, is limited for two main reasons. Firstly, data in these languages is not defined explicitly, making it challenging to express where information is stored or how operations are done. As the ICR framework has demonstrated, information flow is as essential as cyborg behavior when it comes to understanding and designing cyborg control algorithms, meaning that an adequate representation of data is required. Secondly, swarm control algorithms often rely on cooperation or communication between cyborgs. A way of representing relationships between behaviors and data of two different cyborgs is needed to account for mechanisms that lead to the emergence of desired macro-level outcomes.

Therefore, due to the shortcomings of the existing modeling languages, a new Behavior-Data Relations Modeling Language (BDRML) is proposed here. Inspired by other modeling languages, such as UML and DisCo, BDRML defines a set of primitives that represent behaviors and data, a set of relationships, i.e., relations, between these primitives and a bunch of operations allowed on the primitives. All these language elements have their visual and textual representations in BDRML.

- Behavior, i.e., a set of processes that deal with a particular situation a cyborg finds itself in, for example, "Scout" or "Rest."
- Internal data, i.e., information that represents a particular aspect of the environment or a cyborg's internal state and is stored in the cyborg's memory.
- External data, i.e., information that is stored by a non-cyborg entity in the environment, for example, by an RFID tag or by the presence of a chemical substance in an ant-inspired swarm.

Note that "behaviors" in BDRML, such as "work" or "scout," can refer to "states" or "sets of states" in finite state machines. In neural network controllers, "behaviors" would not be programmed explicitly but manifest through the network dynamics.

Also, a crucial difference is noted between internal and external data. Internal data is readily available to a cyborg at any point, while external data must be found in the environment. Moreover, when information between cyborgs needs to be exchanged, data stored internally can only be passed from one cyborg to another when they meet. On the other hand, one cyborg can deposit external data into the environment and read by another cyborg later.

Since both behaviors and data are primitives, BDRML allows the relations between cyborg actions and information to be formulated. There are sevens types of connections possible:

1) Transition: a behavior-behavior relation, where the cyborg transitions from one behavioral mode to another.
2) Read: a behavior-data relation, where internal data, stored in the cyborg's memory, is used by the cyborg when it is engaged in a particular behavioral mode.

3) Write: a behavior-data relation, where internal data is stored into the cyborg's memory when it is engaged in a particular behavioral mode.

4) Receive: a behavior-data relation, where external data, stored in the environment, is used by the cyborg when it is engaged in a particular behavioral mode.

5) Send: a behavior-data relation is sent, where external data is stored by the cyborg into the environment when it is engaged in a particular behavioral mode. Alternatively, internal data of another cyborg is written in when a cyborg is in a specific behavioral model.

6) Copy: a data-data relation, where information is copied from one data primitive to another (for example, from an external to an internal data structure that represents the same information).

7) Delete: a data operation, where data is disposed of.

It is also necessary to define a set of conditions under which a particular relation or operation occurs. A state is visually represented as an annotated triangle at the beginning of a relation or operation arrow. A condition set follows a relation or operation signature in a textual representation and is separated by a colon. A condition may be annotated as a name of a Boolean function or a probability, as existence or non-existence of a data structure, or as a simple and unambiguous textual description. A particular type of condition is an "always" condition, represented by a star (*). Visually, a relation or an operation with an "always" condition may be described without the condition triangle symbol. Multiple conditions can affect a single link or operation. The "or" logical operator is assumed when requirements are combined unless otherwise specified.

Note that there are three types of lines used in BDRML. Single solid lines represent transitions between behaviors and read/write relations between behaviors and internal data structures. Double solid lines represent some form of communication and link external data structures with behaviors (in the case of the "receive" and the "send" relations) and with internal data structures (in the case of the "copy" operation). Double solid lines can also link behavior with an internal data structure, i.e., during the "send" operation, signifying that a cyborg engaged in a particular behavioral mode sends information to another cyborg that stores the data in its memory. Finally, dashed lines are used for annotating relation and operation conditions.

A design pattern representation in BDRML consists of both a visual and a textual specification. A set of primitives (V) is defined, followed by a list of their relations and operations. Each box and arrow in the visual representation must have a corresponding line in the textual representation and vice versa.

It is essential to point out that while the design patterns are not implementation-specific, by default, it is assumed that:

- The swarm is homogeneous.
- The cyborgs can sense their environment locally. In particular, they can feel the presence of worksites. They can also sense the presence of other cyborgs and obstacles nearby and resolve collision conflicts.
- The cyborgs have a read/write internal memory.
- In the case of some design patterns, it is expected that cyborgs are capable of communicating with other entities.

These requirements are satisfied by the majority of cyborgs currently being used in swarm cyborg experiments, such as the e-pucks, the eSwar-Bots, the kilobits, the s-bots, and the marXbots. Future extensions to design patterns could accommodate heterogeneous swarms or swarms with other non-standard properties.

1.10   Design Patterns Updating in Cyborg

This section presents seven design patterns belonging to one of the design pattern categories: transmitter, exchange, and update. The design is an example of a design pattern specified in BDRML. The design pattern consists of three primitives: behaviors B1, B2, and an internal data structure D1. A cyborg changes its mode from B1 to B2 when a Boolean function f returns true. The cyborg transitions from B2 to B1 with a probability p(G). While engaged in behavior, B2 writes to and reads from D1. Patterns are primarily based on the control strategies used in experiments throughout, and relevant chapters are mentioned in the design pattern descriptions where appropriate. In some cases, the author's previously published work is also referenced.

The patterns are defined in the following format. First, the pattern's name and category are given, followed by a list of applications for which the design is suitable. The cyborg behaviors and data structures that the mark represents are described in plain text and BDRML. A list of the pattern's dependencies, behavior parameters, and consequences follows.

It is important to remember that a design pattern is not equivalent to a complete cyborg control strategy. Depending on the pattern's category, only a particular aspect of the cyborg control algorithm is described, such as how information is obtained, transmitted, or updated. How multiple design patterns can be combined into cyborg control strategies is formalized and demonstrated.

1.10.1 Behaviors and Data Structures

- Information about worksites is easily obtainable; for example, when worksite density is high.
- It is strongly recommended if, in addition, new information is generated in the environment over time and continuous exploration is thus important.

A cyborg scouts the environment and can find a worksite with a probability p(F). Upon seeing a worksite, the cyborg begins work and stores the information about the worksite, such as a local vector towards it, in an internal data structure. The data structure may be updated periodically while the cyborg works.

The cyborg ignores any information and actions of other members of the swarm.

An overview map of design patterns: Design pattern categories are indicated on the left. Design pattern parameters are shown in italics below each print. Daines joins design patterns that can be combined.

- Leads to a low information gain rate, which is the reason why information needs to be readily available to cyborgs.
- The spread of cyborgs across worksites only depends on their movement pattern. If the movement of cyborgs is random, an even spread across the environment is achieved.
- Prevents spread of erroneous information.
- Minimizes any misplacement and opportunity costs.

1.10.2 Basics of Cyborg Swarming

A cyborg scouts the environment and can find a worksite with a probability p(F). Additionally, it can receive information about a worksite from other cyborgs while engaged in the "Work" behavior. When an informed and an uninformed cyborg meet, they form a temporary peer-to-peer connection. The uninformed cyborg gets recruited to the worksite, stores information about it in its internal data structure, and begins work. Similarly, a scout remembers and starts working on a worksite that it discovers on its own. The cyborg's internal data structure may be updated periodically while the cyborg works.

- Cyborg communication range: A more extensive communication range causes a higher information gain rate and increases misplacement and opportunity costs. Consequently, performance can decrease due to congestion and overcommitment to worksites.
- Information about worksites is more easily accessible by uninformed cyborgs.
- Information is carried and transmitted by cyborgs, meaning that the information gain rate depends on the probability of cyborgs meeting, i.e., on their movement algorithm and the structure of the environment.
- Causes the cyborgs to incur misplacement costs associated with traveling to worksites after being recruited.
- Increases the probability of cyborgs incurring opportunity costs as a result of outdated information being spread across the swarm.
- Can lead to spread of erroneous information.

1.10.3   Information Exchange at Worksites

Uninformed cyborgs are likely to encounter information transmitters, i.e., other cyborgs or non-cyborg information storage devices near worksites, for example:

- In the consumption task, during which cyborgs remain at worksites until they are depleted.
- When a combination of worksite density, the cyborg scouting strategy and the communication range of the transmitters and the uninformed cyborgs leads to the probability of information exchange that is likely to be higher than with alternative exchange design patterns.

Cyborgs only exchange information near a worksite that an informed cyborg is working on. Note that in the BDRML syntax, the conditions of the two relations that connect the "Work" behavior with the "Worksite data int." and "Worksite data ext." data structures have an "and" operator. This notation assures that both "at a worksite" conditions always have to be met when this design pattern is combined with other ways.

- The information gain rate depends on the structure of the environment and the communication range of transmitters.

Parameters

- Proximity threshold: a maximum distance at which a cyborg is considered to be "at a worksite."
- After an initial worksite discovery by a cyborg, the range at which other cyborgs can find the worksite is enlarged, increasing the swarm's scouting success.

1.10.4   Information Exchange Center

- Static and dynamic environments where worksite density is very low.
- Environments with mediocre worksite density, where the swarm task requires cyborgs to become misplaced from worksites (e.g., the collection task), provided that the Information Exchange Center is identical to the place where cyborgs need to travel to periodically as a part of their task.

Cyborgs meet at the Information Exchange Center (IEC) to exchange information. There are two types of cyborgs found at the IEC: informed cyborgs that provide information and uninformed cyborgs that search for information.

An informed cyborg pauses its work and returns to the IEC when its boolean transmission initiation function, t, returns true, to begin providing information at the IEC. The cyborg leaves the IEC based on a transmission expiry function, r, and resumes work.

An uninformed cyborg outside the IEC, i.e., a scout, periodically returns to the IEC based on a scouting expiry function, to check whether new information is available. If the cyborg finds information about where work is located, it transitions to the "Work" behavior and leaves the IEC. If no information is available in the IEC, the uninformed cyborg goes to the IEC and resumes scouting according to a scouting initiation functions.

- The swarm's scouting efficiency decreases because scouts return to the IEC based on a scouting expiry function. This function must fit the nature of the environment (for example, enough time must be given to scouts to explore a large or a highly dynamic working arena); otherwise, the swarm might be unable to discover worksites.
- Transmission initiation function, t: a rule that causes informed cyborgs to return to the IEC. For example, the need to drop off resources in the base during the collection task.
- Transmission expiry function, r: a rule that causes informed cyborgs to leave the IEC. For example, if the IEC pattern is combined with the Broadcaster pattern, the expiry of a recruitment time can trigger the cyborgs to resume work.
- Scouting expiry function, u: a rule that causes scouts to return to the IEC. For example, the expiry of a maximum scouting time.
- Scouting initiation function, s: a rule that causes uninformed cyborgs in the IEC to become scouts. For example, each second, cyborgs might become scouts with a certain scouting probability.
- Information gain rate depends less on the environment's structure than on the cyborgs' communication range and on the cyborg movement algorithm. The variance in information gain rate is slight across different environment types.
- Promotes spatio-temporal coordination between cyborgs. This is advantageous when a single worksite exists in a static or dynamic environment. On the other hand, the swarm performance is poor when the swarm needs to concentrate on multiple worksites simultaneously.
- Incurs high misplacement and opportunity costs relative to the other exchange patterns. The amount of incurred costs depends on the structure of the environment, especially on the worksite distance from the IEC. A more considerable worksite distance generally leads to higher prices.

1.10.5   Working Features of Cyborg

A cyborg continues to work from a worksite that it discovers and does not abandon the worksite until it is depleted.

- The swarm behavior is relatively easy to design and predict.
- Opportunities for a better swarm performance might be missed.

1.10.6 Highest Utility of Cyborg

Environments where it is essential to extract rewards from worksites with the highest utility:

- Static environments, where there is a time limit on how long a swarm can work.
- Dynamic environments.

A cyborg continuously evaluates the utility of its worksite. It compares it to the utilities of all other worksites that it can obtain information about (as a result of scouting, communication with other cyborgs, or discovery of a lead in external data storage devices). The cyborg abandons its worksite and subscribes to a new one when a Boolean switch function, w, returns true.

- Unregulated information exchange can lead to a high increase of the displacement and opportunity costs incurred by the cyborgs and poor sampling of the environment. For example, if Opportunism is combined with the IEC pattern, that promotes a high information gain rate, overcommitment of the majority of the swarm to a single worksite can occur, significantly decreasing the swarm performance
- It is recommended to combine the Opportunism pattern with a transmitter or an exchange pattern where information flow is regulated to some extent, for example, the Information Exchange at Worksites pattern.
- Switch function, w: a rule that a cyborg switches from working on a worksite W1 with a specific utility U1 to a worksite W2 with a "better" utility U2. For example, a real-value threshold can specify how much U2 should be greater than U1.
- Promotes preferential exploitation of high-reward worksites.
- Requires sampling of the utility of all worksites that a cyborg encounters while working. This can imply additional energy costs to the cyborg.

- If Opportunism is combined with another design pattern involving communication between cyborgs, additional data packets about worksite utilities must be exchanged during communication. In addition, more frequent communication between cyborgs is required, as worksite utilities of other swarm members need to be evaluated whenever possible. This can imply additional energy costs and data error accumulation and propagation.

1.10.7   Gain Extra Reward

Environments where it is essential to extract reward from worksites with the highest utility:

- Static environments, where there is a time limit on how long a swarm has to work.
- Dynamic environments.

– A cyborg continuously evaluates the utility of its worksite and abandons the worksite when a Boolean abandonment function, a, returns true.
– Worksite abandonment leads to information loss and thus to a higher amount of the swarm's higher uncertainty cost, therefore abandoned worksites must be able to discover new information relatively quickly.
– It is recommended to combine the Anticipation design pattern with another pattern that leads to a high information gain rate, e.g., the Information Exchange Center pattern.
– Abandonment function, a: a rule according to which a cyborg abandons its worksite. For example, the worksite might be left when its utility falls under a specified threshold.
– Promotes frequent sampling of the environment.
– Prevents overcommitment to worksites and congestion.

1.11   Property of Design Cyborg

An essential property of design patterns is that they can be combined into a specific cyborg control algorithm, i.e., a control strategy. A BDRML representation of a control strategy can be created by following six design pattern combination rules:

- Copy all sets of behaviors, B, from all patterns into a new behavior set, B′, i.e., B′ = {B1 ∪ B2 ∪ ... ∪ Bn}.
- Copy common data structures from design pattern data structure sets D into a new data structure set, D′, i.e., D′ = {D1 ∩ D2 ∩ ... ∩ Dn}.
- Add additional data structures that have a genuine relationship with behavior and do not already belong to the set D′ into D′. This allows one pattern to extend the information processing routines of another.
- Copy all relations between the primitives that belong to sets B′ or D′, including their conditions. If otherwise specified by a relation condition, assume the "or" operator when combining shapes.
- Copy all operations on the primitives that belong to sets B′ or D′, including their conditions. If otherwise specified by an operation condition, assume the "or" operator when combining shapes.
- Delete all relations that belong to shorter relation paths between behaviors and data structures (but not between behaviors).

A relation path specifies a set of links that lead from a primitive V1 to a primitive V2, including those relations that pass through other primitives and create an indirect connection between V1 and V2. If multiple relation paths exist between a behavior and a data structure after multiple design patterns have been combined, removing relations that belong to shorter relation paths allows one design pattern to redefine communication routines of another. For example, imagine that a direct-write link between "Work" and "Worksite data" exists in design pattern P1. Another design pattern, P2, defines that there is a transition between the "Work" and a "Stay home" behavior and a write relation between "Stay home" and "Worksite data," but that "Work" and "Worksite data" are not directly related. When P1 and P2 are combined, the relation between "Work" and "Worksite data" should be deleted so that P2 can redefine the communication routine suggested by P1.

Broadcaster and Information Exchange at Worksites can be combined to create the "local broadcaster" control strategy. First, a set of behaviors that belong to both patterns is found. This set includes the "Scout" and the "Work" behaviors. Next, the "Worksite data int." data structure that belongs to both patterns is included in the control strategy. The "Worksite data ext." data structure and its relations are not copied since the system does not have a read relation to any behavior. The ties between all primitives that belong to the control strategy and their conditions are also included. The requirements of the connection between "Work" and "Worksite data int" are combined using the "and" operator, as specified by the Information Exchange at Worksite pattern.

The "local broadcaster" control strategy results from combining the Broadcaster and the Information Exchange at Worksites design patterns. Primitives and relations of the Broadcaster pattern are shown in black. Additional primitives and links drawn from the Information Exchange at Worksites pattern are green. Primitives and relations not copied are established as rough text, but they are not shown visually.

The "bee swarm" control strategy combines the Broadcaster and the Information Exchange Center design patterns. Primitives and relations of the Broadcaster pattern are shown in black. Additional primitives and relations, drawn from the Information Exchange Center pattern, are green. Primitives and relations that were not copied or deleted are shown as strikethrough text, but they are not shown visually.

Combining the Broadcaster and the Information Exchange Center design patterns results in the "bee swarm" control strategy. The control strategy has four behaviors and one data structure, "Worksite data int.". Similarly, as was the case with the "local broadcaster" control strategy, "Worksite data ext." is not copied from the Information Exchange Center pattern since it does not have a read relation to any behavior. The send relation between "Work" and "Worksite data int.", defined in the Broadcaster pattern, is deleted since a longer relation path that passes through the "Provide data in the IEC" behavior, inherited from the Information Exchange Center pattern, exists.

Three design patterns can be combined by following the same combination rules. It shows how the Broadcaster, Information Exchange at Worksites, and the Opportunism patterns form a "local broadcaster with opportunism" control strategy. The "Scout," "Work," and "Work data int." primitives are shared among the patterns and are a part of the control strategy. The write relations between "Worksite data int." and the two behaviors inherit conditions from all three design patterns. Note the condition that belongs to the read relation between "Work" and "Worksite data int": *, w. According to the Broadcaster pattern, the "Worksite data int." is continuously (*) updated while the cyborg is working. Additionally, the Opportunism pattern suggests that a new worksite should be adopted while a cyborg is in the "Work" behavior and finds a "better" worksite, based on the switching function, w.

Apart from a BDRML representation of the cyborg behavior, other characteristics of design patterns should be considered together when design patterns are combined. The "local broadcaster with opportunism" control strategy results from combining the Broadcaster, the Information Exchange at Worksites, and the Opportunism design patterns. Primitives and relations of the Broadcaster pattern are shown in black. Additional primitives and links are drawn from the Information Exchange at Worksites pattern shown in additions drawn from the Opportunism pattern, which are shown in magenta. Primitives and references not copied are established as strikethrough text, but they are not shown visually.

The list of suitable applications becomes more specific when multiple patterns form a control strategy. Or, from a developer's point of view, a more detailed specification of the swarm's environment and task allows for a higher number of design patterns to be combined with greater confidence. For example, suppose a swarm is required to collect easy-to-find rubbish from a city square but has no specific constraints for its operation. In that case, the design patterns catalog suggests implementing a cyborg control strategy by combining the Individualist and Blind Commitment patterns. On the other hand, an application may be more specific; for example, a swarm may be required to collect minerals that are difficult to find and appear in mineral veins of varying richness, while the cyborgs can only operate with enough sunshine provided for their solar batteries. In this case, the design patterns catalog would suggest combining the Broadcaster, the Information Exchange Center, and the Opportunism patterns.

Secondly, the list of control strategy parameters grows when multiple patterns are combined. To avoid creating a cyborg control algorithm with an ample parameter space that needs extensive optimization, it is advisable to prefer more straightforward control strategies based on several design patterns that are as small as possible. Similarly, design patterns with smaller parameters should be selected unless there is a reason for using a more complicated way. The problem with parameters is that they require decisions made by cyborg designers when the swarm is being built. Unless an exhaustive list of situations is considered during the optimization phase or a suitable online parameter learning algorithm is implemented, each new parameter can lead to undesirable results. For example, the Information Exchange Center pattern requires a parameter set for the "scouting expiry function" to specify when a scout should return to the IEC. Setting this parameter to an inappropriate value can prevent the swarm from discovering worksites when not enough time is given to scouts to explore the environment or communication between cyborgs when scouts spend too much time outside of the base do not meet with recruiters on the ground.

Before discussing how the design patterns proposed here have been used in the existing literature, it is essential to consider the level at which they describe cyborg behavior and its categorization. It has been suggested that design patterns for swarm cyborgs should represent multiple levels of behavior. For example, "local-level" or "basic" patterns should describe how cyborgs interact, while "global-level" or "composed" patterns should describe swarm-level behavior, such as "labor division." On the contrary, all design patterns presented here represent the same cyborg behavior level, equivalent to the "local-level primitives" of the "basic design patterns." The control strategies, for example, "solitary swarm with anticipation," represent a combination of design patterns and are similar to the "global-level primitives" or the "high-level patterns." The control strategies, however, do not design patterns themselves. Instead, they are particular design pattern realizations in swarm applications that fit specific mission requirements.

It is proposed here that information and cost-based description of the individual, "local level," cyborg behavior is an appropriate level at which design pattern should be defined. A detailed, lower-level description that deals with a particular object-oriented or functional implementation on a cyborg would have to include details about a specific experiment or special cyborg hardware that would potentially not be useful to a developer with slightly different hardware or application. Similarly, a description of macroscopic, "global-level" swarm behavior, for example, a "flocking pattern," would be a re-description of a combination of cyborg behaviors that fit a particular swarm mission. Such a global-level description would also potentially contain a lot of parameters. On the other hand, describing parts of cyborg behavior that deal with particular problems without providing too many implementation details allows for modularity and reusability.

While they describe the same level of behavior, the design patterns presented here are categorized based on what particular aspect of cyborg behavior they represent concerning obtaining, sharing, and updating cyborg information. They thus follow the categorization methodology of object-oriented design patterns and multi-agent systems design patterns. Each design pattern belongs to three categories: transmitter, exchange, and update.

Various combinations of these patterns can be found throughout the literature. The Individualist and Blind Commitment patterns are often used when simple foraging algorithms are needed for cyborg behavior. In contrast, swarm behaviors, such as self-regulation or task allocation, are explored.

The Individualist pattern is also often used when the performance of swarms without and with communication is compared. It is usually the case that hives in such experiments forage from difficult deposits, resulting in better swarms that utilize communication.

A combination of the Broadcaster and Information Exchange at Worksites patterns has been explored. Confirming the design pattern characteristics presented here, the authors showed that increasing the strength of interaction between cyborgs (e.g., due to a giant swarm size or an extensive communication range of cyborgs) leads to sub-linear performance improvement. In other words, in the ICR framework terminology, a high information gain rate often leads to high misplacement and opportunity costs that prevent the performance from improving linearly with the amount of information that the cyborgs can get. Similarly, it is argued that recruitment in swarms that used the Broadcaster and the Information Exchange at Worksites patterns leads to increased congestion (i.e., a higher misplacement cost) and the propagation of old information through the swarm (i.e., a higher opportunity).

The work of swarms that used a combination of the Broadcaster and Information Exchange at Worksites patterns did not outperform swarms that used the Individualist pattern. The authors proposed that the relatively poor performance of swarms that utilized communication resulted from communication noise. However, the characteristics of the Broadcaster design pattern point to two additional possible explanations. Firstly, only four cyborgs were used in the experiments, and it is possible that they did not meet often enough for communication to make a positive difference to their performance. Secondly, the cyborgs were collecting pucks that were pretty far apart from one another, considering the size of the cyborg body. A cyborg recruited to a puck thus searched to locate another puck nearby. In such a setup, it is possible that the negative effect of misplacement and opportunity costs outweighed the positive impact of recruitment.

The Broadcaster pattern has also been combined with the Information Exchange Center pattern, often in bee-inspired cyborg swarms and agent-based simulations. In these experiments, cyborgs collect items from the environment and return them to the base, where they also recruit in a peer-to-peer fashion. Since the Information Exchange Center pattern is the most suitable when items of interest are difficult to find but need to be collected into a central place, swarms that use it outperform other, non-communicating, swarms in foraging experiments where items of interest are clumped in a small number of patches. Interestingly, in their simulations, contrary to the characteristics of both of these patterns, they did not find any adverse effects of communication, such as the increase of congestion or fast depletion of resource deposits. They thus claimed that the swarm performance increases linearly with swarm size. A closer inspection of their algorithm reveals that their agents were allowed to occupy the same space, meaning that the physical aspect of agents was not fully modeled, preventing misplacement costs from being incurred due to congestion. Furthermore, their simulations could not incur opportunity costs since resource deposits had unlimited volumes.

Cyborg control algorithms that contain the update patterns can also be found throughout the literature. The Opportunism pattern has been used in foraging simulation experiments where agents preferred to head towards resource deposits closer to the base, i.e., residues that allowed a faster collection of resources. It showed that Opportunism causes the majority of a swarm to concentrate on a single resource deposit when the information spread in the swarm is not regulated.

Opportunistic behavior, where a swarm prefers to forage from more profitable resource deposits, can also be achieved when cyborgs that utilize the Information Exchange Center pattern and recruit in the base, recruit for a more extended amount of time when their deposits are more profitable. Even though the mechanism of achieving opportunism is different than when unemployed cyborgs prefer to be recruited to better promises, the results of such behavior are similar. In line with the Opportunism design pattern characteristics, Schmickl *et al.* demonstrated that a sufficient amount of scouting in a swarm where cyborgs behave opportunistically is significant for the ability of the swarm to react to environmental changes appropriately.

Finally, the Anticipation design pattern has been used in a control algorithm that allowed cyborgs to decide which type of puck they should search for to maintain the desired density of puck types in a drop-off location. The abandonment function, which caused a cyborg to stop foraging for a particular puck type, was related to the locally perceived behavior of other swarm members.

Design patterns allow us to consider a broad range of experiments with different cyborg hardware and identify building blocks of cyborg behavior that fit specific swarm mission requirements. For example, other design methodologies exist, probabilistic finite state machine models and evolutionary algorithms. Unlike design patterns, these methodologies are more suitable for parameter optimization than behavior selection. Therefore, design patterns complement these methodologies when developing cyborg control algorithms.

1.12   Extending the Design of Cyborg

The transmitter design patterns presented above did not communicate or rely on local, peer-to-peer communication between cyborgs. Another type of communication, called stigmergy, involves exchanging information between agents through the environment. Algorithms that utilize stigmergy are often inspired by the pheromone-based touch characteristic of ant colonies. To help their nestmates search for food, ants leave chemicals called pheromones on the ground. An extended overview map of design patterns shows the new ways in green. Design pattern categories are indicated on the left. Design pattern parameters are shown in italics below each print. Lines join design patterns that can be combined, and any extra parameters required for the pattern combination are shown next to the bars.

They travel back and forth between the nest and the food, forming trails in the environment. Other ants can sense pheromones and thus use the pheromone trails to navigate foraging. The evaporation rate of pheromones assures that a path no longer being used, for example, because the food source has been depleted, eventually disappears and does not recruit more workers.

There are two aspects of stigmergy that are interesting from the design pattern perspective. Firstly, it involves a stationary and external medium to the cyborgs and holds information relevant to the swarm's work. Secondly, it is the fact that information is available in many locations across the work arena, rather than only being exchanged in the base or near worksites. Two design patterns can be created to capture these aspects of cyborg behavior A transmitter pattern, called Information Storage, according to which information is stored in data storage devices, and an exchange pattern, Information Exchange Any Time, according to which data can be exchanged anywhere in the work arena. This section formalizes these two patterns using information from experiments found in the swarm cyborgics literature. Their description is not as detailed as the patterns presented since no experiments that could thoroughly test the suggested cyborg behaviors have been performed yet. Nevertheless, it is demonstrated here that the new design patterns can easily be combined with the other design patterns according to the design pattern combination rules defined, which shows unique ways on an extended design pattern map.

1.12.1   Information Storage in Cyborg

A cyborg scouts the environment and can find a worksite with a probability $p(F)$. Additionally, it can receive information about a worksite if it finds a data storage device located in the environment. Once a cyborg discovers information about a worksite, either as a result of scouting or when seeing a data storage device, it stores data about it in its memory and begins work. The cyborg's internal data structure is updated periodically while the cyborg works.

An informed cyborg stores information about its worksite into a data storage device(s) when appropriate. For example, when the design pattern is combined with the Information Exchange Any Time pattern, special data storage devices, such as RFID tags, may be dropped into the environment and updated by the cyborg. Chemicals that mimic ant pheromones, such as alcohol, can also exist. Alternatively, stationary cyborgs that do not directly participate in work can store information. On the other hand, when the Information Storage and the Information Exchange Center design patterns are combined, data is stored in a central location, for example, in the cyborg base.

The information is deleted from the storage device(s). According to an evaporation function, the data deleted from the storage device(s) is how long the information about worksites remains available in each storage device, i.e., the life span of the stored data. The function must consider the dynamics of the environment. If the information life span is too long, cyborgs follow information to depleted worksites and incur a high opportunity cost. On the other hand, a brief information life span prevents cyborgs from finding and utilizing the stored data.

- Evaporation function, e: a rule according to which information in the data storage device(s) is deleted or considered too old. This function plays a similar role as the evaporation rate of ant pheromones. For example, information might have a pre-defined life span. Upon life span expiration, the storage device deletes the information if such an ability has been programmed into it. Alternatively, cyborgs that read the report also evaluate its age and death there and decide whether it should exist.
- Detection range: a range at which a cyborg can find a storage device.
- Information about worksites is more easily accessible by uninformed cyborgs.
- Information is stored in the environment, meaning that the information gain rate depends on the probability of cyborgs detecting the information storage devices, but not on the likelihood of cyborgs meeting each other.
- Causes cyborgs to incur misplacement and opportunity costs due to recruitment to remote worksites. The extent of these costs increases with an increasing swarm size due to

congestion. However, the expenses paid may be smaller than when the Information Exchange Center pattern is used since data storage devices may be closer to worksites.

1.12.2 Information Exchange Any Time

Maximum storage device density: When the Information Exchange Any Time pattern is combined with the Information Storage pattern, the maximum allowed information storage device density must be specified to prevent the environment from being cluttered with storage devices. For example, the minimum distance between two RFID tags should be set. This could be related to the frequency at which the chemical is deposited into the environment in chemical trials.

1.12.3 The New Design Pattern Rules in Cyborg

The new design patterns can be combined with other ways from the catalog by following the design pattern combination rules.

Using the Information Storage and the Information Exchange Any Time patterns together results in an ant-inspired cyborg control strategy, resulting from combining the Information Storage and the Information Exchange Any Time design patterns. Primitives, relations, and operations of the Information Storage pattern are black. Other relations, drawn from the Information Exchange Any Time pattern, are green. Relations that were deleted are shown as strikethrough text, but they are not shown visually.

Cyborgs utilize their energy to find information about worksites in the environment. Cyborgs are designed by combining the Information Storage and the Information Exchange Center patterns to store information about where worksites are located in the base. Unsuccessful scouts arrive at the bottom to read the news and begin work.

Combining the Information Storage and the Information Exchange Center design patterns is a control strategy. Primitives, relations, and operations of the Information Storage pattern are black. Additional primitives and references drawn from the Information Exchange Center pattern are green. Links that were deleted are established as strikethrough text, but they are not shown visually.

Combining the Broadcaster and the Information Exchange Any Time design patterns is a control strategy. Primitives and relations of the Broadcaster pattern are shown in black. Additional primitives drawn from the Information Exchange Any Time pattern are green. Primitives and deleted links are established as strikethrough text, but they are not shown visually.

The Information Exchange Any Time pattern can also be combined with the Broadcaster pattern, leading to behavior where cyborgs exchange information when they meet anywhere in the work arena.

1.13   Bee-Inspired Cyborg

A design pattern represents a particular aspect of cyborg behavior that addresses a specific swarm mission requirement, such as finding worksites given a particular density of worksites dealing with specific environmental dynamics. A design pattern is created by considering the results of experiments with a particular behavior of cyborg, for example, a bee-inspired information exchange in a central "base" location, and by generalizing knowledge learned during the experiments using the Information-Cost-Reward framework.

Each design pattern presented here belongs to three categories: transmitter, exchange, and update. Transmitter patterns identify entities that should transmit information. For example, a transmitter pattern might suggest that cyborgs share information or exchange information via RFID tags placed in the environment. Exchange patterns dictate where data should be exchanged, such as whether cyborgs can communicate when they meet each other or whether a specific meeting place should be designated. Update patterns deal with how individual cyborgs update their information, such as whether they continuously search for "better" worksites or decide to abandon and forget them when certain conditions are satisfied.

A description of a design pattern includes its name, category, a list of suitable applications, definition of cyborg behaviors, including their parameters, dependencies on other behaviors of the cyborg, and the consequences of the design pattern on the swarm's scouting efficiency, information gain rate and tendency to incur the misplacement and the opportunity costs. Cyborg behaviors are described using the Behavior-Data Relations Modeling Language (BDRML). A BDRML-based report consists of the visual and textual representation of cyborg behaviors and data structures used by the behaviors and conditional relations and operations between and on them.

Using BDRML, multiple design patterns can be unambiguously combined into a control strategy by following the design pattern combination rules. The design patterns catalog introduced here provides cyborg designers with knowledge about suitable applications, parameters, and consequences of various cyborg behaviors. It thus allows them to devise practical cyborg control algorithms based on known mission characteristics.

1.14   Conclusion

Characterization of movements provide remarkable similarities: groups of people seem to remain nearly fixed from their neighbors; they are aligned with their closest neighbor, showing a definite inclination to stay with their neighbors. Indeed, this definition may readily be extended to many other species, such as salmon and songbirds, which travel in groups. The motives for their united activity, however, differ significantly. It is essential to stay with the swarming for solitary bees in the swarm as a single bee cannot live. The intricate structure of the microenvironment induces cohesive locomotion in locusts.

2

Foundation of Swarm Intelligence

Abstract

Swarm Intelligence (SI) is a pretty recent technology for the monitoring and administration of many interactive objects, such as telecommunications, computer and sensor networking, spacecraft constellations, and much more, in various research contexts. However, initiatives to use this framework and mimic the behavior of insect swarming often lead to numerous diverse SI applications. Due to its somewhat broad self-organized ideas, it is harder to precisely establish what SI is and completely appraise its capabilities. This chapter sets forth a set of basic concepts for SI R&D. A clear description of self-organized behavior is given instead of the traditionally popular ad hoc method to use SI terms. It offers the foundation for a much more fundamental, sensible solution to study and innovation. The Pareto optimization idea is used to grasp the concepts of effectiveness and adaptation. In a novel notion, Pareto template matching is considered, which involves symmetry links and invariance in scales in the context of changing system states that preserve Pareto correctness. The idea of the smooth deterioration of effectiveness so commonly sought in complicated systems is therefore described as a mathematics approach to express ethical trade-offs across distinct scales.

Keywords: Social behavior, optimization, simulation ant, machine intelligence, genetic algorithm, artificial life, chip, IQ test

2.1 Introduction

This chapter starts to lay the scene for the "particle swarm" evolutionary computing concept, the subject of the book's second chapter. Since the gold standard for intelligence is human cognition, we will build our model on people's perceptions as artificially intelligent investigators have done before us. Unlike most other earlier cognitive psychologists, however, we do not adhere to the idea that the intellect is equal to the brain, a private organizational culture, or a certain amount of mechanical dynamism. The present cognitive perspective has taken the dominant role in public and scientific thought, despite its radical expectations. We thus anticipate that many

Kuldeep Singh Kaswan, Jagjit Singh Dhatterwal and Avadhesh Kumar. *Swarm Intelligence: An Approach from Natural to Artificial*, (37–64) © 2023 Scrivener Publishing LLC

people will enjoy the background information on our fresh approach. This fundamental discourse emphasizes and provides algorithmic techniques that encourage life's adaptable and dynamical character in general, specifically human intellect. We believe that thinking is a part of our social character, and we take this very much to heart. We also prefer to highlight the parallels between humanity and other animals' social behaviors. The primary distinction is that in a highly dimensioned multidimensional space, the individuals, that is, minds, "move." People traverse a universe of numerous significant contrasts and similarities. This chapter will next examine some ideas on the adjustability of living objects and computer models and the adjustability of human cognition [11].

2.2 Concepts of Life and Intelligence

The specific difference between living and non-living things has been speculated about from the dawn of time. And though the difference is clear, it is hard to place a finger on it. Aristotle assumed: What has a soul in it is different from what it doesn't have because the former shows vitality... Living, in other words, might imply cognition or perception, or local mobility and repose, or nutritional movement, decay, and increase... This self-nutritional strength... is the original power that causes us to talk of life as life [12].

In the days before genetic manipulation and "artificial life," this list of traits was believed to describe the properties of living beings. Computer software was conceivable; and the black and white psychology of Aristotle characterized and impacted orthodox thinking for a thousand years.

The concept that living beings were inanimate continued until William Harvey recognized, in the 17th century, that the blood circulating through the body did not seem significant. Immediately, the heart was pumped, like any other pump, and the blood circulated like any other fluid. It had an immediate and tangible impact.

The year after Harvey's work, *On the Motion of the Heart and Blood in Animals*, was published, Descartes stated: "After examining the possible activities in this body, I discovered all those in someone without the capacity to think and so without our soul—that is, this portion of us, apart from the physical, of which it has been claimed that its essence should be thought." Descartes, therefore, established the connections among living beings and other physical stuff, possibly the actual transformation of the last few decades, in the same way that he noted—or invented—a renowned contradiction between mind and bird. Like anything else in the world, our live bodies are. Where earlier philosophy had seen the epithelial surface, body, and intellect as a dynamic unity, separate from inorganic material, the Cartesian way of thinking allowed the field of cold substance into the organism and pressed the soul back into a less known abstract cosmos dimension which, though essentially different from the one it was, was in some way—although nobody knows how—linked to the physical. The Cartesians didn't come up with the concept that mental things were separate from material things—all people were thinking that. Instead, they proposed that living beings would be the same as all the other things in the universe. Where they have been, minds remained.

Even Isaac Newton found it challenging to believe, even if he knew it was true, that the living matter was constantly inanimate: "No one with an impartial spirit is to examine every person or animal without being touched enthusiastically by the wonderful structure or qualities of the organism that is far higher than the inanimate dust below our feet." It appears that an unbelievable intricacy is a characteristic of existence. Even the smallest, most basic microorganism has only astonishing methods and architectures. These occurrences are so dissimilar to how we usually conceive of creation and implementation that many can't imagine that life might have originated in this way. However, suppose they know that it is accurate when we study a subtle element of the universe, such as the differences between items alive and not living. In that case, it may seem that it is desired to know if our differences are based on characteristics or identifications of things. It may prove unattainable. One of the main obstacles is that we are used to conceiving ourselves over and above nature; However, we should not belittle human achievement; we must admit (if this conversation continues) that many of our sensations of greatness are delusive—and that we cannot always discern which aspects [13].

One of the fundamental pillars of our experience of being exceptional is the taxonomy separation between natural processes and another physical system. We believed that we were heavenly, and our flesh proved it alive. Just as Galileo has pumped our small planet out of the middle of the world and Darwin has degraded our species from the divinities to the beasts, these days we are witnessing contemporary science chip away even in this final and long-lasting expansion. Today, ethical considerations are made in the light of the viability of unborn fetuses, the brain dead, donor organs, tissues that develop in the test tubes, and stem cells. Is this stuff alive? Where is the true frontier between life and physical inanimate objects? And what about those researchers who claim that the planet is a live spacefaring civilization itself? Or an insect colony is a superorganism? Is it nothing like making clothes or fixing a dent that creates the so-called death of one ant rather than loss of life? On the other hand, the development of computer programs of adaptive robots and lifestyle creatures with behaviors self-reproductive, educational and reasoning-capable behaviors and the development of their digital contexts confounds the boundary between the living and non-living systems. Humans can accomplish all that living organisms can in artificial life programs. In *Mind and Nature*, Gregory Bateson explained what he saw as the criteria and traits needed to designate anything as a mind:

- A mind is an element or component group of interacting elements.
- Difference triggers the communication among mental components.

Perception, for example, depends on stimulus modifications.

- The mental process needs energy collateral.

Both systems each contribute to an interaction; as Bateson argues, "You can take a horse to water, but you cannot make him drink. The drinking is his business."

- In the mind process, the determination chains must be circular (or more complicated).

The notion of mutual cause or feedback is crucial for cognitive processes and is essential.

- The impacts of difference should be considered in the mental process as transformations (i.e., coded versions) of the primary difference. The effects are not identical to their cause; the map is not similar to the area.
- The characterization and categorization of such transformations reveal a hierarchy of intrinsically logical categories.

2.2.1   Intelligence: Good Minds in People and Machines

We explored when something falls into one area or another. We examined whether someone is ineffective. The next subject may be the most well-known example. Intellectual ability is used to characterize human cognitive skills, even if it may be employed in other species, particularly communication and computing programs and inorganic things. Psychologists are highly unanimous, and computer scholars believe little regarding the meaning of this word—and there is practically no understanding between two different disciplines. Since computer science is the evoking of consciousness in electronic equipment, the idea's definition and background in contemporary times should be considered. It's not always a swarm and comfortable narrative. Again, we see that genetics and cognition are closely related to the great probabilistic systems [14].

2.2.2   Intelligence in People: The Boring Criterion

The intelligence-inheritance relationships are very controversial and disagreeable. Much of the situational leadership on IQ test success concerns are related to statistical disparities across different groups. In this context, it is noteworthy that the current idea of intelligence emerged in conjunction with inheritance and that efforts have traditionally linked intellect and genetic inheritance. Following Darwin's global wave of evolutionary declarations in the 19th century, in the first half of the 20th century eugenicists held the concept that human beings were defined by molecular markers. According to the individualist theory, the mechanism by which species are transformed is genetic modification; environmental selection forces drive adaptability. Therefore, selective breeding would be a method by which human authority would determine which of their peers could and would not reproduce. As Victoria Woodhull, who in 1872 was the first woman ever nominated for president of the United States, said, "To wish to have higher people, they should be produced, and if they are unwanted citizens, murderers, poor men, and unfit, they should not be raised." Thus, the contemporary idea of cognitive ability came into being; the selection criteria for who to propagate. "Better" individuals have always been distinguished from "bigger" by the idea of intellect. The knowledge of what is a "good" mind may be described by a set of criteria that support the judgment of the experts. The concept includes standard features in European and American civilization in the 20th century, such as memory, problem-solving abilities, and linguistic and mathematics skills. However, the reality is that intelligent people, even information specialists, have different skills; in the end, they describe their favored traits when they try to define intelligence—so there is an unavoidable discrepancy.

We stated earlier that the definition of knowledge is quite unanimous. In psychology, Edwin G. Boring gave the most cited (off the record) definition of intelligence: "intellectual is whatever an entrance exam assesses." In intelligence studies in psychology, the focus on examination, techniques for evaluating features, and the lack of ambition in defining what it is have been overshadowed. Intellectual ability was traditionally seen as a personal characteristic; one of the underlying assumptions is, for example, a measure of the competence of a person would be done at about the same time at various times (the "trustworthiness" component of measurement). This chapter is concerned with community adaptability, in which we tend to see people's intellect. While disparities exist among people, the accomplishments of exceptional people are incorporated into their communities for the benefit of all members. Not all of us can be Sir Isaac Newton, but every institution of physics and calculus provides courses, and we all profit from the discoveries of Newton. The successes of exceptional people make us all smarter—all of us can't ascend to the intelligence level of Einstein, but we increase our functional independence substantially by assimilating their thoughts [15].

2.2.3   Intelligence in Machines: The Turing Criterion

We have discussed the psychology phenomena of the intellectual ability of humans to date. However, a comparable debate was held in the computing world throughout the last half-century or more. It soon became evident that many mental activities might be duplicated using electronic computer systems; concepts and statistical relationships needed to be processed, stimuli needed to be reasoned and remembered. Perhaps we would construct machines that would be more powerful than the human brain if they could accomplish things like our physical minds and be trained to tackle issues that the brain can't handle. The idea was even put forth that computers may be more intelligent than people.

In a nutshell, that didn't happen. Personal processors did not work very well when it came to thinking and solving actual problems. Perhaps part of the explanation is how computer programmers define intellect, which differs from how psychiatrists describe it, and how their ideas about intelligence were carried out.

It is safe to assume that every computer intellect discussion inevitably ends with the Turing test (Alan Turing, 1950). The Turing test sounds relatively straightforward. A participant is put into a room with a computer screen and monitor, while a computer and the other participant are located in another room. The question(s) are typed into the computer and answered from the opposite side. A simple explanation of the test is this: if the respondent cannot distinguish between human replies and those of the machine created by technology, it is thought that the computer is intelligent.

It sounds like an odd IQ test in the first place. It is different from our IQ testing! Interestingly, a cognitive gathering test could outperform the computer very well.

2.3   Symbols, Connections, and Optimization by Trial and Error

Today, certain technological principles form the basis of our sociological and microprocessor theorization synthesis. Thinking about individuals and creatures in evolution will address issues by testing approaches, generating positive changes, and attempting once more. Although it is a "higher" or more complex way to problem-solve by applying logical principles, the "lesser" methods perform incredibly effectively. In this chapter, we create a language and conceptual framework for describing cognitive functions and optimizing challenges faced during testing. What alternatives are there? Can this be accepted? What did informatics do in artificially intelligent programs, and how did it work? Human vocabulary is a significant, good problem! Human communication! How can people (including those who are not bright otherwise) travel through a semanticist jungle of millions of comments and new sentence construction frameworks globally? We explain some critical issues and significant types of remedies [16].

2.3.1   Problem Solving and Optimization

Mind development is a particular type of business: an offensive commercial design that satisfies a complicated set of limitations. One example is a collection of characteristics that best matches a dynamic niche of ecology and, in the other, a structure of ideas, emotions, and conduct that minimizes conflicts with personal, societal, and physical limitations. Although the subject matter of regional characteristics has diverse tendencies, such as intellect, social awkwardness, imagination, etc., there is some inclination to develop specific mental features that seem to have been inherited. While a predisposition to learn may be hereditary, learning can only be done in a lifetime; there is no genetic transmission of gained information from generation to generation. As we have seen, the two main stochastic algorithms have distinct ways of working, but both rely significantly, if not entirely, on the experimentation variant. This subsection covers several problem-solving elements when the aim is to fit as many as several practicable restrictions. There may seem to be an odd use of the word "trouble."

The term has unique significance for particular communities which utilize it. We use this to define circumstances—not exclusively mathematics scenarios—where some facts exist, and other realities must be found following these conditions. An evolving species might have problems with a changed habitat. A moral individual is faced with an ethical issue. For most individuals, making a profit is a challenge.

A mathematician has difficulty with an equation containing certain unknowns. In other situations, the facts sought may be more accurate concerning how the information we currently know can be arranged or connected. Optimization is yet another phrase that is interpreted differently by diverse people. This phrase often refers to a system adjustment procedure that achieves the optimum result. Sometimes, even though a "good" result is good enough, a futile or wasteful hunt continues for the best result. Since we have described a challenge as a scenario where specific facts are sought, optimizations are defined as the application process that modifies the system to find the missing information. In a computational intelligence take on this, we propose that social connections between people enable complicated behavioral and cognitive patterns to be optimized [17].

2.3.2   A Super-Simple Optimization Problem

An issue has certain features that make it possible to evaluate the quality of the solution. This evaluation usually starts with an assessment of a system that provides an error. For example, the issue of finding a value (a pattern that consists of only one component in this simplistic example) for x that leads to best performing or fitting could contain some unknowns, such as $4 + = 10$. The discrepancy between some of the real and the intended outcomes is the mistake of the suggested solution; in the scenario where we want $4+x$ to equal 10, we could have to estimate what x should be, and find that, for example, $4+$ equals 20, for example, while we have been trying $x = 16$. So, if $x=16$, the mistake might be said to be 10.

Error is a decreasing element in increased goodness. An optimization issue may be presented with the same outcome to minimize error or maximize worth. However, sometimes it is better to talk about the quality or suitability of a solution to the crisis (note the links with evolution). Fitness is the evaluation of the hereditary or morphological pattern's quality. It is not always easy to convert mistakes; there are a few typical techniques, but none are perfect. The counterpart error (e.g., $1/e$) is one estimation of cleanliness. This specific measure is approaching infinite since the error is near zero and not defined if the numerator is equal to zero, but that is not necessarily an issue. We know that we have resolved that difficulty if the denominator is nil. Furthermore, we will probably not happen so near a perfect answer in precision floating-point accuracy that the computers believe it to be null and crash. The regression line of the error (multiply by −1, then the higher the values are, the better) is another transparent approach to assess the effectiveness of the possible solution.

We may utilize those specific arithmetic issues mentioned above to show the basic ideas of trial and error optimization. Our strategy, in general, is to test out some alternatives, i.e., values for x, and pick the best answer. When we try to find answers, the search itself gives us some indices of what we might do next. First, when 4+x less than 10, we may examine how far it is from 10 and utilize the mistake to help us offer a more significant amount. If the error is enormous, then perhaps we should make a substantial jump to attempt the next possible solution; if the mistake is tiny, we're presumably near the answer and should take incremental steps. The search procedure provides different kinds of helpful information. If we tried to choose a unique number, say 20 for x (10−24) =14, we'd find that the reply was not very good.

We could determine if we were trying to enhance productivity or worse if we attempted another number. When you are 12, you notice that 4+12 is still incorrect, but with error=6, the outcome is closer to 10 than 4+20. If, say, we attempted x=1, if we wandered past x=6, the signal of the difference has moved and we need the orientation to move up again, even if an error has increased to 5. Since there are different types of information, they can assist in solving an issue by trial and error: The quality or mistake of a solution provides us with an indication of how far we are from the best solution (which may be a minimum or a maximum). The fitness of two or more points is compared, and the signs of the difference are indicated to enhance our guessing of the route forward by graduating slope. A pitch is a multifaceted pitch. A programming language that can identify a gradient may travel in the direction of the peak. That information can be beneficial if the rise shows the slope of the peak is sufficiently good; nevertheless, it is occasionally only the pitch of a low cliff. Therefore, a method based on filtering algorithms can be fixed in a poor result [18].

2.3.3   Three Spaces of Optimization

Three linked number domains can be conceived of as optimization. The space parameter holds the permitted values of all arguments to be inserted in the test function. Since x is the one component in the following straightforward mathematical equation, the single-dimensional space parameter may be seen as a numerical line ranging between negative and positive endlessness, i.e., x lawful values. The most intriguing issues with optimization have increased the complexity of parameters, and the difficulty may be to play off numerical quantities. Sometimes inexpensive areas in the parameterization area are counterintuitive, contradictory, or nonsensical input data patterns.

A functional is a collection of arguments, and the space of the function includes the outcomes. For example, in instances of multi-objective optimization, the typical one-dimensional practical universe is a particular case because a new automobile might be evaluated concurrently with respect, for instance, to its price, attractiveness, performance, and security by assessing a multitude of components. Each of these metrics results from specific characteristics being combined; examples include color, aerodynamics design, chromium content, etc., in the judgment of attractiveness. The fitness area is one-dimensional; it consists of success levels, which allow parameter sequences to maximize values as quality or error in the functional area. The fitness is the value to proceed with the analogy, which decides if you purchase the automobile. You will have to integrate these capabilities into a single decision-making magnitude after assessing their price, appearance, energy, etc. You will more likely buy your automobile if it is significant. Each point of the space variable maps the interactive application because it then maps the performance area up to an end. In many situations, a characteristic may be mapped to the fitness area immediately from the universe, i.e., the fitness degree related to each characteristic pattern can be calculated directly. If one central communication result is maximized, the fitness area and the functionality environment are the same; they may be vice versa in function minimization. Wellness and effect produced are typically handled the same, but the differentiation is often helpful. The optimization should involve finding maximum fitness characteristics.

2.3.4   High-Dimensional Cognitive Space and Word Meanings

It may seem strange that we have departed from the intriguing subjects of mind and civilization to a mathematical discussion of everything. Before examining this subject more deeply, let us provide an example as to why we think it is a question of optimizing complicated functions.

The development of computer techniques, which can identify the meanings of words, has been one of the fascinating breakthroughs in knowledge science in the last decade. Two sets of researchers have devised distinct techniques to determine the definition of a sentence from its environment statistically. In the 1950s, Osgood, Suci and Tannenbaum studied the narrative of the position of words and thoughts in a multidimensional feature space. Their approach, termed the memantine divergence, put a word on the top of a page and asked users to assess it over many scales. For example, the term may have been "radio," and individuals were asked to evaluate it on scales like chilly to hot, harsh to kind, etc. (see Figure 2.1). (The first revelation was that it was typically not very difficult for individuals to accomplish this.) The known effect happens when a person or thing is presumed to have another favorable attribute. In other words, evaluations of various sizes are usually correlated. The main component or analysis methods are used to identify these numerous relationships. Osgood and his collaborators explained that by utilizing these quantitative procedures, their research revealed three critical characteristics that most influenced the words and ideas. According to them, the most essential aspect by far was called the "assessment." People rank things as excellent vs. poor according to their likes and dislikes, and their views on other elements follow these assessment ratings. Two other perpendicular elements were considered essential but not as crucial as the assessment, which they referred to as "power" and "activities." In the 90s, the study was

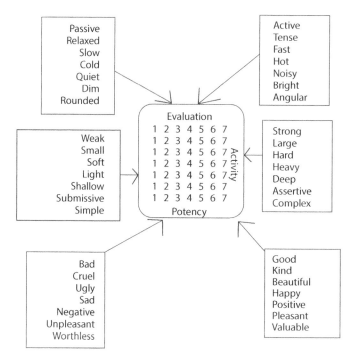

Figure 2.1 Optimizing cognitive function.

re-examined and expanded by academics from the University of Colorado and the University of California, Riverside. At first, they noticed an inherent unfairness in selecting target phrases and structured observations out of the blue. For example, the scientists' selections for rating scales might be impacted by their very own precepts. The researchers decided to try something basic. They wrote a great deal, termed a corpus, and examined the professional and non-professional terms therein. If you've read Internet news, you know there's lots of text and a handful of assumptions. Usenet is a series of Internet-based group discussions; nobody knows how many there actually are, although there are indeed over 30,000 separate groups, many of which are pretty busy with members who write and post to each other's posts, who respond to each other and who answer the answers. Again, if you've ever visited Usenet you will understand that it's not the place where you will find the King's Language being used. There is much slang and, yes, darkness, with flaming battles and other digressions mingled with the flamenco discourse of love and programming and philosophies and animal care. Their program called "Hyperspace Analog to Language," acquired 300 million words of Usenet conversations for analysis.

Their software spanned the whole corpus, examining each word utilizing a "window" on one side of its ten closest neighbors. A matrix included each word as rows or column headers (around 170,000 different words) in the whole corpus. When a word came right before the destination, the next column included a 10 in the target word line. A comment three characters ahead of a target had a 9 in a row corresponding to the word sequence, etc., appended to its column. In the word paragraphs, they were beginning to follow the word correctly. The matrix, therefore, included large numbers in the cells determined by the rows or columns of words most frequently used and small numbers for pairs of words, which did not commonly occur in Usenet conversations.

It was exceedingly unusual to delete words that occurred. This technique resulted in a matrix of 70,000 to 70,000—still too large for usage. Burgess and Lund combined the columns vectors of talks with the row vectors such that the whole set of correlation intensities of words preceded it, and each word observed those which followed it in the collection. Some of the phrases were not words; they appear in a standard computer vocabulary; additionally, there was minimal variation in specific terms, and little research contributed to them. By eliminating small columns, the researchers determined that the matrices for each of the 70,000 words could be cut to the highest 200 columns.

A sharp difference of two words implies that they are commonly linked to the same terms: incomparable contexts they are utilized in. When

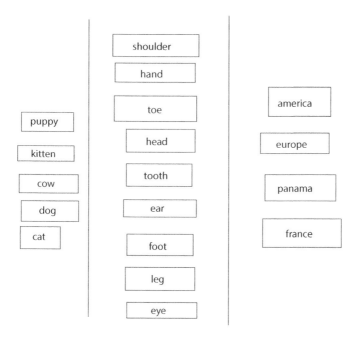

Figure 2.2 Multidimensional scaling analyses.

Gibbons and his colleagues painted two-dimensional subsets of phrases using a multivariate scale method, they saw that those words comparable in significance were close to each other in the semantical space (see Figure 2.2).

2.4   The Social Organism

Although human phenomenology tends to enhance the contributions of the individual, behavior and performance may be seen through many "zoom angles" and reference frames, which can give insights into and clarify mental life and cognition. These viewpoints extend from the minuscule to the cosmic and take into account life genesis, continental ecological processes, and the development of social behavior. Contemporary thinkers have often tested the effects of these varied zoom degrees on computer models, automation, and other design projects, and we comment on some of these experiences. The development of such models gives the Global Optimization Paradigm detailed later in quantity an essential background [19].

2.4.1 Flocks, Herds, Schools and Swarms: Social Behavior as Optimization

Mutagenesis and reproduction, together with selection and perhaps self-organization (covered in a later chapter), enable the development of optimal environments in challenging areas. Genetic mutation and combination are crucial if population variety or originality is introduced and alternative treatments are selected over time. More than one human nature observer has claimed that creativity demands some mutagenesis, some means of creating new answers at randomness. For example, the psychologist Donald Campbell (1960) defined cognition skills concerning "blind change and observational learning" and claimed that mental innovation might be comparable to biological evaluation of alternatives.

Learning by trial and error must involve creating new solutions. Spontaneous behavior production in the animal world is omnipresent. All of these factors suggest that the capacity to create unexpected, random actions is an animal adaptation, due to the chaotic activity of a caught fish, the head shake of a dog playing tug-of-war, the bucking of a broncho or a bull, or the zigzagging of a hunted rabbit by a meadow. A randomized experiment is essential for avoiding predators and is suitable for an organism looking for food, a mate, a place to build a nest, or a safe refuge. Konrad Lorenz (1973) highlighted the relevance of random fluctuations in creature search movements and escaping risk in an intelligent paper entitled "Modulation and Perturbations as Cognition Capabilities." For instance, (he adds) the sea bird waves its long urinary catheter to detect the

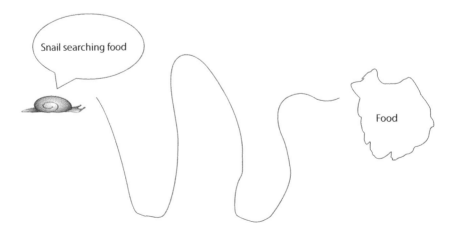

Figure 2.3 Snail moving toward a searched for target.

fragrance of something to be eaten, moving indiscriminately from across the water [43]. The snail senses the variations in the intensity of ascent at the two ends of the movements of the respirator tube. Such disparities are most significant if the snail is rotated to the perfect distance, such that the food is on either side. But rather than turning straight towards the stimulation, the snail performs a quick revolution similar to an exhaust reaction, which continues to crack so that the scent strikes the receptors on the opposite side. Consequently, the snail continues its objective on the repeated zigzag course (see Figure 2.3). Lorenz relates the typical marine snail hunt to individual opinion variations.

2.4.2   Accomplishments of the Social Insects

In insect research and especially social insect behavior, the optimization potentials of simple behavior have been particularly emphasized. An insect may have just a few thousand mental faculties, but insect organizations can achieve architectural wonders, sophisticated systems of communication, and have remarkable resilience to natural dangers.

After hearing the lectures of Konrad Lorenz at Harvard University, E.O. Wilson began a systematic study of the social behavior of ants in 1953. Lorenz is perhaps primarily remembered as the scientist who revealed the phenomena of animal "pair bonding"; newborn birds develop an attachment to a mother and follow her all around. Some of Lorenz's renowned pictures show a line of joyful fledglings who took him as their mommy. Lorenz had the impression that this is a kind of instinctive behavior which data calls a fixed sequence of activity. An organism's response to the initial, typically exact stimuli, is a set action sequence. For example, in the summertime, singing, posturing and fighting other males are behaviors a male western robin uses to establish his territory. The specific behavior stimuli for these actions have been demonstrated to be the crimson breast. The male will disregard it if a cutout of a bird with an emerald green breast is placed next to the nest; however, a whole range of territorial threats arises from tufted red feathers placed on a wireframe [20].

Wilson speculated that the blinding achievements of ant civilizations could be made clear. He acknowledged that fixed repeated actions, which included the top pheromone behavioral response to compounds that have a certain kind of odor, could have been detected. In addition to the descriptors from Lorenz's characterization of the fixed structures of actions, Wilson demonstrated that ants release certain hormones and characterized the compounds and emitting glands. He also determined the reactions to each of the many pheromones with much effort. He observed that hormones constitute a means of communication between ants that enables the cooperation of a predetermined activity, resulting in collective adaptive behavior where individuality does not exist.

For Wilson, the critical issue in insect evolutionary biology was the question of building mass behaviors from the actions of single ants. Given that a single ant's behavior is distributed unequally and tends to stochastically go along routes trampled by other ants, it is astonishing what the swarming of ants accomplishes. A solitary ant's action leads to the individual's swift death, while the mass behavior of an ant settlement supplies the overall population with nourishment and defense.

The study of complicated systems and the development of virtual environment software models of these structures have provided scientists with the necessary tools to shape simple ant colonies which can interact to form an influence far greater than the sum of its parts. These words of wisdom have led to a greater understanding of the nature of individuals and society and the natural universe. Insect sociality is a famous important part of international consequences resulting from dynamic interplay.

2.4.3 Optimizing with Simulated Ants: Computational Swarm Intelligence

How to optimize the bicycle messenger issue using basic hormone behavior was revealed.

The "ant optimization of the colony" is founded on the fact that ants take the shortest way to get their nest away from candy on a summertime pavement. They leave pheromone tracks that fade over distance and time as the ants travel about. There are strong pheromones at a place where, for example, a traveling ant has just crossed the site with more ants or when more ants have crossed the area with more ants. Ants following neighboring nodes tend to be assembled because with each new ant following the route, concentration of the pheromones rises as shown in Figure 2.4.

It believed that ants wandering from nest to nest to sweets and back return faster and pass the same places more regularly while taking a quicker route. They will give a thicker pheromone path more frequently. As more ants use the reinforced course, it is improved more and more. By adopting these characteristics to your computer, a community of the "anti-salespeople" seeks quantum mechanics for the traveling salespeople map, enhancing the chance of connecting two cities depending on the number of other simulation ants currently pursuing that connection. This method may tackle complicated nonlinear equations by utilizing the positive responses

Figure 2.4 Ants find the shortest path to food.

mechanism, i.e., reinforcing the trail with every subsequent ant, to discover a solution to complete one of the fewest tasks.

Mathematical equations of swarm and collective intellectual ability dynamics were created at the Santa Fe Institute and Los Alamos National Laboratory based on a straightforward ant's pheromones detection. Investigation with live ants showed that when food was put some distance from the nest and two uniform pathways travel to the nest, the swarm ends on the shortest path.

If a shorter way is provided, however, they cannot switch to it if, for example, an impediment has been eliminated. The ants will pick one or the other if both pathways are of similar length. If two natural habitats, one richer than the other, are provided, a swarm of ants will pick an excellent experience. If, after the selection, a more prosperous component is supplied, most species cannot switch for trust reasons, but other species may modify their pattern. If two identical sources are available, an ant will randomly select one or the other.

Like parallels the network of communications between ants to the highly linked neuronal architecture of the brain. Both instances may be described in terms of three features:

- Their structure includes a collection of nodes and links.
- They dynamically modify the status of the node variables.
- The strengths of the links between the nodes are modified.

2.5   Evolutionary Computation Theory and Paradigms

We discussed consciousness and development, which are regarded as the two main natural stochastic models. These four leading algorithms have given some of the fascinating problems in the history of computer science as if to validate Bateson's statement. Naturally, the goal of the machine intelligence organization is to model knowledge processes in the mind. It was an enormous challenge to model the complex adaptation mechanisms of biological development. The many evolutionary computing paradigms give insight into nature's tools and provide a toolkit for architects and others who need to resolve exceedingly difficult issues, frequently unspecified.

In many instances, evolutionary programming concepts are closely linked with the swarming methodologies at the center of this chapter. This chapter examines the area of developmental calculation in some detail, including artificial intelligence and categorization frameworks approximately based on evolution, such as physiological genetics, selective breeding, and emerging adaptive behavior. Evolutionary computing paradigms offer tools to create intelligent systems which simulate innovative behavior.

2.5.1   The Four Areas of Evolutionary Computation

Many organizations have proposed the use of evolutionary computation in four areas:

1) Genetic Algorithm

Anthropologists utilized computers to model genetic modification systems to carry out the creation of simulated annealing in the 1950s. One of those who did these simulations was the Australian, Alex S. Fraser. He started writing on this subject in the late 1950s and was intimately connected with our present notions of simulated annealing. Thus, our evolutionary calculation history (arbitrarily) begins with him. Fraser worked in the epistemic field (repression of the impact of a gene), and each of the three epistatic system parameters was made up of a 5-bit string of the 15-bit length. He then chose the lines with variable values that generated function values between -1 and +1 to pick the fathers. Fraser worked with ecological systems. While his work resembled the improvement of functions presently performed by genetic algorithms, he had no consideration of the possibility of using his technique for computational agents. At the individual level, the GA metaphor is a genetic heritage. An individual's chromosomes, or the pattern of genetic alleles, are viewed as a specific task, and low-level activities such as those in the nucleus of cells are offered to generate new solutions. Chromosomes consist of twisted DNA strands of adenine, cytosine, guanine, and thymine proteins. The DNA sequences include instructions on how and what to develop, which are now considered computer software that offers education for the cells you are composed with. While modern computer systems encode programs and data using a two-base or binary numbering system, chromosomal domains employ a four-based approach represented in the kinase domain order. Generally, genetic algorithms use two sets of chromosomes. However, Fraser and his supporters may utilize methods created for any group of raw numbers, including precision floating-point decimal. Starting in the 1960s, Dutch students frequently employed their techniques for selection, crossover, and mutagenesis. In his doctorate, J.D. Bagley (1967) coined the phrase "genetic algorithm" and then used evolutionary systems to determine system dimensions for the hexpawn in actual gameplay, which is played on a 3×3 chessboard, with each player beginning with three bishops. The genetic algorithm of Bagley was similar to the many now employed with crossover, selection, and mutations.

2) Evolutionary Programming

Darwinian computing utilizes the fittest, but since there are no crossovers, mutations are the only structurally modifiable operation permitted. Fogel and his collaborators, who were primarily interested in artificial intelligence, experimented with finite state machines, and solved some issues that were extremely tough for simulated annealing. Fogel (1994) characterized evolution computing as having an approach diverse and complicated to genetic algorithms. The technique summarizes the development as a top-down appropriate assessment process rather than a bottom-up artificial immune method. It is more suitable since natural selection does not occur in isolation on different pieces but rather on the entire collection of organisms' manifested behaviors due to their interactions with the world. Two critical extensions have been added to generate continuous parameters and personality since the initial evolution computing was first developed. (Evolutionary programming's first version operated with discrete parameters only.) The integration of self-adaptation permits the development of the strategic criteria which govern the change.

3) Evolution Strategies

Currently, we're trying to discover an ideal physical arrangement in a wind turbine and a liquid-supporting tube all across the ocean. The standard approaches for gradient descent have not solved the set of the wind impedance equation. An experimented with mutagenesis, which disturbed their best solution for random searches in the neighboring problem areas. Rechenberg and Schwefel simulated a technique called evolution strategies in its original iteration. The first computer can be accessed at the Illinois Institute of Technology. Rechenberg wrote a book regarded as the cornerstone of this method in the early 70s, and evolutionary strategy continues to be crucial, particularly for Europeans. In Germany and the Western Hemisphere, research advancements continued in tandem, with one group ignoring the findings of the other until the 1980s, even though they might have known each other.

4) Genetic Programming

Systems biology is the fourth most significant field of adaptive calculation (although, as previously mentioned, others regard it to be a subset of genetic algorithms). Computing courses are designed directly in biological evolution. Some of the first associated works of Friedberg (1958) and Friedberg, Dunham, and North (1959) dealt with software applications having a fixed length program written by another initiative to maximize the performance of information format. They each had 64 instruction sets, called "Herman" and "Ramsey," and each operation was 14 bits long. The algorithms have been defined so that any 14-bit scheme is a valid command and every package of 64 instructions is a legitimate one. The outcomes of their efforts, however, failed to meet expectations. In retrospect, three primary explanations were probably found for this. First, the program was limited to 64 commands: if the program was not adequately terminated after the 64th instruction, the "failure" was determined (even if there was a loop). Second, just one software had been developed, and hence only one population had emerged. Third, the usage of the fitness value is not apparent. Stanford's John Koza (yet another Holland student) created genetic programming in its present version toward the end of the 1980s that effectively addressed these constraints. Although the other three techniques for evolutionary calculation employ string chromosomal in a population of trees, Koza developed software programs. Lisp symbolism formulations, which are developing mechanisms, were utilized for crossover.

Mr. Koza has been a developer of one of the most fast growing and intriguing combinatorial optimization fields for documenting, including books and genetically programmed videotapes. The notion of developing software programs has already become a reality for generations.

2.5.2   Evolutionary Computation Overview

- In principle, evolutionary computation (EC) paradigms are differentiated in three key ways, with the help of a community of points (possible solutions) from the classic search and optimization paradigm.
- They directly utilize information based on "fitness" rather than derivatives of functions or another relevant knowledge.
- They use transitional rules that are more opportunistic than prescriptive.

Moreover, EC implementations frequently encode binary or other parameter representations instead of using parameters themselves. We now look further at these distinctions and see how optimization algorithms may be used.

2.5.3   Evolutionary Computing Technologies

Not with standing the paradigm used, evolutionary computing technologies typically follow the same procedure:

1) Initialize the population;
2) Calculate the fitness for every person in the population;
3) Reproduce a fresh population of specific participants;
4) Carry out evolutionary procedures on the organism, such as crossover and mutation;
5) Loop to step 2 until certain conditions are fulfilled.

Setting the population at random values is the most frequent way of initialization. This means only producing the random strings of the one and zero strings (with probability proportional for each value) for the fixed-length previously mentioned if the parameters are represented using binary strings. (While most optimization techniques employ fixed population length, biological systems also develop the structure of the general population, including the size of each individual.) People with prospective values reasonably near to the optimum in a hyper-special region, can occasionally be seeded.

The overall number of people selected to compose the population depends on the topic and paradigm but is generally between a few dozen and a few hundred. Fitness comes equipped with the resulting value of the optimized function; optimization may also be calculated from several function outputs combined. The fitness (evaluation) system accepts one or more functional outputs as its input and results in some reproductive probability. To obtain a suitable fitness metric, it is often required to modify the function performances. The algorithm requires just a tiny proportion of the computing time; most of the calculation time is used to evaluate the fitness.

A new population (also referred to as a younger breed) is generally determined based on fitness metrics. The better the fitness, the more probable it is for the future generation to be chosen. However, some of the paradigms, such as artificial neural networks, are considered adaptive and can hold all population members from time to time. In a Bentley (1999) population, members preference for confident parents instead of others is not required for development. (If there is no operator of the selection, then all community segments generate equally likely offspring) The end of the algorithm generally depends on a population individual with a specific fitness or the process running for a certain number of generations. In many, if not most, instances, an optimal global exists at some point in the spacetime of choice. In addition, stochastic or chaotic noise can occur. Sometimes, the maximum quality varies dynamically; local optima is usually extremely good. For these reasons and other considerations, it is generally unrealistic to expect any objective function to achieve (even when it exists) a global optimum in a limited time.

2.6   Humans – Actual, Imagined, and Implied

Since minds cannot be viewed directly, the sensation of considering an emotion can be expressed only in metaphorical terms, and individuals have utilized symbols for this. Individuals throughout history have tried to explain their cognitive processes. At various periods of time the mind has been widely imagined as working with humor, deity interference, the activities of stars and related earthly things, demonic possession, and the pneumatic and hydraulic activities of glands and other physical laws during the last few millennia. The metaphors used to explain mental functionalities prescribe proper functions and therefore co-construct the paradigm and its reference. The prevalent description is that the conscious mind is like a computer algorithm and that the neurons are like technology. While the beginning of this now widespread notion is not a particular moment, it was thought feasible in the 1950s with the emergence of probability theory. By proposing that information might be mathematically conceived as a type of reverse function of probabilities, Charles Babbage (1948) changed contemporary thinking, including no technologies. The question is how the understanding depends on the possibility of things. If information depends on the probability of different events, reflection may somehow be described as pattern recognition. Claude Shannon conducted intriguing and highly valued experimentation on communication and showed how the information from our surroundings is extracted in computations. He was interested in the alphabet's characteristics as utilized in English. Shannon took a database of the probability of letters being written in an English language and created specific random text by choosing letters in a stochastic way, as detailed in his article "A Mathematical Theory of Communication," published in the 1958 volume of *The Bell System Technical Journal*. He documented the letter he discovered there and then proceeded to a random article in the volume to run his finger down the comments until he located the letter. He was able to go to a blank location in the book. Then he grabbed the next letter and went to another empty place and searched for the letter, etc.

2.6.1 The Fall of the Behaviorist Empire

At least in the USA, serious academic psychiatrists studied the mind for most of the twentieth century. In the 1920s, the behavioral impact was significant and pervasive, and "the ghost in the machine" was discussed. The behavior of the early twentieth century was logical positivism, which stated that research could only create events that could be seen. It was apparent that nothing could immediately be observed in the mental health field; consequently, thought was not a list of essential study subjects. The one element that could be seen was a creatures' behavior; and so psychiatry, whose name comes from the ancient Greek soul deity Psyche, was called the study of open conduct. During bachelor's degree psychological training, lectures from instructors derided ideas such as mind and awareness ("Show me mind!"), as it is not observable and hence unworthy of scientific research. Most behavioral genetics were carried out, particularly on rats and pigeons, while human conclusions were made based on great limitless possibilities. One such generalization was Skinner's interpretation of language, and its spectacular thrashing was partially attributed to the demise of the behaviorist monarchy.

The two streams of conduct doctrine accurately mirrored the polarization that prospered during the Cold War. The traditional Russian paradigm, which originated in the laboratory of Pavlov, concentrated on the organism's response to glands and smooth muscles. An animal's response is visceral, and activated by the autonomous nervous system, whether faced with an unconditional stimulus like the scent of food or the appearance of danger. The Pavlovian examples of glandular reactions, such as salivation, increased cardiac rate, suddenness, etc., are all traditional responses. When a new stimulus is frequently combined with one that causes an answer, it will also be generated by that conditioned activity. Hence, classical and operant conditioning considers the organization to react quietly to environmental events; stimulus that preceded it "drink the organism's behavior." (It is worth noting that all behaviors have been characterized as "responses," removing curiosity, playfulness, and other behaviors.) On the other hand, in the United States, behaviors prioritized functional programming in which the creature works to strengthen the surroundings. The body here is pushed in the direction of a behavioral input. The operating behavior employs striated musculature, which moves the skeletons, which are loose motions or activities of the body. After Watson, Hull, and Richardson, the American idea of behavior was like a commercial business, where animals of all types did whatever was needed for the all-powerful enhancer. American lifestyle commonalities throughout the 20th century were mirrored in the common usage of the term race to characterize everyday life.

Behaviorism was, in many respects, a Behaviorism 19th-century introspective psychology. Although the ancient psychiatrists found several essential truths about how the mind worked, their techniques were susceptible to mistakes. Trained watchers noted their feelings and recorded them as thoroughly and accurately as possible in Wilhelm Wundt's laboratory set up in 1879.

Working as both experimenter and subject, Hermann Ebbinghaus pioneered the study of memory upon which his whole hypothesis was constructed. Alternatively, the single-subject research approach was not suitable to identify hidden, universal, and individual processes. His persistence in attaining results contributed to memory and learning literature.

The relevance of observational science in psychological studies was highlighted by behavioralists (which also depended on single-subject research methods). Comportments were operationally defined and thoroughly recorded. The behavioralists constructed sophisticated formulae from these data, which relate stimuli to reactions. Although the behaviorist approach has just fallen out of the conceptual environment, we may credit that paradigm for holding up the procedural grindstone with empirical psychology. The conductors did not employ complex measuring methods, inferential statistics, or observational studies themselves but set a high bar for empiricism that still influences researchers today.

Even as health informatics grew in other university disciplines, behavioral orthodoxy endured. Councils may be persuaded to strive for reinforcements constantly; if you've taken water from them for an extended period, they could do practically anything for a drink. Behaviorism fits in exceptionally well with the viewpoint of the times. It provides academics with an autonomous philosophy, which demands a minimal explanation. It has taken everything except stimuli and answers from the debate to reduce behavior to several essential factors.

2.7   Thinking is Social

There is a popular narrative of blind men and an elephant based on a parable that originated in the ancient Indian subcontinent; the problem with it is that it is supposed to be deaf. The parable, as retold in the poem written by John Godfrey Saxe in the in the mid-nineteenth century, depicts the experiences of six blind men who go to see an elephant but the complete elephant resembled that particular portion each of the men happened to encounter by chance: The first man approached the elephant and fell against its broad, sturdy side: "God bless me! – but the Elephant is very like a wall!" The second man feels the tusk and shouts "Ho! – what have we here, So very round and smooth and sharp? To me 'tis mighty clear, this wonder of an Elephant is very like a spear!" and so on. Of course, the moral of the narrative is that people are not convinced of their inadequate knowledge of the world. Suppose several blindfolded men took turns and announced a presentation of their specific element of the elephant. In that case, it is evident that hearing each other means that all the blind men would grasp the various features of the elephant quite fully and correctly. All the group should know that the monster has a wall-like side, tusks like spears, legs like a tree, etc. They might even understand how the pieces are linked and how they work together during the conversation. The objective of this creative criticism is that communities can share the incomplete understanding of people that leads to a corpus of facts and tactics far beyond what a single person could have learned individually.

The subject of this chapter is that thought is a group activity; human culture and understanding are facets of one process. Not just information but strategies for interpreting these things are learned among people. The topic is not new: Bandura has, for one, hypothesized clearly on the acquisition of one person's behavior.

2.7.1 Adaptation on Three Levels

Not only does it teach about the importance of each other, but the community converges to optimize procedures as information and abilities pass from one individual to the next. This subsection depicts a system that functions on three levels concurrently:

- People learn regionally. People are aware that they engage with their neighbors and that they adopt origin insights and, in turn, share their views; local socialization is easy to quantify and record.
- Diffusion of information via social learning leads to emerging groups. People in a population experience this social, political, or economic level of phenomena as constants in beliefs, attitude, behavior, and other qualities. A social system of self-organization has global characteristics that cannot be anticipated by the people that make up it.
- Culture enables cognition to be optimized. While all contacts are local, ideas and innovations are transmitted from culture to remote people; the synthesis of various inventions leads to even better techniques. This significant impact is usually evident for system operators who profit from it.

2.8 Conclusion

We need to seek innovative and inventive solutions to predicted challenges in managing these SI systems by expanding telecommunications and networking technologies. To use the SI paradigms successfully, specific structures are needed to construct the appropriate theory and then conduct research towards practical application. This chapter studied three parts of a meta-formalism to build a more comprehensive and academically sound framework for analysis to investigate SI further. The three meta-formal parts are 1) a set of basic concepts based on natural laws, 2) a dynamic environment, and 3) a framework of problems. Scientific processes are linked to evolutionary theory and the consequences of survival of the fittest. Evolution theory justifies the description of efficient behavior in the colony of social insects. This efficiency may be identified and linked to Pareto optima analytically. Thus, the autonomous behavior typically connected with SI may be represented in operational locations along the Pareto optimum border as a parameterization. A cross-border operation also defines behavioral responses, one of the characteristics of SI, using mathematics. The complex structure ultimately offers a recital for the abstraction of the problem and supplies the modeling clay used to mold SI research to conform to the first two main components of formality. The problematic application provides swarm state-controlled machinery models to represent a complexity continuum seen in the SI displayed by various animals. Finally, the author hopes that this meta-formalism concepts make fundamental research easier by utilizing SI. In many fields of study, complex systems theory can be applied. Enhancing the efficiency, scalability, and autonomy of these increasingly complex systems helps to assure their successful future performance.

3

The Particle Swarm and Collective Intelligence

Abstract

Social philosophy has typically concentrated on processes that are thought to be individually internal or personal, while the social world is often seen as an "environmental" element. A recent cross-cultural psychology study demonstrates basic variations in how cognition works in persons from other cultures. This shows that the social surroundings influence and contribute to generating thought. The researchers who explore ways of obtaining intelligent behavior from robots are continually turning to new models to analyze individuals intimately intertwined with the social environment. These new models diverge dramatically from classic AIs, which approach cognition as a collection of processes in an isolated brain. This chapter will address this dichotomy regarding the particle swarm optimization algorithm, the model of cooperatively connected intelligence. Improvements of the particle swarm paradigms in terms of lifestyle and cognitive interactions will be defined.

Keywords: Collective intelligence, socio-cognitive, binary decision, parameter selection, IQ scale, cognitive, behavior model

3.1   The Particle Swarm and Collective Intelligence

This chapter presents the binary and exact numerical optimization algorithm. The book has thus far prepared the background, explaining relevant informatics and social scientific paradigms, talking about culture, norms and languages, and other advancements in science and philosophy, which, if successful, would make the search space appear apparent.

The Adaptive Cultural Model for which the simplest possible interactions with the simplest conceivable agents can lead to what can happen if they are even termed "agents." Due to a wide range of options, people can often find multivariate alternative structures that solve issues through a type of social contact that has been removed. It should be emphasized that

Kuldeep Singh Kaswan, Jagjit Singh Dhatterwal and Avadhesh Kumar. *Swarm Intelligence: An Approach from Natural to Artificial*, (65–88) © 2023 Scrivener Publishing LLC

people do not strive to resolve problems in the cultural model. They obey the fundamental algorithm rules, which do not tell you anything about the presence or fix a problem. But each person increases their "fitness" via reciprocating social impact, the term being less suitable here than when discussing evolutionary algorithms, and the community performs better. We wouldn't argue that the adaptive culture algorithm is a powerful means of solving issues but an excellent introduction to sociological computations. However, in terms of linguistic and academic conduct, the particle swarm algorithm is extensively employed in computer science and engineering as a problem-solving approach. The original version of the optimization algorithm here was meant to function in a binary solution space. Along with addressing binary issue encoding, later in the chapter, we will present the most often used variant that works in actual quantities [21].

3.1.1   Socio-Cognitive Underpinnings: Evaluate, Compare, and Imitate

The Adaptive Cultural Model with Particle Swarms is a relatively simple socio-cognitive hypothesis. This process of adapting cultures contains a high-level element, which can be observed in developing individual characteristics and solutions to handle issues. A low-level feature is the current and likely universal behavior of humans.

- Appraise: Perhaps the most widespread behavioral feature of living beings is the ability to assess stimuli—to rank them as pleasant and unpleasant, appealing and repellent. Even if the surroundings are not harmful, the bacteria run and collapse. Appreciating the characteristics of the surroundings that attract and the factors that repel them, identifying good from evil cannot be learned until the organisms can assess it. Learning may also be described as a change that will allow the organization to enhance the average environmental assessment [22].
- Compare: Festinger's idea of cultural comparisons (1954) has outlined several ways in which individuals use other individuals as standards to evaluate themselves and how similarities with others may act as motivators for learning and changing. In the original version, Festinger's theory was not expressed in a readily verified or refuted fashion, and a few of the current theory statements were not validated.

Still, they were usually used as a foundation for future social psychology theories. In almost anything we think and do, whether assessing our looks, wealth, humor, or intellectual ability (note that a median number of people is a piece of digital information and its assets according to the IQ scales; that is, your scoring system tells you how you compare with others—which is the whole point, isn't it?). We evaluate ourselves through comparative analysis to others *or* different views and ability characteristics. Persons in the Evolutionary Culture Model—and optimization algorithm—critically evaluate themself with neighbors and only copy their superior neighbors. They compare themselves with others to determine norms for social behaviors.

- Imitate: Imitation is a highly efficient technique to learn how to perform things. You would assume that emulation is ubiquitous. However, as Lorenz mentioned, very few creatures can imitate others; actually, he claims it can only be done by humanity and a few birds. There are differences in social learning among many other creatures, but none compare to the ability of humans to imitate one another. While "monkey see, monkey do" aptly defines our cousins' imitative conduct, human imitation consists of absorbing the other person's views, not just mimicking a behavior but fulfilling its goal and carrying out its action when appropriate. In The Cultural Origins of Human Cognition, Michael Tomasello argues that social learning of several kinds occurs in chimpanzees, but true imitation learning, if it occurs at all, is rare. For example, a person can draw awareness to an object while using it as a tool; This second person may utilize the same thing, but otherwise. True imitation is essential to human sociality and fundamental to gaining and maintaining mental capacity.

Even in oversimplified human groups like software programs, the three concepts of evaluation, comparison, and imitation may be used to adapt them to critical environmental obstacles and to solve exceedingly difficult tasks. From a cognitive standpoint, our perspective is that there is nothing other than assessment, comparison, and copying in the individuals; the mind is not located on the inside of the person in hidden secret compartments, but it exists openly; it is a public phenomenon.

3.1.2 A Model of Binary Decision

Take a naked person, an elemental creature, a series of decisions to be made, yes/no or true/false, binary choices, but highly nuanced ones, where it is difficult to discern which alternatives you can choose. This super-simplified person can either be in one condition or the other concerning the yes states we depict with one or the no=0 state for each decision. It visits many places that do not want to decide. Do I have to say yes? Do I have to say no? All of them desire to choose the best alternative [23].

These primitive creatures have two essential types of knowledge accessible. The first of them is their very own knowledge; they have attempted options, and they recognize the better position thus far and how nice it has been. They know. However, these social entities have a second concern; they understand how others are accomplished. Indeed, they're so essential that all they know is the most favorable decisions their neighbors have made to date and the most excellent option pattern. They understand how they have done, if these scrubbed entities are like humans, by seeing them and discussing their encounters with individuals. Both of these forms of knowledge reflect the cognitive and cultural transmission of Boyd and Richerson. The likelihood of the person choosing "yes" for each of the options depends on how effective the "yes" choice was concerning "no" in the past. Although there is no definite rule in humans, social influence also impacts choice. Social theory of effect argues that the unilateral selections of the particular tend to agree with, weighed by intensity and closeness, the view representing the majority. Yet, given the uncertainty of power and intimacy, that criterion is pretty ambiguous.

In the current introduction concept, we will mention that the most successful persons in their sociometric neighborhood have been affected by the best successes of any associated persons. Although we accept that this task is too easy, it has a grain of truth that warrants the parsimony it carries with it. One of the two simple sociometric concepts is used to implement most particle swarms. The first, best known one, theoretically ties all the people to each other. This results in every particle being affected by every individual of the whole population's most excellent efficiency. The next one is the best-known neighborhood of each individual (and 1 stands for the worldwide and locally), which comprises oneself and its nearest neighbors. For example, if k=2, the optimal performance between a group composed of particles−1, I, and i+1 depends on each individual. Various geometries in the area could have somewhat significant consequences, except where indicated in Figure 3.1.

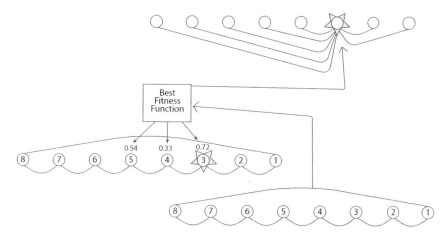

Figure 3.1 Good binary decision types of neighborhoods.

Otherwise, optimal neighborhoods with k=2 ("neighborhood=3") will assume the following talks. The individuals must make a variety of selections or judgments in a socio-cognitive example such that they all fit everything properly, which is called "thinking clearly" or "comprehension." Several binary options must be contemporary to be evaluated, compared, and imitated by the individual [24].

How can we enhance cognitive fitness? There are, of course, many hypotheses. In the planned behavior model of Ajzen and Fishbein (1980), the purpose is viewed because of two sorts of items that need now be made known (see Figure 3.2). On the one hand, the intention is influenced by the behavioral position of the individual; for example, when they consider violence terrible or immoral, they may be prepared not to behave aggressively. In the theory of planned behavior, these two aspects readily reflect the elements of Boyd and Richerson's culture of propagation; that is,

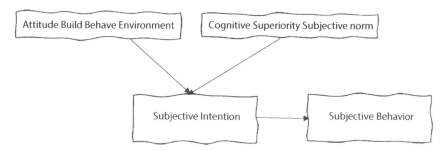

Figure 3.2 Intention and behavior model.

a single word (personal education or behavior) and a social term are used (cultural transmission or subjective norm). These two sorts of ideas are also prevalent in other concepts, and in our choice of model, they are given as the two terms to make up the storyline of transformation. We believe that the convergence of these two forms of knowledge, namely, information gained via sensory experiences in the environment and information gathered achieved through others, provides humans with a cognitive superiority and is the basis of our brilliance.

3.1.3   The Particle Swarm in Continuous Numbers

Ideas have progressed from a qualitative methodological, social optimization algorithm—the adaptive cultural model—to a qualitative data collection model—a binary nanoparticle swarm [25].

This section contains a simple numerical algorithm called the "actual" crossover operator. The particle swarm method looks optimum in a searching area that frequently is symbolic of the dimensional space of real numbers. (This is really searching in computer space, of course. And we use PCs, so warning about things like round-off mistakes is reasonable.) In actual numeric particulate swarm, the characteristics of a function can be visualized as a location in real-time space. Then, if we consider a study as a method of processing tasks by computer, any measure, such as a psychotherapist's MMPI, a public opinion survey, a risk-seeking inventory, a Myers-Briggs report, or a "What's Your Love-Q?" questionnaire in the back of *Cosmopolitan* magazine, will produce real numbers. It is usual to see system conditions as points in multidimensional space in industrial applications. Based on the circumstances, the dimensional space is known by many names; state space, stage space, and subspace are used to describe these concepts.

It's a short conceptual jump to believe that numerous persons may be displayed within a given possible destination, with the measurements on a gathering of participants producing a community of dots (see Figure 3.3). Individuals who are physically close to one another in space are comparable in the necessary measurements; if the test is legitimate, there may be fundamental similarities between them. We would anticipate locations in the same region with associated functional output and fitness if multiple vectors of mathematics system parameters were evaluated.

The challenge is to create rules that manipulate the particles in the direction you want so that tests are best allocated while looking for optimum results. The optimization algorithm method samples the search area by changing the velocity term.

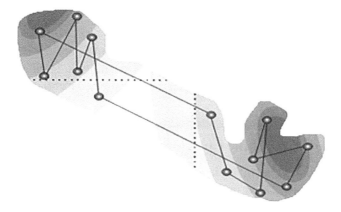

Figure 3.3 Search space topological neighbors.

3.1.4 Pseudocode for Particle Swarm Optimization in Continuous Numbers

In short, the optimization algorithm technique for actual numbers is nearly the same as the binaries, other than that the accompanying pseudocode shows motion increases rather than plausibility:

```
Loop
    For i = 1 to number of individuals
        if G(x̄ᵢ) > G(p̄ᵢ) then do              //G() evaluates fitness
            For d = 1 to dimensions

                pᵢd = xᵢd                       //pᵢd is best do far
            Next d
        End do


        g = i                                   //arbitrary
        For j = indexes of neighbors
            If G(p̄ⱼ) > G(p̄g) then g = j         //g is index of best performer
                                                  in the neighborhood

        Next j
        For d = 1 to number of dimensions
            vᵢd (t) = vᵢd (t − 1) + φ₁ (pᵢd − xᵢd (t − 1)) + φ₂ (pgd − xᵢd (t − 1))
            vᵢd ∈ (−Vₘₐₓ, + Vₘₐₓ)
            xᵢd (t) = xᵢd (t − 1) + vᵢd (t)
        Next d
    Next i
Until criterion
```

3.2 Variations and Comparisons

Since its development in 1994, the particle-swarm hypothesis has undergone several changes. Several experts, mathematicians, engineers, physicists, microbiologists, and psychiatrists have examined it and experimented with it [26].

3.2.1 Variations of the Particle Swarm Paradigm

There has been a considerable amount of knowledge that provides a theoretical framework and guidance for implementations. The sound itself changes with a greater understanding of the algorithm. The theorists discuss the nature of the interacting components and the surprising development of programmers' serendipitous experiments and bugs. A discussion of some of the principal aspects of contemporary algorithm operation research is given below.

3.2.2 Parameter Selection

Many particular variables in the optimization algorithm may change the algorithm's look for space. The most significant are Vmax and which directly engage throughout the test in the beginning. Modification of these three features alone can, as will be seen, create unexpected changes in the structure's response. In addition to the explicit characteristics, if we considered the terms weighed by the formulae in their previous version by 1.0, the system may hold a combination of implied ones. We may, of course, modify these implied characteristics; for example, by assigning a phrase 0.0 weight or increasing its influence by a higher weight, we can erase the mark. The system may be subtly changed in this approach, and essential behavior can be controlled, such as concurrent and explosive. Changing the significance of different explicit and implicit factors may maximize the proposed algorithm's performance [27].

3.2.3 Vmax

The mechanism of the particle swarm changes the amount each component moves every repetition in each dimension. Velocity fluctuations are unpredictable, and an undesired outcome is that unchecked, the particle's path might spread over the issue area to more extensive cycles, ultimately drawing near to infinity. Something needs to be done to dampen the oscillations if the particle is to search.

3.2.4   Controlling the Explosion

The path of the non-random particles with some specific values of μ is fully cyclic, but it usually weaves back and forth with distinctive but not repeated values. If μl has a, but instead, the particle's track stretches into infinity, what can be performed here to regulate the detonation?

It examined the system of determinism is outlined by

$$\begin{cases} v_{t+1} = v_t + \varphi y_t \\ v_{t+1} = -v_t + (1-\varphi)y_t \end{cases}$$

where you = p–xt. Where are you? In terms of applied mathematics, this system may be updated. With such a portrayal

$$P_t = \begin{bmatrix} v_t \\ y_t \end{bmatrix}$$

3.2.5   Simplest Constriction

The lowest contraction parameter, Type 1″, demands that the coefficients be applied to both terms. The streamlined system describes this restriction approach:

$$\begin{cases} v(t) = \chi(v(t-1) + \varphi(p - x(t-1))) \\ x(t) = x(t-1) + v(t) \end{cases}$$

where ϕ must be greater than 4.0.

A straightforward method for calculating the values of restriction is:

$$\chi = \frac{2k}{\left| 2 - \varphi - \sqrt{\varphi^2 - 4\varphi} \right|}$$

The variable κ can range in $[0,1]$; a value of 1.0 works fine, as does a value of ϕ=4.1.

3.2.6 Neighborhood Topology

Human social contact happens within a group or colonial architecture frequently represented as a network of relationships between pairs of people by psychologists. Research since the 1940s has demonstrated that the organization of the social media platform is changed by communications within a group and eventually by its effectiveness. Particle swarms have relied, while alternative power institutions are conceivable, on many simple social institutions, particularly the development of individual people with their near surroundings and the engagement of all people with the most successful individual within the community. It has proven that persons with separated particle swarm work very poorly: the algorithm works because of the charged particles. Is there a better social particle structure? The solution to the issue is relevant for human organizations when the parallel between particle swarming and human activities is established [28].

3.2.7 Sociometric of the Particle Swarm

Nanoparticles were previously examined in two types of broad neighborhoods known as the best and greatest. In the finest community, each person is driven by every citizen to the most excellent solution. Therefore, this structure is like a fully linked social media platform; everyone may compare and imitate the most effective behavior of each other. The maximum enhancement of their direct neighbors in the topology population in the best network is influenced by every person — a regular ring bar. In one typical l best instance, k=2, its nearby neighbors impact the individuals. The selection of social structures was often an issue for each artistry, with little information helping the researcher adopt a method. The report shows that the best communities converge faster with the best people and are more likely to connect with local optima than the best neighborhoods. A trial was done with 20 people structured into circles (l best), with individuals linked solely to their near neighbors in the wheeled arrangement while in the circle, where one is attached to all the other people (see Figure 3.4). There was also a decent condition. Segments of the population that are far apart are independent of one another under the circle architecture, while neighbors are intimately linked. As a result, one section of the community may find a local maximum, whereas another segment finds separate optimality or continues to search. In this topology, attraction spreads from neighborhood to neighbor until, if an optimum is the best discovered by any section of the population, it ultimately draws all of the particles in; k=2 was used to define circles.

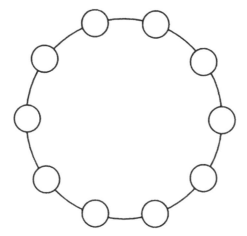

Figure 3.4 Circle cell interacts with k nearest neighbors.

Individuals are effectively isolated in the wheel architecture because all knowledge must be transmitted through the care recipients. This focal person analyses the performance and trajectories of all individuals within a population towards the best among them. If changes enhance the performance of the focuser, this performance is conveyed to the rest of the people. Thus, the focuser functions as a barrier or filter, reducing the speed with which excellent suggestions are sent through the populace. (It is worth noting that a very centralized wheel is a frequent design for many businesses and governmental bodies.)

The focal particle filtering function [29] is an attempt to maintain the many possible solutions to issues. Although it was predicted that the capacity of the populace to interact might be destroyed, it should avoid rapid convergence to local optima. Standardized test measures, including De Jong's f1 sphere, Griewank, Rastrigin, and Rosenbrock functions, were derived from evolution calculation literature. All functions have been constructed in 30 dimensions, and after 1000 iterations, the dependent variable utilized performed best on the data set. The populations of 20 persons with μ=4.1 were used in all the experiments using functions as shown in Table 3.1. Additional parameters in the research were adjusted; this chapter will solely report impacts on functionalities of the self-reported health structure.

Variance results reveal that the relationship between the neighborhood type and the performance was quite strong. Individuals were shown to perform better in three of these measures than the wheeled arrangement while

Table 3.1 Experimental functions.

Function	Formula
Sphere	$$f(x)^n + \sum_{i=0}^{n} x^2$$
Rosenbrock	$$f_1(x) = \sum_{i=1}^{n} \left(100(x_{i+T} \widetilde{x_i^{-2}}) + (x_i - 1)^2 \right)$$
Rastrigin	$$f_2(x) = \sum_{i=1}^{n} (x_i^v - 10cos(2\pi x_i) + 10)$$
Griewank	$$f_3(x) = \frac{1}{4000} \sum_{i=1}^{n} x_{t_{i-1}}^{2^n} cos\left(\frac{x_i}{\sqrt{i}} \right) + 1$$

in the circle. But the effectiveness with Rastrigin was quite the reverse, as the wheel topology showed higher results for Rastrigin communities.

3.2.8 Selection and Self-Organization

In particle swarm optimization, selection isn't usually a role. Singular mortality dictates the character of the next generations in evolutionary groups; whereas, in particle swarms, all inhabitants remain. The term "learning" is occasionally used to refer to evolutionary groups, as learning addresses a difficulty independently. However, learning is more commonly referred to as development in an individual through time.

Learning is the process of acquiring and retaining information. The term "adaptation" appears to be a better fit for evolving communities. A metaheuristic optimization simulates alterations in people over time rather than their elimination. The metaheuristic optimization method varies from all the other evolutionary computation (EC) applications described in this chapter in this crucial aspect. If you try to fit particle swarming into the creationist theory, you might claim that those change each iteration's nanoparticles from the next. In this approach, particle jamming is analogous to evolutionary computation in which each community member is modified to generate a (candidate) community member for the upcoming generations. In evolutionary programming (EP), like in an optimization algorithm, each item in the population has a distinct "ancestral" route through time. However, some individuals may leave no progeny, and others may live to the next generation accompanying their kids. There is a one-to-one correlation between people in one iterative process and those in the next within magnetic field swarms. As a result, EP lineages die out, which is impossible in a fitness function. Each parent generates one kid who substitutes it in the following generations in the (1,1)-ES method (rarely utilized in availability sampling but a viable alternative). This replacement method, like that used in nanoparticle swarming, may be compared to the (1+1)-ES, in which the survivor is either the kid or the parent (now considered to be a clone of the parent).

One significant distinction between particle swarming and standard convex optimization techniques is that particle velocities are changed when evolutionary individuals' locations are reversed; it's as if we were changing the "fate" rather than the "state" of cuckoo search for individual people.

The variation of the step, not its orientation, is optimized in EAs that self-adapt step sizes. Even if people were thought to endure through generations, talking about their "trajectory" in evolution are meaningless. The resemblance between component swarms and evolving techniques, notably EP and (1,1)-ES, would be much stronger if the gradient descent was set to 0.0 in the model above. The optimization algorithm acted just on position. The key distinctions are the unidirectional element of the "mutation," recurrent contact with the same neighbors, and the fact that EP and ES step sizes are developed in response to the fitness of the present characteristics. The velocities of the particle swarm are changed in relation to a previously found approximately optimum location. When selection is used, an explicit rate is impossible to achieve since it presupposes preserving an object's identity across time [30].

The primary subject is the differences and commonalities between evolution and social cognitive functions. If we look for analogies and parallels, we can see that vast particulate numbers use a kind of operator that combines the effects of mutation and crossover, as well as sharpness and functionality that is comparable to momentum—the particle's tendency to continue in the direction it was heading in the previous layer.

3.2.9   Ergodicity: Where Can It Go from Here?

Genetic algorithm (GA) chromosomes may potentially reach any position in the computational complexity through recombination. However, it's improbable, especially at the end of a run. Getting to a distant point will almost certainly need a sizeable somatic mutation. Because genetic mutations are generally low (0.1–1.0 percent), numerous generations of beneficial alterations may be required. When the community has consolidated and the general fitness value is sufficient near the end of a run, mutations will almost always result in low-fitness chromosomes that do not survive the selection procedure. As the centuries pass, the likelihood of survival drops exponentially. So, even though many mutations may put the chromosomes into a high-fitness area, they never do since they do not survive selection.

So, while a GA is conceptually ergodic (a chromosomal can inhabit any state with a nonzero likelihood), it is not stochastic in practice due to the many steps necessary. Because there is a limited chance an individual may reach any point in problem space with a single leap, a human evolutionary programming (EP) system is ergodic (in one generation). In this sense, optimization algorithm systems lie somewhere between GA and EP systems. It's feasible that a particle can't reach any location in problem space in a single iteration. However, this might happen throughout the run if the velocity is high enough. However, given enough repetitions and the right combination of parameters, any particle may finally move anyplace. As a result, particle swarms have a stronger case for ergodicity than GAs.

3.2.10   Convergence of Evolutionary Computation and Particle Swarms

Many of the modifications being tried using the proposed algorithm have a socio-cognitive or "persisting-individuals" element to them, as we explore the literature of contemporary evolutionary computation (EC) research. Various academics have used proposed algorithms to communicate with accessible populations, such as "group recollections." A subset of stronger people is permitted to remain throughout generations. We prefer to conceive of these collective-memory approaches as explanations on exclusivity in GA, which is a word for retaining the best-fit person from one generation to another. Effective issue solutions and representations can also be maintained for future contact with the general population using the site and population movements like the "virus" algorithm. Several separate scholars have devised techniques for preserving people through the centuries.

3.3   Implications and Speculations

This section describes the reasons presented thus far and offers some theoretical implications, including suggestions for future study and reflections regarding the work and its role in the scientific community. The particle swarm concept provides a framework for sociological practice and a set of tools for science and engineering; in this section, we start to think about this new study's conceptual and applied consequences.

Some issues that do not worry researchers in other disciplines hinder a scientific framework for thinking about the brain. The first issue is the well-known and extensively debated fact that brains are impenetrable. This was the justification for behaviorism's repudiation of mental objects, but it hasn't deterred other disciplines. Dinosaur feeding habits are unmeasurable; subatomic particles are unmeasurable; electricity is unknowable; gravity is unobservable—yet all of these are regarded as suitable study topics. Many scientific events are assumed numerically or quantitatively rather than seen; this is not a valid reason to dismiss them from scientific inquiry. More significantly, because we are thinking beings, studying minds is challenging. We have our thoughts to keep and defend, and we may not want to learn truths that compel us to change, that cause us to doubt our existence in the world, or contradict our notion of good and evil. Facts contradicting our Christian convictions, notably if those views are deeply held, are extremely dangerous. Furthermore, scientists have aspirations and ethical beliefs, and they, like anyone else, do not want to be shown to be wrong. For example, accepting that people are animals is one thing; following that idea to its rational conclusion that thousands might exterminate them is quite another when animals are undesirable, such as domestic animals, or when consumed, such as cattle and poultry. Why then should humans not be bred for food? Several of them have a lot of flesh on them. Even for researchers, it is difficult to think objectively about humans, and perhaps this example shows that this is a positive thing! However, this is precisely what must be done to "do science" on brains. Scientists must set aside their romantic notions about brains, sympathies, inclinations, and assumptions about humanity and, more importantly, what it should be, and observe objectively. The "ought to be" should not overshadow the "is." Pure impartiality is unattainable in any circumstance due to the intimate coloring of observation by interpretations, but this complexity is amplified when considering someone as close as the intellect.

3.3.1   Assertions in Cuckoo Search

The cuckoo search concept has been described as a multidisciplinary project, a software program, and a method of thinking about carbon- and silicon-based brains, life, and intellect. This section looks at various counterarguments to socioeconomic and information processing science claims. To begin with, what are the claims? There are two primary ones, with lesser proposals reliant on them: 1) Minds are social. 2) Swarm Particles are a useful computational intelligence (soft computing) methodology.

3.3.2   Particle Swarms Are a Valuable Soft Intelligence (Machine Learning Intelligent) Approach

These two statement in section 3.3.1 encapsulate the book's core concepts. We highlight the social communication elements of cognition from a linguistic and academic scientist attempting to understand human behavior better. Then, as previous cognitive psychologists have done, we aim to tap into clever human methods by incorporating the mind as we know it—as a social phenomenon—into computer systems. This novel problem-solving strategy has shown to be a very effective method for optimizing complicated functions. Some universal applicability that has given the meat of the arguments filled are hierarchical structures dependent on these two primary assumptions. I am a social being. We reject the functionalism view of consciousness as an inner, private entity or process, arguing that both functionality and phenomena are derived from human encounters in a social environment. Even though it is fundamental to conventional social science, the assertion must be made clear in an age where the behaviorist viewpoint dominates both social and government thinking.

- Social contact is the source of human intellect. People can adapt to complicated situations by finding generally optimum patterns of mindsets, attitudes, and actions by assessing, comparing and mimicking each other, and through learning from mistakes and replicating the effective behaviors of others. Our species' innate intellect has developed because our species prefers a specific type of social interaction.
- Human sociality has inextricably linked culture and intellect. Communities grow increasingly identical because of reciprocal observational interactions, and culture evolves. Culture influences individuals to adopt more universal cognitive and behavioral tendencies. Emergent and immigration phenomena coexist and are inextricably linked.
- Particle swarms are a valuable soft intelligence (supercomputing intelligent) approach. Algorithmic understanding and computer engineering are defined in a variety of ways. Machine learning and intelligent systems are combinatorial optimizations, fuzzy logic, machine learning, and scientific

visualization. Computer adaptability, which permits or promotes intelligent human behavior, is complicated, and evolving contexts are central to the idea of cognitive computing.
Soft computing includes the relaxing "approximation" of
operations like AND, OR, and NOT.

- A helpful paradigm for creating essential concepts is
  swarmed cognition. It is an extension of combinatorial optimization. The application fields covered are modeling, control, and healthcare products in architecture and computing
  science.

- The optimization algorithm is a parametric design modification and a possibly important new manifestation. We're
  talking about geometrically organized systems in which the
  topographical locations of the members don't change. Each
  cell, or site, simply carries out the most basic computations.
  These statements are compatible with results in social psychology and computer science, as well as conventional intellectual theory, with just a slight tilt of the head necessary
  to see any of the consequences we've discussed throughout
  the whole book. We confess that we contribute practically
  no new data to the table; our interpretations and computer
  algorithms are the only things that are novel. Behavioral
  psychologists have long believed that the self and others are
  part of a more extensive system. No credible thinker would
  argue that studying the person in isolation would provide
  significant results. As previously stated, archaeologists have
  known that cultural heritage and public persona are two
  perspectives on the same hypothesis since at least the time
  of Ruth Benedict; and they have a thorough understanding
  of the adaptiveness of consumer characteristics, even if the
  advantages are not always apparent to an investigator from
  outside the society.

Lately, a reductive approach to cognition research has been a trendy way
to explain consciousness in terms of low-level brain processes. Researchers
can now detect physical and magnetic damage to the brain as it does different tasks thanks to new techniques. It is anticipated that the mind can
be described in terms of neurotransmitter plasticity and cerebral modularity. This is akin to forecasting the climate based on known gas molecular
behavior. While it is true that the atmosphere is a system of circulating
particles, the prediction must be predicated on air mass molar patterns.

The status of the weather predictions is considered in the context of the dynamics of weather systems in other areas when forecasting local weather. Human behavior may one day be explained in terms of neuronal firings and brain structure. Still, it will never be fully comprehended in those terms, just as the climate will never be fully comprehended by analyzing gas molecules. To understand people, you must first understand how they interact with others. If you want to learn their ideas and behaviors, you must first understand who they care, trust, and want to be like. You must also understand who educated them in what they know. The optimization algorithm view, or MM, is a technique to show the motions of many people in a single geometric frame. It would be absurd to forecast or characterize the trajectories of psychological components without accounting for the courses of elements they depend on and interact with; it is essentially a multidimensional perspective of dynamic equations, especially human behavior. A logical endpoint, for example, will vary if the premise shifts. Not the premises or the conclusions, but the pattern of assertions must be optimized.

Some readers might find it a touch insulting or dry to reduce warm-blooded, creative humans to points in space. Let us emphasize that this is only a heuristic. Questionnaires like the Myers-Briggs Type Indicator reduce people to patterns on a printout that translate directly into points in the space of personal characteristics. Assessment tools typically reduce people to points on a one-dimensional political scale; personality tests like the Minnesota Multiphasic Personality Inventory reduce people to trends on a printout that translate directly into locations in the space of personality traits. We are just opening a perspective on the human evolving, looking for knowledge in a complicated area of ideas, deeds, feelings, and other people by seeing persons as nanoparticles.

3.3.3 Information and Motivation

Skinner (1986) highlighted two primary benefits of copying models: informational and motivating aspects of social learning. The model's repercussions tell the observer their implications if they took the identical behaviors. However, to infer correctly, the observer must examine various factors. For example, if the model is like the observer, some results could be predicted to be comparable. Some aspects of the setting are likely to indicate if imitation may produce similar results. When the needs of a scenario are unclear, that is, when individuals are curious as to what to do, the advantages of the behaviorist approach significantly outweigh any benefits of the observer's primary method of acting, and the new one may be accepted. Surprisingly, it seems that when the rules are pretty complicated, viewers are far more prone to mimic others. People can learn a penalized modeled action—in fact, they are more likely to learn penalized conduct than activity with no adverse repercussions. They are less likely to execute the behavior right away; however, they are more inclined to enact the behavior with time. People are more likely to recall the act but forget the repercussions, culminating in the belated repetition of bad habits.

Vicarious outcomes can inspire observers in addition to giving knowledge. According to Bandura, the regularity and size of results produced can impact the persistence of actions learned through observation. More enormous incentives are more motivational, particularly when putting in a lot of work to get a rare prize. Resemblances between the spectator and the model mitigate these effects; if the two are highly dissimilar, the observer is less likely to predict comparable results.

3.3.4   Vicarious vs. Direct Experience

Finally, Bandura looked at the differences between vicarious and directly received consequences. One reason he did this is that other people's outcomes serve as a benchmark for determining whether your own are right or fair. According to many scholars, observers learn too much and more quickly than those whose own achievements are reinforced, particularly on intellectual tasks rather than physical ones and complicated tasks rather than essential ones. Unlike learning from direct personal experience, vicarious or observational learning may occur in a vast number of people simultaneously; that is, one learner's example can teach a significant number of people. Part of the risk perception of classical conditioning, according to Bandura, stems from the fact that an agent must pay close attention to the execution of their activities. Still, a spectator may devote immediate attention to the behavior and attitudes of a third-party player.

3.3.5   The Spread of Influence

Bandura does mention that witnesses who mimic a model's conduct may become models for other watchers, culminating in the propagation of task performance across society. Still, he doesn't detail the implications of this impact. The present story's socio-cognitive theory proposes that the spread of adaptable sentiments, actions, and cognitions across a community result in the predominance of adaptable perceptions, activities, and cognitions. Individuals' paths across the issue space bring them closer to one another or to one another's accomplishments, which are more likely to be shared simply by self-consideration. What models transmit to investigators is more inclined to tell others about their successful excursions than unsuccessful ones. (Choosing which traits to publicize about oneself puts a bias into social search; morally objectionable and perfectly viable issue solutions may be hidden from others.) Behavioral troubles throughout a population cause people to cluster or converge inside a problem space region. This grouping includes the creation of norms in the near term and civilization over a long period.

3.3.6   Machine Adaptation

As utilized in metaheuristic optimization computer systems, cognitive technology encompasses practical adaption principles, paradigms, algorithms, and representations that enable or promote appropriate behaviors (intelligence behavior) in complicated and changing contexts. Read Holland for a description of complex systems that apply to expert systems. Many machine adaptability applications can benefit from particle swarm, such as developing fuzzy AI techniques, which use non-programmed emergence behavior to create fuzzy inference sets. In turn, the particles swarm's properties (such as constricting factors) may be adjusted using fuzzy rules. The resultant system resembles a self-referential Gordian knot that can't be classified as Darwinian or unclear, thus the name computing intellect. Control, diagnostics, categorization, and optimization may all be accomplished with the help of a fuzzy expert system. Using particle swarm technique to evolve such a system can result in condensed systems (low number of regulations) that deteriorate smoothly. And these systems are developed in a fraction of the time that typical computer algorithms take to create. They need computer science to obtain all required rules from experts and are naturally "brittle," failing spectacularly when confronted with scenarios outside their rule area. The use of particle swarming to evolve software programs like biological systems is presently classified as hypothetical (although this is a chapter headed "Implications and Speculations"). A feedforward network may be built utilizing each member of the terminal set (input parameters and constant) as an embedding layer node and each member of the functional group as a remote unit's component. There might be more than one weight matrix, and the terminating set could be included in all except the last output neuron. The binary particle swarm might then be used to find the best (or near-best) restoration hardware, which would describe a programmer to resolve the problem. A possibly more powerful method would be to evolve software that weighted each link using the particle swarm in actual numbers. The answer would then be expressed in a standard computer program language, similar to a regular feedforward neural network.

3.3.7   Learning or Adaptation?

The terms "knowledge" and "adaptive" signify different things. For example, psychology uses them slightly differently from engineering and computer science; according to Webster's New Collegiate Dictionary (1975), it is defined as a) the act or process of trying to adapt: the state of being acclimated, adaptation to external factors, such as the strength or quality of stimulus received by a sensory organ; b) a change to an organism or one of its components that makes it more suited to its surroundings.

Adapts is defined as follows by the same source: to adapt (for a specific or new purpose or circumstance) often via alteration (to befit as appropriate, fitted to survive, and acceptable from a particular perspective). These principles that fundamentally describe evolutionary computing systems are described as radical (and adhered to). Learning describes changing structures such as machine learning, genetic algorithm tools, and evolutionary algorithms. This use is consistent with the findings of most studies.

However, the first approach to learning is "information or skill obtained by teaching or study," and understanding is listed as a synonym for knowledge. Similarly, "to obtain experience or awareness of or proficiency in by study, instruction, or encounter" (Webster's New International Dictionary, 1975); "to acquire expertise or awareness of or skill in by study, instruction, or experience."

Learning is what an integrated system accomplishes from the standpoint of computer science. Learning is for the whole expert agent, whereas adaptation mainly pertains to the part of the system we're talking about in this book—the evolutionary computing piece. Many obstacles, such as optimal solutions and uncertainties, must be overcome during adaptability. The subspace terrain (topographical, surroundings) is likely to change regularly. We're dealing with complicated adaptive (researching intelligent) systems. The fitness or productivity metric is frequently complex and changes over time.

Adaptive systems address this problem by gradually altering population structures using a collection of operators that develop (adapt) over time. When contrasted to exhaustive search techniques, which must search substantial sections of the problem space, these adaptive procedures dramatically reduce the time necessary to arrive at a solution. To summarize, adaptability is likely the most suitable phrase for what computer vision systems perform from the standpoint of applied mathematics. Computed intellectual ability and system adaptability are almost interchangeable terms in computer engineering. This chapter does not attempt to characterize acquisition or adaptation, we're merely pointing out the many ways these terms are used, notably the variations between how they're employed in psychology and the social sciences vs. science and engineering. Psychology may prefer not to use "knowledge" to describe intelligence, mainly when it refers to artificial intelligence.

The term "intelligence" denotes both conscious awareness and the implementation of those ideas or storage of data. Developmental theorists look at the concept of "feeling of understanding," which is a subjective sense of being able to recall a fact that isn't the same as actual recall ability—and isn't the same as knowledge. Historically, psychiatrists have studied learning as an empirical phenomenon defined by Webster's second definition: "modification of a change in behavior by experiences (as exposure to conditioned)." The difficulty of measuring subjective experiences is recognized by scientific psychology; the idea of "knowing" can only be operationally defined in terms of behavior and hence cannot be investigated objectively.

As a result, "learning" can only be examined as a quantifiable change in attitude; these multidisciplinary disparities in the definition of a frequently used term, philosophically on one side and experimental on the other, may cause misunderstanding, which we hope has not occurred in this book.

3.4 Conclusion

According to this chapter, cognitive processes are based on social relationships. Why is this significant? Because it focuses the explanation of the mind on the relationships connecting individuals rather than the inner mechanics of the individual—mainly reason, which is an entirely isolated piece of equipment. The statistical information regarding what cognition is contradicted the sensation of reasoning. We accept as truth the myth of thinking like an interior activity, the myth of the given, the mythology of awareness. We must debunk the misconception as researchers; it is our responsibility to examine the facts objectively to comprehend human behavior. The metaheuristic optimization concept operates based on dynamics comparable to human civilizations. Humans' cognitive architecture is improved as they engage with and are impacted by others. Sustaining the social relationships that allow for this optimization takes a lot of human work. There is no cause to suppose that nature would have equipped us with a method for overcoming the viewpoint that goes with our physiological bundle. There is no reason to think that contemplation should be medically legitimate. While it may be challenging to envision people in ways that are at odds with our daily lives, it is vital to have an accurate empirical knowledge of human behavior.

4

Algorithm of Swarm Intelligence

Abstract

Evolutionary programming through contemporary gray wolf optimization and several swarm optimization techniques was introduced in the early 1960s. The potential of all these methods to tackle various optimization issues has been shown. This chapter thoroughly examines well-known optimization methods. Studies carried out with 30 well-known benchmarking functions are briefly described and compared with selected plans. Next, several statistical studies are presented that confirm significant results. The outcomes demonstrate the overall benefit of differential development (DE) and carefully contrast with other proposed techniques followed by particle swarm optimization (PSO).

Keywords: Ant behavior, shortest path, pheromone, optimal solution, bee summing, model-based search, optimization

4.1 Introduction

Like bees and termites, ants are classified as social animals because they live and operate in well-organized colonies or groups of the same species. Ants form small to large colonies with populations ranging from a few hundred to thousands of individuals, mostly sterile females forming several classes. Because of their social nature, these colonies are referred to as select different. Ants are almost invisible insects that successfully seek food. It's fascinating to learn how this species, although essentially individuals, recognizes the value of cooperation in determining the quickest path connecting their nest and providing nutrients [31].

> "Many entomologists prefer to view ant colonies and the societies of other social insects as more like superorganisms than communities of individualized organisms." – Robert L. O'Connell

In the early 1990s, ant colony optimization (ACO) was presented. Artificial ants were used to mimic the ant colony's social and optimum behavior.

Kuldeep Singh Kaswan, Jagjit Singh Dhatterwal and Avadhesh Kumar. *Swarm Intelligence: An Approach from Natural to Artificial*, (89–112) © 2023 Scrivener Publishing LLC

An ant is a primary, autonomous, and asynchronous agent in an artificially generated population that collaborates to discover the best solution to complex real-life optimization issues. Ant colony optimization is a population-based metaheuristic optimizing approach inspired by the fossilized remains of a horde of insects, such as an ant colony. It refers to a group of model-based search (MBS) approaches. These MBS techniques are very good at finding the best answer to combinational optimization difficulties. The MBS methods are classified into two categories based on probabilistic modes: a) methods that use a specified prediction algorithm without restructuring the model specification during the run; and b) algorithms that use a specified probability distribution without restructuring the model specification during the pass [32].

4.1.1   Methods for Alternate Stages of Model Parameter Reform

The approaches based on ant colonies belong to the first category. The ACO approach adjusts the probability photographer's model parameters during the run to produce a high likelihood of making high-quality outcomes over time. This chapter covers the fundamental concepts of ant behavior and the ACO procedure and uses them.

4.1.2   Ant Behavior

Ants are sociable animals who like to live in colonies. They utilize sensory information to find the quickest path between their territory and a food source. These insects can adapt to changes in their surroundings. Each ant performs relatively simple group activities in these ant colonies without knowing what the other ants are doing; nevertheless, everyone recognizes that the result is highly social and organized. Even if the current path becomes contaminated or hindered by a barrier, they can quickly locate the another way to their blocked goal. Figure 4.1 depicts this occurrence. It can be seen from the diagram that, a) the ants are moving in a horizontal line and find the shortest way; b) a barrier interrupts their trip and divides the path; c) the ants search for the following fastest distance; and d) ultimately, the ants find the shortest direction.

According to ethnographers, this ability of ants is attributed to a phenomenon known as pheromone trails, which ants use to converse with one another. This knowledge also aids the ant colony in deciding whether to stay on the same hunting path or alter it. Initially, ants enjoy the view encircling the nest at random when searching for food. They transport food back to their colony after searching for food sources, leaving a chemical substance called

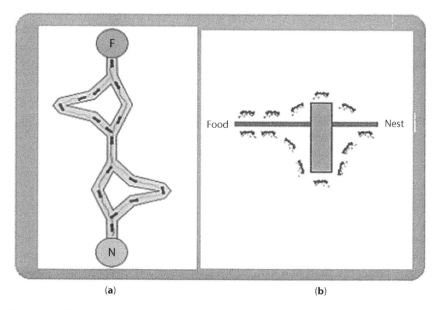

(a)   (b)

Figure 4.1 Traveling behavior of an ant colony: a) ants following the shortest path, b) an obstacle in their path.

a pheromone on the ground when they return with food. While returning with food, they typically release more pheromones and generate less when looking for food. This chemical that has been deposited on the substrate directs their colleagues to a food source. Ants in the area prefer tracing the trail with the highest signal concentrations. The pheromone trail provides a constant and indirect method of communication among ants, assisting the ant colony in determining the quickest path between their colony and food supply. Ants walk in a straight line since it is the shortest distance between two sites, namely the colony and the food source.

The exploring and food-carrying ants are on the same path. Because it is believed that all ants walk at the same pace, most ants will arrive at the shortest distance in the least amount of time. As a result, the pheromones concentrations will rise along the shortest path, as most ants take it. The differential in the quantity of pheromones levels on these pathways will be easily detected by fresh ants joining the ecosystem after some time. These young ants will choose to go along the shortest, most pheromone-rich path, which is a horizontal line between both the colony and the food source. If a barrier has stopped the nearest neighbor pheromones trail, the ants cannot take the quickest route in this circumstance and must choose differently. They turn left and right at random, looking for a way to their objective because they have no idea where they are going. After some time, it has been shown that certain ants discover the quickest paths around the barrier and swiftly build the disrupted pheromones, as opposed to the ants who took a longer journey. As additional ants take the shortest route, the pheromone concentrations will rise. As previously stated, the increasing pheromone intensity will aid the new ants in following the next discovered shortest path. This molecule, on the other hand, has a bias towards evaporating. The ant colony can use this constructively auto-catalytic mechanism to find the fastest route to their objective [33].

4.2 Ant Colony Algorithm

The feeding behavior of an ant colony, which was covered in earlier sections, inspired the ACO method. An ant's behavior is mathematical, and it may be represented in a series of equations to discover the best answer to evolutionary computation issues. Since its inception, this approach has tackled various real-world architectural optimization issues. The ant system (AS) is the most widespread, prolific, and oldest of these techniques. Marco Dorigo invented the technique, which has become the most used operation in ACO methods. One of the essential features of this procedure is that the ant's pheromones quantity is changed at each cycle. What was involved in the construction of the solutions during the repetition? Following is a description of the AS: In the starting step, all ants are randomly started, and then these mechanical ants are placed on the vertex of the construction frame with a consistent quantity of pheromone trail intensities, i.e., $(i,j) = 1$ (i,j); "allowed" is apportioned at all vertices, whereas "permitted" denotes the set of viable neighbors of the ant.

Each mechanical ant has the following personality traits:

1) It likes to walk on the frame with the most excellent pheromone possibility; previously visited borders are forbidden until the circuit is completed.
2) It prefers to travel on the frame with the highest pheromone plausibility.

At each visited edge, the material known as the trail is updated after the voyage is completed [34].

Each ant progressively contributes its share of the material to the partially developing answer frame at each resolution command level or step. Assume that during the construction step, the kth ant of ith edge does a normal distribution from ith border to the next periphery of the building j. Ants make stochastic judgments to pick the next node or cut at each edge. These judgments are based on the possibility of one advantage transitioning to another regarding the ant's current edge bite. The statistical likelihood of the kth ant at the ith edge traveling to the jth edge can be calculated using the spontaneous approximately equal state transition law [5], which is defined as

$$P_k(i,j) = \begin{cases} \dfrac{[\tau(i,j)]^\alpha \cdot [\eta(i,j)]^\beta}{\displaystyle\sum_{c_{il} \in N(s^P)} [\tau(i,l)]^\alpha \cdot [\eta(i,l)]^\beta} & \text{if } c_{ij} \in N(s^P) \quad (4.1) \\ 0 \end{cases}$$

Where $\tau_{ij}(t)$ is the strength of the pheromone trail on edge (i,j). Eq. (4.1) describes how the heuristic value, also known as visibility of path (i,j), is calculated for edge (i,j). Its value is usually inverse to the interconnection or the distance between two points. Ant k has not yet explored edge l. If the length of the path (i,j) is represented by $d(i,j)$, then the quantity of (i,j) may be computed as $1/d(i,j)$. N(sp) is also a collection of viable components or convenient neighbors of the kth ant on edge i.

When the colony's ants have all achieved

$$\tau(i,j) \leftarrow \zeta.\tau(i,j) + \sum_{k=1}^{m} \tau_k(i,j) \qquad (4.2)$$

The coefficients [0,1] are represented here, so that (1) means the disappearance of the pheromones between identify important (the time taken to complete a cycle). The value is smaller than unity to prevent infinite pheromone buildup in the route. Likewise, the $k(i,j)$ refers to the number of pheromones deposited by the kth ant per unit length of the structure (i,j), which is written as follows.

$$\Delta\tau_k(i,j) = \begin{cases} \dfrac{Q}{L_k} & \text{if ant } k \text{ travels through the path } (i,j) \\ 0 & \text{otherwise} \end{cases} \qquad (4.3)$$

where Q and L_k denote the total journey length of the kth ant and constants (typically, $Q = 1$), respectively, the heuristics value provided in (4.1),

(i,j) is generally used in this approach to prefer the cost-effective borders of the frame with a high pheromones level, whereas the first term simulates the evaporating material. Due to pheromones' fading effects, this implies a decreased trail level. It's worth noting that the trail of unattractive edges will fade with time. The second election represents the strengthening of the number of clusters. This will make it easier for freshly recruited ants in the ant infestation system to recognize the path of increased pheromones intensity. The amount of material deposited on the route is greatly dependent on the cleanliness of the solution obtained thus far. The pheromones trail update algorithm aids in modeling the variation in the frequency caused by fresh ants depositing extra scent and the quantity evaporating from the path. There is a basic mathematics model for better comprehension. It depicts the routes of two ants as they walk between the four places denoted by bold and dotted lines. The ants' beginning and stopping points are considered at the margins, indicated by stars. The cost graph depicts the expense of going between two points, whereas the pheromones chart shows the estimated pheromone value among two points. The probability of pathways is now computed for a fresh ant starting its trip from the edge star to choose the quickest route. According to the calculations obtained

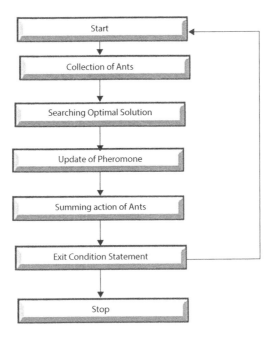

Figure 4.2 Flow chart of ant colony optimization.

from the Figure 4.1, a new ant starting its journey from the border star will travel towards the edge indicated by the triangle since this path contains the maximum concentrations of the pheromones, 0.1. it was compared to two alternative routes to the nodes, the rectangle, and the circular, with pheromones concentrations of 0.07 and 0.03, respectively. The ant will select the path towards the circle after accessing the triangles node since it contains the highest material concentration, 0.07. It will also travel towards the square edge before returning to the star [35]. The ACO optimization flowchart is shown in Figure 4.2.

4.3 Artificial Bee Colony Optimization

The aggregate behavior of social animals is modeled by swarm intelligence. Responsibility distribution, self-organization, and adaptability to new conditions without global oversight are the sources of intellectual capacity. To avoid stagnating states, personality is accomplished by repeating rewarding acts (positive feedback), discarding repeated behavior patterns (negative feedback), talking with neighboring agents (many interactions), and discovering unknown connections (fluctuation) [36].

Honeybees are social insects that display dynamic programming in various behaviors, including nest project planning, mating, and foraging. There is a task allocation among the bees in the foraging conducted to identify lucrative sources to increase the honey amount transported to the hive and the other tasks. The bees are separated into three groups to efficiently do this critical task: employed bees, onlooker bees, and scouts. Employed bees are in charge of transporting nectar from newly discovered blossoms to the hive. Once they return to the hive, they perform a dance through which they provide information about the quality and location of the food source to the onlookers. Onlooker bees observe the dancing and fly to possibly beneficial blooms depending on the info gained from the dances. An onlooker bee is more likely to choose a potentially excellent option. Because of these constructive comments, the bees engage in foraging and dancing. When a bee chooses a flower, the amount of nectar it produces diminishes until it runs out with each extraction. A scout bee searches for a new source (fluctuation) when the depleted source is deserted (negative feedback). The qualities of positive and negative feedback, interaction, and change indicate that a bee swarm may self-organize and adapt to inner and external situations without the help of a higher level. Inspired by honeybee foraging behavior, Karaboga introduced the Artificial Bee Colony (ABC) algorithm in 2005, which replicates job division and personality in a bee colony.

The algorithm is divided into three phases: employed bees, onlooker bees, and scout bees. Bees seek sources of food (solutions) in their surroundings (search space) to optimize nectar yield (fitness of the answers). The employed bee phase, like actual bees, examines the area around the sources found thus far, while the spectator bee phase uses the data acquired from the cluster centers to attract the awaiting bees to good supplies. The employed bee phase aims to locate new blooms that have yet to be found. The algorithm's effectiveness has been examined in single-objective uncontrolled, restricted, and multi-objective optimization, and it has been effectively utilized in various study fields. The ABC algorithm is a robust and straightforward concept, which according to the research may be used effectively on muscular and multi-modal issues. The method was tweaked for hybridization and compound situations to increase its local search capabilities and premature convergence. It used Deb's rules to modify its selection method on local issues; and used non-dominated filtering to rank answers and create a community of influenced and non-dominated solutions on multi-objective challenges. It's an excellent option in optimization techniques since it has fewer process variables and a more matched experimentation capability [37].

4.3.1 The Artificial Bee Colony

The Artificial Bee Colony (ABC) method is an optimization technique that mimics dynamic honeybee programming in foraging. Each answer represents a food source location in the computer, and the system seeks to identify the source with the most nectar. Figure 4.3 contains the ABC computation pseudo-code.

In the initialization phase of ABC, an SN number of solutions (food sources) are generated.

$$x_{ij} = x_j^{lb} + \text{rand}(0,1)(x_j^{ub} - x_j^{lb}) \qquad (4.4)$$

where $i \in \{1,..., SN\}$, $j \in \{1,..., D\}$, D is the problem dimension. x_j^{lb} and x_j^{ub} are the lower and upper bounds in jth dimension of design parameters, respectively.

The employed bee, onlooker bees, and scout bee phases evolve the food supply population depending on global optimization features. The nectar exploitation behavior of employed bees is replicated by a random optimum between each supply [84].

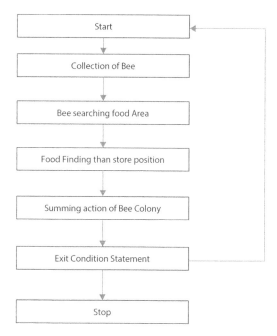

Figure 4.3 Artificial bee colony.

A selection approach in which each answer is allocated a likelihood proportionate to its quality simulates selecting valuable resources based on the knowledge received from the hired bees. The resolution suitability (Eq. 4.5) is used to determine the excellence, and the possibility may be calculated using (Eq. 4.6):

$$p_i = 0.1 + 0.9 * \frac{\text{fitness}_i}{max(\overrightarrow{\text{fitness}})} \tag{4.5}$$

Fitness (Eq. 4.6) is roughly related to the optimization problem. When an onlooker bee chooses sources of food, Eq. 4.2 is used to perform a search engine from around suppliers.

$$\text{fitness}_i = \begin{cases} \dfrac{1}{1+f_i}, \text{if } f_i \geq 0 \\ 1+\left|f_i\right|, \text{if } f_i < 0 \end{cases} \tag{4.6}$$

Suppose the existing source can be enhanced by a different opportunity generated by the feature selection. The number matching the number of exploitations is incremented by one in the cluster centers and onlooker bee phases. If the counter reaches a predetermined number (management variable, limit) by modeling food supply depletion, the answer is removed from the population. The bee renounces the extremely tired source and searches queries for a different opportunity by Eq. 4.6, just like natural scout bees.

4.4 Cat Swarm Optimization

Cat swarm optimization (CSO) was introduced by Chu and Tsai, who proposed the initial iteration of the CSO algorithm. The primary source of inspiration for the CSO method is cat behavior, and the algorithm optimizes the search for a solution in an M-dimensional space using a fitness function. Cats represent the answer sets. Each cat has several dimensions, velocities for each size, a flag indicating whether the cat is searching or tracing, and a fitness value. The cat with the highest fitness value represents the best solution. The seeking mode simulates a situation in which a cat in a resting position searches for a new place to go, whereas the tracing mode simulates a condition in which the cat tracks some targets. The literature shows that numerous modifications of the CSO method have taken place, including CSO for clustering, parallel CSO, a similar version of CSO based on the Taguchi method, a modified version of the CSO algorithm called Crazy-CSO that introduces the concept of craziness, multi-objective binary cat swarm optimization (MOBCSO), a grey image segmentation algorithm based on CSO, harmonious cat swarm optimization (HCSO), discrete binary cat swarm optimization (DBCO), and a quantum cat swarm optimization clustering (QCSOC) algorithm. The CSO method is commonly used to solve many engineering issues, and we successfully used it to generate menus for the elderly [38].

4.4.1 Original CSO Algorithm

Figure 4.4 presents the pseudo-code for the global version of the cat swarm optimization (CSO) algorithm, which is based on the one given in [12]. The process measures are fed into the algorithm, where represents M - the number of dimensions of the search space, $P_{i,j}^{min}, P_{i,j}^{max}$ - the range of variability for the positions of the cats, the number of dimensions in the search space; R is the range of variation in the cats' locations; SMP stands for seeking memory pool; and MR stands for mixture ratio, which is a percentage that specifies how many cats are in seeking mode and how many cats are in tracing mode. And CDC is counts of dimension change; SRD is seeking range of selected dimension; and SPC is self-position considering, which is a term that refers to the consideration of one's position. N is the total number of cats, max denotes the number of iterations, and c1 represents the first iteration. In tracing mode, this constant is used to update the cat's movement. The personal optimum reflects the output, a cat's highest ranking. This chapter provides a modified version of the original CSO method, which assumes that the flag SPC equals 0. The location to move to in the seeking mode is picked arbitrarily from the SMP copies, with each copy possessing the same possibility of being chosen. In step 1, an initial population of N cats is generated at random, with each cat symbolized by an M-dimensional real-valued number. The Gbest, or global best, is updated

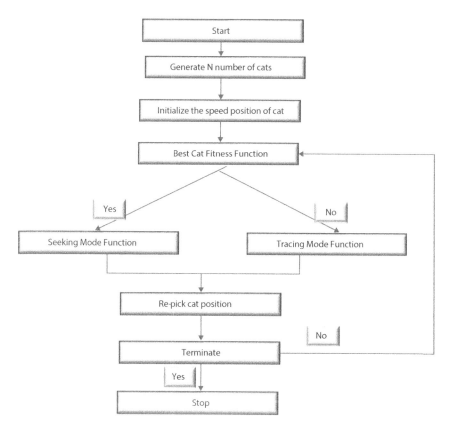

Figure 4.4 CSO flowchart.

to include the best cat (step 3). A sequence of steps is repeated until the halting condition is not met or the convergence rate is less than the maximum number of iterations. Some cats will be in trace capacity, while the remainder will be in seeking mode, according to MR (step 5). After computing the function value of all cats (step 6), the Gbest cat is changed, and the value of the new areas is calculated for each cat based on whether the cat is in searching or tracing mode. When the cat is in seeking mode, SMP copies are generated, the copies' locations are updated based on the value of SRD, and the new position to move to is chosen randomly. The speed is changed first (step 6) in the tracking mode, and the new department is calculated using the changed velocity (step 7). Finally, the optimal Gbest is provided as the application's final result in steps 8 and 9.

4.4.2   Description of the Global Version of CSO Algorithm

The worldwide variant of the CSO algorithm is presented in this section. The method begins by setting its parameters, after which the cats' initial locations and velocity are created at random. The cats are divided into tracing and seeking modes based on the value of an announcement as MR (mutation ratio). The cats' fitness levels are calculated using an optimization problem, and the ideal option so far is the best cat's position (Xbest). The seeking or tracking steps are then applied based on the indicator readings. The procedure is stopped if the terminating conditions are fulfilled; or else, the steps that follow activation are restarted. The proposed algorithm, the running duration, and the percentage of improvements are all typical CSO completion criteria. The following sections go through the seeking and tracing modes in further depth [39].

4.4.3   Seeking Mode (Resting)

When a cat is sleeping, it is in the seeking phase. When a cat detects a threat, it walks carefully and slowly. The cat examines the M-dimensional space of solutions in the seeking mode to determine the next step. The cat is aware of its surroundings, circumstances, and options. The following parameters are used in the CSO algorithm to describe these facts: (a) seeking memory pool (SMP), (b) seeking range of selected dimension (SRD), (c) counts of dimension change (CDC), which is the number of altered measurements, and (d) self-position consideration (SPC). The following stages outline the seeking mode procedure: (1) SMP copies are produced for each cat Xi, and if the flag SPC is true, the cat's present location is one of those SMP copies; (2) According to the CDC, each cat's new location is calculated using the accompanying approximation:

$$X_{cn} = X_c \times (1 \pm SRD \times R) \tag{4.7}$$

where Xcn is the permanent project, Xc is the actual situation, and R is a random number between 0 and 1; (3) compute the strength training values of the new locations for each situation and set the original CSO algorithm likelihood for all of the applicants' points to 1 if all of the objective functions are equal, anything else uses the approximation mentioned in the next step; (4) Choose a point to relocate to at random from the list of possible sites, and use the following formula to substitute the position of the cat Xi:

$$P_i = \frac{FS_i - FS_b}{FS_{max} - FS_{min}} \tag{4.8}$$

where 0 I j, P_i is the applicant cat Xi's likelihood, FS_i is the cat Xi's fitness value, FS_{max} is the strength and conditioning function's highest voltage, FS_{min} is the fitness function's minimum value, $FS_{max} = FS_b$ for asymptotic analysis, and $FS_b = FS_{min}$ for optimization problems, and $FS_{max} = FS_b$ for solvent regeneration.

4.4.4 Tracing Mode (Movement)

The tracing mode resembles a cat hunting its prey. Following are the calculations for changing the cats' velocities and leadership roles:

$$vk,d = vk,d + R \times c1 \times (Xbest,d - Xk,d) \tag{4.9}$$

and

$$Xk,d,new = Xk,d,old + vk,d \tag{4.10}$$

4.4.5 Description of the Local Version of CSO Algorithm

In the international variation of the CSO method, each cat gravitates towards the swarm's greatest cat. In the special version of the CSO algorithm, each cat seeks the strongest cat in its vicinity from the other side. As a result, the method:

$$vk,d = vk,d + R \times c1 \times (Xbest,d - Xk,d) \tag{4.11}$$

is replaced with the formula:

$$vk,d = vk,d + R \times c1 \times (XLbest,d - Xk,d) \qquad (4.12)$$

where *XLbest* denotes the greatest in the local area, and *Xbest* distinguishes the finest in the world.

Another option is to add the momentum component to the equation:

$$vk,d = \omega \times vk,d + R \times c1 \times (XLbest,d - Xk,d) \qquad (4.13)$$

A hysteresis component is a quantitative number used to govern the pace at which the velocity drops in value. Its starting value is generally more prominent than 0.9 and falls with each node of the network with a fixed numerical value of 0.01, 0.001, or 0.0001. A neighborhood can be either geometric or social. Simple geometric areas may be calculated using a variety of distances, including the Euclidean, Manhattan, and Chebyshev distance and time. The cat's rating determines the sociological neighborhood. The token ring, wherein the conservative and liberal neighbors are addressed, and the network system, in which a central component is linked to all other vertices, are two frequent topologies. The neighbors of the ith cat in the token ring are found by solving the following formulations:

$$\text{Left}_i = \begin{cases} i+1 & \text{if } i < N \\ 1 & \text{if } i = N \end{cases} \qquad (4.14)$$

$$\text{Right}_i = \begin{cases} i-1 & \text{if } i > 1 \\ N & \text{if } i = 1 \end{cases} \qquad (4.15)$$

The optimal option amongst the value, Left and Right, is used to update the local best for cat i.

The star topology considers the relationship between the mother cat and her offspring. The original swarming of cats is split into multiple smaller swarms, each containing one mother cat and her progeny. The local best for each cat in the swarming is modified in this scenario, taking into account the best value earned by a kitten or the parent cat. An illustration of these two topologies is shown in Figure 4.5.

The fact that these algorithms may investigate multiple locations and discover different optimal solutions is one of its benefits. However, because

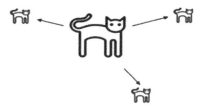

Figure 4.5 Star topology of CSO.

the community groups will have fewer individuals, this unique feature of the program may fail to discover the optimum solution.

4.5 Crow Search Optimization

The crow search algorithm (CSA) for the restricted engineering optimization technique is a unique metaheuristic presented for use in solving constrained engineering optimization issues. Its primary source of inspiration is the behavior of pigeons, which are considered among the world's domesticated creatures. The algorithm's main principles are the institution of pigeons into flocks, memorizing hidden rooms for stashing surplus food, continuing to follow one another when they steal, and the safeguards of their caches. These ideas led to the creation of a novel algorithm that differs significantly from previous algorithms based on natural bird behavior, such as chicken swarm optimization (CSO), cuckoo search (CS), bird swarm algorithm (BSA), bird mating optimizer (BMO), and peacock algorithm (PA). Particle swarm optimization (PSO), genetic algorithms (GA), and harmony search (HS) are some of the methods that may have inspired CSA; however, CSA has fewer adjustable variables than other algorithms, reducing the effort of parameter setup, which is a momentous task. CSA may be used to solve various architectural optimization problems, and numerous examples are given in the original paper that introduce the method, such as the three-bar truss, welded beam, and gear train design challenges.

The CSA solution is evaluated as crows, each with a D-dimensional location, a memory, and a fitness value. Even though CSA is a new bio-inspired algorithmic, it already has several versions in the literature, including the multi-objective crow search algorithm (MOCSA), binary crow search algorithm (BCSA), and chaotic crow search algorithm (CCSA). Hybrid cat swarm optimization–crow search algorithm (HCSO-CSA) and hybrid grey wolf optimizer–crow search algorithm (GWOCSA) are two examples of CSA

hybrid algorithms. Communities that depend on electrostatic standardization, parameter estimation of software reliability growth models (SRGMs),
identity verification of photovoltaic parameter values, foreign investment
dispatch, efficiency improvements for inverter-based distribution networks,
and augmentation of the productivity of inverter-based distributed generators have all been solved using CSA in the literary works [40].

4.5.1   Original CSA

The pseudo-code of CSA is presented and adapted after the original presented version. The computation inputs are N is the number of ravens, D
is the number of state space directions, and [$Cmin$, $Cmax$] is the range of
variance of the crows' locations, AP is the attentiveness likelihood, and fl is
the flight duration, and itermax is the maximum number of variables. The
ith item from memories M for which the value of OF(Mi) is minimum
in the reduction case or maximum in the maximizing case is the result of
CSA. The input sequence of N crows is started in steps 1–5 of the method
as follows: for each crow, the D-dimensional vectors Ci that specifies the
location is populated with arbitrary integers from the range [$Cmin$, $Cmax$],
and the memory Mi's initial value is populated with Ci's value. At first,
Memory(M) = Flock(C).

$$Flock = \begin{bmatrix} C_{1,1} & & \cdots & \cdots & C_{1,D} \\ \cdots & \cdots & \cdots & \cdots & \cdots & \cdots \\ C_{N,1} & & & \cdots & \cdots & C_{N,D} \end{bmatrix} \tag{4.16}$$

$$Memory = \begin{bmatrix} M_{1,1} & & \cdots & M_{N,1} \\ \cdots & \cdots & \cdots & \cdots & \cdots \end{bmatrix} \tag{4.17}$$
$$MN,1 \ldots MN,D$$

The performance index defined by Eq. 4.5 measures Ci's competence.
The number of the present incarnation is set to 0 in step 6.

The following stages are performed from step 8 to step 32 for the specified epochs. If the number of a probability distribution r from [0,1] is
higher than or equal to AP, the input sequence of N crows is established
using Eq. 4.18, alternatively using Eq. 4.19. The first instance relates to the
scenario in which the crow Ci follows another crow Cj from the group
with the primary goal of discovering that crow's memory Mj. The second

scenario correlates to the circumstance where the current hires in the D-dimensional solution space are arbitrary.

$$Ci,j = Ci,j + ri \times fl \times (Mk,j - Ci,j) \qquad (4.18)$$

$$Ci,j = rj \times (Cmax - Cmin) + Cmin \qquad (4.19)$$

The value of ri in Eq. 4.18 is a random value between [0,1], and k is an integer between 1,..., N chose randomly before revising the crow position. The value of rj in Eq. 4.19 is a particular variable between [0,1] for each dimension j such that j 1,..., D.

For each crow, the viability of Ci is assessed. A location Ci is deemed viable in this chapter if all elements of the D-dimensional vector Ci fall within the range [$Cmin$, $Cmax$]. The crows' locations are changed in steps 20-24 to take numbers from the domain [$Cmin$, $Cmax$] as follows:

if Ci,j $Cmin$, then $Ci,j = Cmin$, and if $Ci,j > Cmax$, then $Ci,j = Cmax$.

Steps 25-31 update each crow Ci's remembrance as follows: Step 26 evaluates the significance of the stance Ci using the formula estimates of the value of the recollection Mi using the same procedure. If the value of OF(Ci) is less than the worth of OF(Mi) (or greater than the value of OF(Mi) for calculation purposes), then Mi is updated to the value of Ci (step 29). The value of the present period t is raised.

Finally, the method returns the storage Mi from the complete set of memory variables. The quantity of OF(Mi) is either minimum or maximum in the minimizing or maximizing cases.

4.6 Elephant Intelligent Behavior

Compared to other animals on the planet, elephants have a sophisticated social and emotional family structure; elephant females establish and lead the family, according to many studies worldwide. Elephants form strong clan bonds and prefer to stay in small family groupings in herds. A herd typically consists of 8–100 elephants, depending on terrain, climate, and family size. Herds are led by a wise older female known as the matriarch, and are mostly made up of females such as mothers, daughters, sisters and their calves. Herd assembly of 500–1000 elephants near a location with food and clean water has occasionally been recorded. According to studies, elephants have lasting emotional bonds with their relatives and friends and even lament the death of prematurely born offspring and loved ones.

Elephants have a distinct walking technique that is highly comparable to people. When baby elephants walk, they usually use their trunks to grasp their mothers' tails, and other females encircle them to defend them from ravenous predators. The entire matriarchal herd raises and protects a new-born calf. Male elephants (bulls) like to be alone; therefore, they leave the family at around 12 to 15 years of age to hang out with other guys. Although the herd is closely connected, the pack can sometimes be divided. Ecology and societal factors can affect the separation. As a result, various herds distributed throughout a broad region might all be from the same family. They use multiple calls to stay in touch with their family group members. The elephant has a keen ability to hear and can make various noises such as roars, snorts, and screams to converse with other elephants, but it excels in supersonic grumbling.

Over five years, O'Connell-Rodwell conducted tests on captive elephants in the United States, Zimbabwe, and India. According to these experiments, elephants respond to low-frequency electrical signals that pass through and slightly above the earth. According to a subsequent study, elephants may respond to charged particles even in the presence of different frequencies of oscillations. Elephants in Sri Lanka and Thailand are said to have fled to higher ground before the devastating tsunami of 2004 because they felt the tension of a faraway herd and heard the impending thunderstorms from a hundred miles away. Elephants' superior cognition and recollection have sparked the development of a new nature-inspired objective function. In 2015, Gai-Ge Wang *et al.* invented elephant swarming optimization, a clustering-based metaheuristic optimal solution approach. Elephant herding optimization (EHO) behavior influenced the development of the technique. As previously stated, the elephant is a pack animal, and a herd consists of numerous elephant clans and young offspring. Each clan is guided by a leader, often the oldest and largest female, known as the matriarch. The recommended algorithm is as follows: The female elephant represents the clan's best option, while the male elephant represents the clan's worst option. Female elephants are used to staying with their family groups. In contrast, male elephants leave when they grow up but stay in touch with their family group members via low-frequency vibrations, per the elephant herding behavior. The number of elephants in each clan is kept constant for simplicity's sake. When the worst male elephant quits the family, replacement elephants might be generated to maintain the elephant population. The following sections go through the fundamentals of EHO.

4.6.1   Elephant Herding Optimization

Elephants' complex herding behavior is modeled using mathematical formulae. As mentioned below, some rules are defined in basic EHO to search for global and regional alternatives.

- Each tribe should have a set number of elephants. If an elephant quits the clan, a new animal or a young elephant might take its place.
- A set percentage of male elephants will leave their family group and live in solitude far away from the main elephant group in each generation.
- A matriarch leads the elephants in each clan.

Figure 4.6 depicts an elephant herd with various lines of elephants. Two placement updates operator, clan updating and separation operators, have been proposed in EHO to update the placement of elephants in each generation. The EHO technique may be split into two halves based on these operations, as outlined in the following subsection.

Figure 4.6 A clan of elephants on the move.

4.6.2 Position Update of Elephants in a Clan

The locations of the surviving elephants in the clan are changed. As previously stated, an elephant's standing in a clan is influenced by the matriarch of that clan. The location of the jth elephant in clan c is defined as follows in EHO:

$$p_{jc}^{t+1} = p_{jc}^t + \alpha \times (p_{\text{best}} - p_{jc}^t) \times r \qquad (4.20)$$

The updated and previous positions are calculated in $t+1$ and t generations, respectively; α is a scaling factor, varied between [0, 1], used.

The elephant herd is organized into clans. The matriarch's effect on a individual elephant of clan c is evaluated. The best individual position (pbest) is the location of the clan's matriarch elephant with the fittest individuals so far. If the proportion is uniform, the status of the matriarch elephant is checked regularly.

$$ptjc+1 = \beta \times center,c \qquad (4.21)$$

where the *center, c* is the scale parameter impacted by the *center,c* and reflects the central place of the clan. The matriarch uses this position to maintain its status by guaranteeing the clan's stability. The center of a clan c can be calculated as follows:

$$p_{\text{center},c} = \frac{\sum_{j=1}^{n_c} p_{jc}^t}{n_e} \qquad (4.22)$$

where n_c represents the number of elephants in clan c.

Separation of male elephants from the clan: As mentioned earlier, male elephants will leave their families when they reach adulthood, preferring to live alone or in male groups. The separation process must be quantitatively described for the suggested optimization approach to work. The elephants in each herd with the worst fitness will quit their specific clans. As a result of this split, the current worst elephants j in the ith clan may be calculated as follows:

$$p_{\text{worst},jc}^{t+1} = p_{min,c} + \text{rand} \times (p_{max,c} - p_{min,c} + 1) \qquad (4.23)$$

In the EHO method source code in mathematics, where *Pmin,c* and *Pmax* are the lowest and upper limits of elephant members in the clan, the distributions are uniform and unpredictable.

4.6.3   Pseudocode of EHO Flowchart

In the algorithm, the standard EHO pseudocode is expressed in the flow-chart in Figure 4.7 below.

4.7   Grasshopper Optimization

In 2017, Saremi, Mirjalili, and Lewis presented the Grasshopper Optimization Algorithm (GOA), an application development approach. It belongs to the swarm optimization strategy category. Human engagement amongst ordinary agents (grasshoppers) and the attraction of the best individual is part of the GOA method. The application's exploratory skills were proven in early trials by the researchers, and they will be investigated further in the duration of our research.

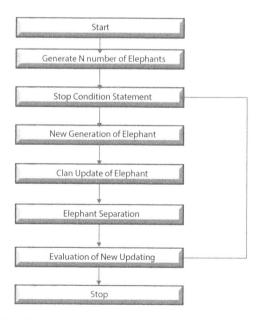

Figure 4.7 EHO flowchart.

According to reports, GOA employs two grasshopper movement techniques. The first is grasshopper communication, demonstrated by sluggish motions (when in the larval stage) and rapid activity (in insect form). The second correlates to a desire to get closer to a food supply. Furthermore, the slow movement of grasshoppers as they approach food and finally consume it is considered. The grasshopper optimization algorithm is described in detail below.

This chapter, like the others in the book, is about continuous optimization, or finding a value for x inside the workable search space S RD – indicated as x, such as $x = argminxS f(x)$. Assume that the aim is to reduce the linear cost function to the smallest value. GOA is an example of a population's metaheuristic. It indicates that the abovementioned issue is addressed by using a population of P agents of the same type. Each agent is described by a solution vector xp, $p = 1, .., P$, which represents a single solution in the domains of the tested function f [6].

The following equation may be used to represent the displacement of member p in iteration k:

$$x_{pd} = c\left(\sum_{q=1,q\neq p}^{P} c\frac{UB_d - LB_d}{2} s(|x_{pd} - x_{pd}|)\frac{x_{qd} - x_{qd}}{dist(x_d, x_p)}\right) + x_d^*$$

(4.24)

The dimensionality of the search space is represented by $d = 1,2, ..., D$. For legibility, index k has been removed. The first component of the equation relates to paired social relationships between grasshoppers. In contrast, the second correlates to wind-driven mobility (in the algorithm, in the direction of the best particle). The effect of gravity is not incorporated in the fundamental algorithm scheme, even though it is crucial for natural grasshopper swarms.

The intensity of social forces is defined by function s, which is contained in the first component of 4.24. The algorithm's authors defined it as:

$$s(r) = fe^{\frac{-lr}{}} - e^{-r}$$

(4.25)

where $l = 1.5$ and $f = 0.5$ are the default values.

It splits the space between the two examined grasshoppers into three distinct zones. In the so-called repelling zone, individuals who are pretty near are detected. At the other extreme, remote grasshoppers are in the attraction zone. The absence of social contacts characterizes the zone (or equilibrium condition), dubbed the comfort zone. The superior and inferior limits of the possible search space are also used to standardize the first component.

4.7.1   Description of the Grasshopper Optimization Algorithm

The parameter c – which appears twice in the formula, is reduced using the continuity formula:

$$c = c_{max} - k\frac{c_{max} - c_{min}}{K_{max}} \tag{4.26}$$

where c_{max} and c_{min} were used as the highest and lowest values, and K as the scaling factor as the algorithm's proven effective. The initial appearance of c in (4.26) lowers grasshopper motions around the target, achieving a

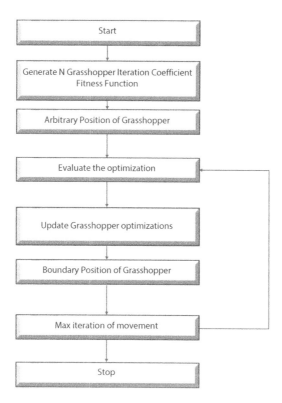

Figure 4.8 Grasshopper flowchart.

balance between swarming exploration and production. The Russell number in the particle swarm optimization algorithm is comparable to this. As shown in the whole element, cUBd2LBd reduces the area that grasshoppers should explore and utilize linearly. The flowchart in Figure 4.8 below presents the pseudocode for the general version of the GOA method.

4.8   Conclusion

This chapter dealt with the total performance of several methods based on swarm intelligence (SI) and compared widely known SI methods. The select thirty benchmark functions used in Matlab for measuring the interpretation of these approaches are taken together with a set of methodologies, including genetical algorithms (GA), ant colony optimization (ACO), particle swarm optimization (PSO), artificial bee colony (ABC) and cat swarm optimization (CSO). These benchmarks include unimodal, multimodal, independent, and inseparable features. The findings showed that differential evolution (DE) could perform or accomplish 24 of 30 features similar to the top algorithm. It performed very well in multimodal functions and was chosen as the best performance in 11 of the 12 parts.

5

Novel Swarm Intelligence Optimization Algorithm (SIOA)

Abstract

In this chapter, a new way to optimize swarm called the water wave optimization (WWO) algorithm, will be given based on group knowledge, forging, and sparrow anti-predation. Studies regarding 19 benchmark problems were done to evaluate the salp swarm algorithm (SSA)'s performance, which was assessed compared to other methods such as brain storm optimization (BSO) and particle swarm optimization (PSO) algorithms. The simulation results suggested that in terms of accuracy, convergence speed, stability, and solidity, SSA is superior to WWO, PSO, and WSO algorithms. Finally, two actual engineering examples show the efficacy of the suggested SSA.

Keywords: Cultural algorithm, power constraint, water wave, refraction, brain storm, economic load dispatch, propagating, oscillations

5.1 Water Wave Optimization

Economic load dispatch (ELD) is a fundamental component of modern power systems' optimum operation and regulation. Though the primary goal of the initial value problems is to lower total operating costs by selecting the best amalgamation of power outputs to meet actual power demands and setbacks, numerous restrictions, such as valve-point loadings, ramp-rate limits, prohibited operating zones and so on, make the optimization technique enormously unpredictable, particularly for larger energy systems.

Some physical constraints, such as machinery or auxiliary failures (boiler, feed pumps), force the units to have certain zones. Impermissible operational zones are areas that are not allowed to operate in prohibited operating zones (POZs). Generations are not permitted in certain regions because higher oscillations in their wheel components may occur, which must be avoided in prevalence estimates. Due to different constraints of

Kuldeep Singh Kaswan, Jagjit Singh Dhatterwal and Avadhesh Kumar. *Swarm Intelligence: An Approach from Natural to Artificial*, (113–126) © 2023 Scrivener Publishing LLC

unit generating outputs, real-time operating units may also have ramp-rate controls.

The concentration on direct searching and simulation models stems from the fact that, due to the non-convexity of the objective function, mixed-integer linear computing techniques are typically ineffective in finding solutions. The objective functions are simulated as a solitary polynomial equation in conventional methods such as lambda iteration, gradation, reference point technique, etc. Even though the dynamic programming has no restrictions on the characteristics of the cost curves, they cause the dimension of the problem to be high which in turn requires more computational efforts to solve the problem. The input-output character traits in thermoelectric electricity stations are redesigned as a partial differential equation with polynomial function. Even if the cost curves' features are unrestricted in feature selection, the problem is complexity is increased, necessitating more significant computing effort to complete. Several years have passed since. AI approaches are used to discover the best answer for portfolio optimization issues, including genetic algorithms, evolution strategies, differential evolution evolutionary algorithms, recurring roles-based enhancement, artificial bee colony algorithm, and online marketplace methodology.

Although there are numerous techniques for solving the equality and inequality constraints, the longer the network, the more complicated it becomes, necessitating the development of effective programs to discover an objective function consistently. In this regard, this research aims to show how a nature-inspired method may be used to solve ELD issues of varied complexities. The water wave concept was initially linked to gravitational influence and other forces through Newton's work in 1687 and subsequently through the creation of computer simulations such as Laplace's. Lagrange and Poisson expanded linear evanescent waves, as did Stokes, Gerstner, and Kelland's work on nonlinear waveforms.

Zheng has presented a novel metaheuristic optimization approach inspired by shallow water wave simulations dubbed the Water Wave Optimization Algorithm (WWOA). The inspiration for this project comes from wave movements, which are influenced by wave and current bottom relationships. The wave instability hypothesis is used to design search mechanisms for high-dimensional combinatorial optimization. The WWOA keeps track of the set of possible solutions, each of which is represented by a "wave" with a height of "h" and a frequency of. The WWOA is utilized in this chapter to find solutions to ELD issues with generating limitations. The suggested technique has the benefit of being simple to execute, requiring minimum population vectors and implementation details, and therefore being highly successful in searching for the optimum solutions in a high-dimensional computational complexity. To demonstrate WWOA's aggressive environment and effectiveness, it is contrasted with some of the more well-known metaheuristic algorithm approaches that have been presented in recent days [41].

5.1.1 Objective Function

The ELD problem's primary goal is to find the best mix of power generators that reduces overall energy consumption while meeting generating limitations. The ELD problem's conventional optimization issue may be roughly expressed as a single probability distribution [42].

Minimizing the overall operational cost:
The sum of manufacturing and changeable operation costs is the operating energy cost. Over the program's nine timeframes, the target functionality of decreasing total overhead expenses is described as follows:

$$Min\ F_T = \sum_{i=1}^{N_g} F_i(P_{Gi}) \tag{5.1}$$

As a result, the optimization algorithm that should be maximized is

$$MaxF_T = -\left[\sum_{i=1}^{N_g} F_i(P_{Gi}) + h_{pp}\left[(P_D + P_L) - \sum_{i=1}^{N_g} P_{Gi}\right]^2\right] \tag{5.2}$$

where $F_i(P_G) = a_i + bP_G + c_iP_G^2, (S/h), i = 1, 2, \ldots, N_g$, F_T is the overall volume of distribution ($/h); F_i is the ith power station cost function; a_i, b_i, c_i are the ith generator's cost parameters; P_{Gi} is the ith power station output voltage (MW); N_g is the number of generations; h_{pp} is the penalties factor; P_D is the maximum power requirement (MW). The total power loss is denoted by P_L (MW).

5.1.2 Power Balance Constraints

The total energy produced should match the actual energy demands (P_D) plus the electrical transmitting loss (P_L).

$$\sum_{i=1}^{N_g} P_i = P_D + P_L \tag{5.3}$$

How Kron's equation may be used to compute the damage utilizing B-loss parameters is given below.

5.1.3   Generator Capacity Constraints

Each generator's produced energy output (P_i) should vary between its minimum $(P_{i,min})$ and highest $(P_{i,max})$ limitations. This limitation on inequity is written as,

$$P_{i,min} \le P_i \le P_{i,max} \tag{5.4}$$

5.1.4   Water Wave Optimization Algorithm

The bulk of populations' optimal control approaches, which execute randomization, have an inspired nature. Typically, the optimization process begins with generating a collection of random solutions. These starting responses are then merged, relocated, or developed over a predetermined sequence of iterations known as an algorithm, which searches the search process for any other optimal solutions and prevents search inactivity (stagnation). Ultimately, these three stages are critical in determining the best or near-best solution to this issue. Each answer will be implemented here as a "wave" with a height (h) and frequency (f). Impermissible operational zones are areas that are not allowed to operate (POZs). Generations are not permitted in certain regions because higher oscillations in their wheel components may occur, which must be avoided in prevalence estimated. Actual production units may also have ramp-rate constraints owing to variation constraints of unit generating outputs.

The concentration on indirect searching and simulation models stems from the fact that, based on the none of the objective function, mixed-integer linear computing techniques are typically ineffective in finding solutions. The objective functions are simulated as a solitary polynomial equation in conventional methods such as lambda iteration, gradation, reference point technique, etc. The input-output character traits in thermo-electric electricity stations are redesigned as a partial differential equation with polynomial function. Even if the cost curves' features are unrestricted in feature selection, the problem is complexity is increased, necessitating more significant computing effort to complete. Several years have passed since discovering the best answer for portfolio optimization issues; AI approaches including genetic algorithms, evolution strategies, differential evolution evolutionary algorithms, recurring roles-based enhancement, artificial bee colony algorithm, and online marketplace methodology are used.

5.1.5 Mathematical Model of WWO Algorithm

The numerical simulation of propagating, splitting, and diffraction is presented first as a precursor to the hypothesized WWO Algorithm (WWOA).

- Propagation

Each repetition, each wave from the wave's populations, is permitted to propagate just once. The propagating operation, in this case, changes the originating wave x in each dimension to create a newly transmitted wave of x's. The continuity formula is used to describe the new generation:

$$x'(d) = x(d) + rnd(-1,1).\lambda. (d) \qquad (5.5)$$

where $rnd(1,1)$ is a random variable in the region $[-1, 1]$, and $L(d)$ is the dth element's duration is wave x's wavelengths, which is modified after each reproduction as follows:

$$\lambda = \lambda. \alpha - (f(x) - f_{min} + \epsilon)/(f_{max} - f_{min} + \epsilon) \qquad (5.6)$$

where λ are the wavelengths reducing percentage, $f(x)$ is the previous wave's fitness, f_{max} and f_{min} are the contemporary demographic's higher and lower strength and conditioning values, and is a very tiny reasonable result to prevent division by zero. Eq. (5.8) guarantees that vibrations with a more significant objective function have a smaller wavelength and propagate over shorter distances.

- Breaking

In WWOA, only a waveform x that began a better optimal answer (i.e., x becomes the new x) is broken. An innovative population is conducted around x using 'k' isolated ripples to mimic a wave breaking using Eq (5.9).

$$x'(d) = x(d) + N(0,1). \beta. (d) \qquad (5.7)$$

where β is the breaking frequency, and N is the number of times, $L(d)$ is the length of the dth column, and N is the special Gaussian variable. If none of the waveform propagation is better than x, x is kept; otherwise, x is substituted by the solitary wave that is the most suitable. At each n dimension, a total of k number of solitary waves x's are created, with the value of k being produced at randomness between 1 and k_{max}.

- Refraction

Suppose the waveform pathway is not orthogonal to the problems faced during propagation. In that case, the wave is distorted, causing the pulse to converge in freshwater lakes and diverge in deeper areas. Refractive index is done in WWOA on wavelengths when amplitude falls to zero. After diffraction, the wave's location is computed as,

$$x'(d) = N\left(\frac{x^*(d) + x(d)}{2}, \frac{\left|x^*(d) - x(d)\right|}{2} \right) \qquad (5.8)$$

where N is a stochastic empty vector, x is the best approach identified thus far, and d is the cause of problem size. As a result, here the wave's new location is a particular variable in the middle between the previous and the present better-remembered location. The wave amplitude of x's is reset to its reference quantity max once the refractive phase is completed, and its wavelengths are set by,

$$\lambda' = \lambda \frac{f(x)}{f(x')} \qquad (5.9)$$

5.1.6   Implementation of WWO Algorithm for ELD Problem

The WWO algorithm has four primary control factors except for the overall demographic. The variables to consider are the significant wave height, hmax, the wavelengths decrease frequency, the breakage correlation, and the most considerable number of breaking directions, kmax. To develop organizational dispatching issues, the variables =1.01, = 0.001, and hmax= six are utilized in all of our test systems. The most significant number of repetitions is regarded as the terminating criteria. The following are the parameter selection range as recommended by Zheng [17] in his literature.

- **Parameter Selection Range**

    Coeff () for wavelengths minimization = (1.001 to 1.01)
    hmax (significant wave height) = 5 or 6

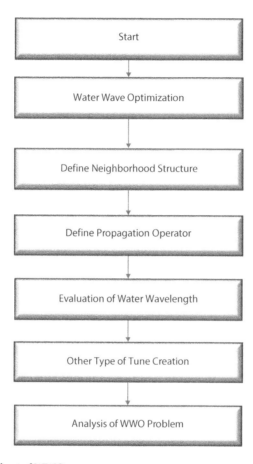

Figure 5.1 Flowchart of WWO.

Initial Frequency () = 0.5 Maximum number of breaking directions kmax = min(12, D/2) where D is the challenge dimensions.

Figure 5.1 depicts the suggested WWO algorithm's process flow used to solve combinatorial problems.

5.2   Brain Storm Optimization

Multi-objective optimization issues have gotten a lot of attention in recent years. The ideal approach to a multi-objective optimization model is a collection of solutions rather than a single answer. The options in the set are all similarly significant, meaning that none of them is better than the others in terms of all of the objectives. Many ecological design methods have been amended to solve multi-objective problems, including the genetic algorithm (GA), evolutionary algorithm (EA), particle swarm optimization (PSO), cultural algorithms (CA), ant colony optimization (ACO), differential evolution (DE), bacterial foraging optimization (BFO), and so on. According to studies, the majority of these methods can enhance the Pareto-convergence fronts and distribution to some extent [44].

Just like birds in PSO, ants in ACO, bacteria in BFO, and others moving collaboratively and individually toward higher and improved locations in the global optimum, individual people symbolize special characters in an international optimization program. Humans are the most intelligent creatures on the planet. After being influenced by the human idea-generating process, a unique optimization method was created, the brain storm optimization (BSO) algorithm. The BSO is further improved in this section to address multi-objective complex problems.

5.2.1   Multi-Objective Brain Storm Optimization Algorithm

The creative process was used to create the BSO algorithm. The idea of creating in a group discussion, known as brainstorming, follows Alex Osborn's previous three guidelines. The team members in the brainstorming group will have to be as transparent as possible to produce more varied ideas. The BSO algorithm's method is illustrated in [8]. The recommended multi-objective brain storm optimization (MOBSO) algorithm consists of six components, three of which would be BSO-specific. Aggregation approach, generation method, and global archives update are the other three. Other evolutionarily adaptive (or swarm cognition) methods share the other characteristics.

5.2.2   Clustering Strategy

One of the approach's key innovations is using a similarity measure in the parameter space. Depending on each aim, we utilize the k-means cluster method [10] to divide the population into k groups in Figure 5.2. Algorithm 1 depicts the procedure. The non-dominated alternatives are in the Archive set, whereas the Elite set and the Normal set are two ephemeral sets created by grouping in each cycle [45].

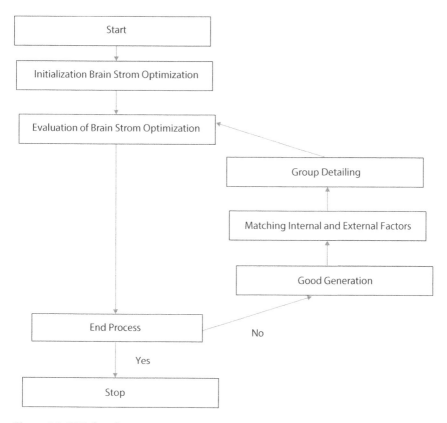

Figure 5.2 BSO flowchart.

5.2.3   Generation Process

Following the clumping stage, the selecting process, dispersion step, simulated annealing, and good at identifying will be used to produce additional humans. The following algorithm illustrates the method [46].

Algorithm 2. Generation procedure

if   rand() < *P1*

   if   rand() < *P2*

      if   rand() < *P3*

      randomly choose an individual from the **Elite_set** as the $X_{selected}$;

       else, randomly choose   the $X_{selected}$ from the **Normal_set**;

       end if

    else, choose an individual as the $X_{selected}$ from the **Archive_set**, randomly;

    end if

  else, dispersal step: randomly generate an individual as the $X_{selected}$;

  end if

where p is the number of people, and *P1*, *P2*, and *P3* are the predetermined likelihood values, selection *X* is the individuals chosen to update the current entity, and new *X* is the innovative ordinary person created by the *X* selected.

A completely random person is the *X* selected in the dispersion stage. The Adam optimizer obtains the new *X* by employing the thresholding technique to the *X* set. *X* picked fresh as the replacement person in the next iteration. Selecting operator: choose the Pareto optimum one from(,) *X* selected young as the developing embryo in the subsequent progeny.

5.2.4 Mutation Operator

From existing remedies, evolution produces new ones. In most traditional evolutionary methods, Gaussian recombination is used. The following representation is open to scrutiny:

$$x_{new}^d = x_{selected}^d + \xi * N(\mu, \sigma)$$

$$\xi = \log \ sig((0.5 * max\_iternation - current\_iteration) / K) * rand \ ()$$

$$\xi = \log \ sig((0.5 * max\_iternation \ current \ iteration \ K-)/) \ and * \ ()$$

$$(5.10)$$

where *selecte*^{d} is the *d*th dimensions of the person to be created, and x_{new}^d is the *d*th dimensions of the recently created individual; $N(,)$ is a binomial distribution function with an average value and; a coefficient that weights the commitment of the binomial phenotype; logsig() is a logarithmic sigmoid integral gain, max iteration, and current iteration are the maximum and current installment numbers, *K* is for modifying the curve of the logsig() function, and rand() is a random value within the logsig() function (0,1).

Cauchy recombination is another significant mutant operator. Due to its long flat tails, Cauchy recombination is more likely to generate more enormous leaps than stochastic evolution [11].

$$x_{new}^d = selecte^d + \xi \ \mu * C(' , \sigma') \qquad (5.11)$$

5.2.5 Selection Operator

The good at identifying is used to determine whether or not a generated resolution should be carried over to the next iteration. Pareto dominance is used to make the decision. The choosing regulations for the case of individual X $selecte^d$ and the genetic mutation individual X_{new} are as follows: if X_{new} continues to monopolize X $selecte^d$, then X_{new} survives; if X set continues to dominate X_{new}, then X $selecte^d$ survives; if X_{new} and X $selecte^d$ are not monopolized by each other, then a new instance is chosen at random from X_{new} and X $selecte^d$.

5.2.6   Global Archive

New non-answers maintain the Universal Archive in each iteration. The best answer is saved in the Universal Archive, restricted by the Max Archive parameter. Each new nonresolution acquired in the current incarnation will be evaluated with all members in the Archive to update the Global Archive. To steer the points forward towards a uniformly spread-out optimal solutions front, the packed with people operator [12] is used.

5.3   Whale Optimization Algorithm

Mirjalili and Lewis created a swarm-based optimizing technique in 2016, known as the whale optimization algorithm (WOA). The moral development and hunting methods of whale sharks are mathematically modeled using this technique. A WOA uses a bubble-net pumping approach to explore the solution's computational complexity [47].

Humpback whales use a circular or '9'-shaped foam cage to deceive krill or small fish schools. Whales utilize two distinct strategies to achieve this task: upward spirals and double loops. More information on those strategies may be found in signals. Surrounding prey, using a bubble-net assaulting technique, and searching for prey are the three major phases of a WOA. The surrounding strategy directs all searching engines to the best-found solution (leader). The bubble-net assault phase (extraction) follows, simulating the whales' path to approach their target. Whales use this method to travel in and around a spiraling pattern simultaneously. Finally, randomly chosen agents alter the placement of the ith search agent during the hunt for prey (investigation) phase. The WOA's success in solving many technical issues has piqued the interest of many in the scientific community. Several modifications and enhancements to the WOA have resulted from this study, including an adaptive vector autoregression WOA (used for handling traffic-aware routing in VANET), a continued focus on improving WOA that uses an enhancing current for upgrading process variables and applies polynomial extrapolation to the leader that helped enhance its

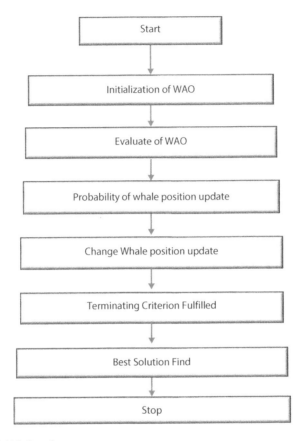

Figure 5.3 WAO flowchart.

ability to handle large-scale optimization problems in Figure 5.3, a Lévy flight velocity vector WOA that prevents convergence speed and helps in avoiding optimal local alternative, an adaptive regression WOA (used for the ability to handle traffic-aware routing in VANET), an improved WOA that uses a dynamic strategy for updating control parameters. The rest of this chapter is structured in the same way [48].

5.3.1   Description of the WOA

The fundamentals of the WOA are explained in a step-by-step manner. The issue formulation is initially formulated as a D-dimensional objective function OF in the first phase (.). Then, for the i-th agent of the j-th variable, boundary requirements are established as follows: j = 1... the number of decision variables in the following stage; the model components of the

WOA algorithm were specified, such as the number of processing agents (SA no) and the number of iterations (MI). A completely random community of Sano search agents has been initiated in the following phases [49]. A leadership was chosen based on two perspectives: the best-found resolution to ensure monetization and a resolution selected at random to ensure exploration. The searching agencies then investigate the solution area surrounding the leadership component. The first mindset of adopting the best-found answer as a leader was addressed in step 5. The existing repetition number is adjusted to zero to begin the WOA algorithm's circuit [50]. An incremental loop changes the location of each i-th search agent. The quantity has been adjusted using a decreasing trend in step 10. In steps 11 and 12, two coefficients' matrices, A and C, are modified. Humpback whales approach their prey by adopting a spiral-shaped route and a decreasing circle (steps 16 and 19). WOA will choose one of these pathways with a 50% chance of success [51]. As a result, a completely random 'p' with a value less than 50% causes the algorithm to use a decreasing circle (as shown in step 14). In step 15, we examine the exact number of the predetermined A. If this condition is satisfied with quantities less than a unit, the best-discovered answer will be used as a leader to update the location using a decreasing circle. Otherwise, one agent chooses personality traits, and the i-th agent's placement changes in steps 18 and 19.

5.4   Conclusion

The search method, which presents foraging and anti-predation behavior, effectively raises many ambiguities. It then offered the computational formula and the algorithm architecture. The SSA's performance in 19 testing functions was ultimately contrasted with WWO, PSO, and BSO algorithms. The findings showed that the suggested SSA may deliver very competitive results compared with existing state-of-the-art algorithms regarding search accuracy, convergence speed, and consistency. In addition, the findings of the two technical issues showed that the SSA is highly effective in many search areas. As the previous research showed, the SSA can explore the potential region of the wpr;d's best, thus effectively avoiding the optimal local problem.

Abstract

Swarm cyborg is a simple paradigm to coordinate multi-robotic systems consisting of several basic robots inspired by social insects. The most striking feature of swarming robots is their capacity to work together towards a common objective. In this chapter, the study of swarming cyborgs categorized according to current research issues and techniques. Recent studies in the main topics are divided into key areas and related subcategories.

Keywords: Swarm cyborg, biological phenomenon, bird flock, inspired immune function, perception, particle swarm optimization, cyborg actuators, microscopic

6.1 Introduction

Swarming cyborgs is a method for organizing and coordinating multi-cyborg systems of very basic cyborgs. Unlike traditional multi-cyborg systems, which use centralized or individualistic communications and control systems to implement cyborg behavior, swarm cyborgs take a decentralized approach, with the required collective behavior emerging from local communication and their ability to interact among both cyborgs and their surroundings. Swarming cyborg systems may exhibit three desirable multi-cyborg characteristics: functionality, reliability, and capacity. A description of these qualities follows [52]:

- Functionality can be understood as the willingness to expand a self-organized strategy to support a more significant or narrower number of robustness is the part of which a system can still function in the presence of partial failures or other abnormal conditions;
- Reliability is the degree to which a test can still operate after the appearance of incomplete errors or other unexpected behavior;

Kuldeep Singh Kaswan, Jagjit Singh Dhatterwal and Avadhesh Kumar. Swarm Intelligence: An Approach from Natural to Artificial, (127–148) © 2023 Scrivener Publishing LLC

- Capacity is the ability to adapt to new and varied changes in the ecosystem.

It is claimed that one of the significant advantages of swarm cyborgs is their resilience to failure. Recent research, however, has revealed that swarm cyborg devices are not as resilient as previously assumed. A basic yet efficient method for emergent swarm taxis (swarm motion towards a beacon) highlights these difficulties. These methods enable the swarm to move collectively towards a more infrared beacon utilizing a simple symmetrical shattering technique without the need for communication among cyborgs to accomplish it. The failed cyborg(s) effect on the entire swarm's functionality was examined to better appreciate the system's dependability, which includes, for example, 1) complete cyborg failure owing to a power outage, 2) malfunction of a cyborg's infrared sensor, and 3) malfunctions of a cyborg's actuators alone. All other functions, particularly detecting and signaling, remain operational. The study found that motor breakdowns can cause the partially failing cyborg to "anchor" the swarm, obstructing the progress towards the beacon. The researchers, therefore, concluded that 1) fault tolerance in swarms must take into account the consequences of complete cyborg failures, and 2) subsequent safety-critical swarms will require built-in mechanisms to mitigate the effects of such incomplete failures. One approach is to imagine (create) a unique cyborg behavior that recognizes that cyborgs with partial failure are "isolated" from the remainder of the swarm: a type of built-in immunological reaction to failing cyborgs [53].

The study presented the failure mode in cyborgs and seeks to solve the challenges of the formation of "anchor points" in the situation of partial cybernetic failing. The cyborg's motors no longer move due to their loss of power. However, it still has enough power for essential signaling. To address this problem. This study suggests and implements a unique immune-inspired approach that allows the swarm to self-heal and continue to function and accomplish the task in specific component failures. As a result, we suggest modifying the existing algorithm that provides a self-healing characteristic that works in particular failure situations. This approach is consistent with previous research, which showed that the fields of AIS and swarming cyborgs, especially, have a lot to offer. We drew inspiration for this methodology from the innate immune system's pituitary adenoma formation process, a procedure of stabilization and repair, from which we deduce a conceptual framework that we use to initialize a technique competent in trying to isolate the influence of the failure and initiating a repair sequential order to allow the barrage to remain operational.

6.1.1   Swarm Intelligence Cyborg

Robustness, self-organization, and adaptability are essential qualities that have fueled computer engineering research. Resiliency is a critical feature of natural processes. Several papers on how durability is engaged in multiple physiological techniques and practices that give birth to robustness in living organisms have been produced, as documented in numerous publications. Robustness is described as "a characteristic that permits a system to continue its function notwithstanding external and internal disturbances" in living organisms. It's one of the most basic and widely seen system-level phenomena that can't be explained by examining various elements. To perform in uncertain situations with inconsistent constituents, a system must be resilient [54].

In addition to resilience, self-organization and adaptability are two biological traits sparked in software engineering studies. Self-organization, or decentralized control, is common in living organisms, such as cells, organisms, and organizations with many components that lack the communications or computing skills, or both, required to execute centralized control.

Adapting is a fundamental biological phenomenon in which an organism improves its suitability for its environment. The word can also allude to the organism's ability to adapt. This is crucial for an organization, such as horses' teeth adapting to grass grinding or their capacity to jump higher and find mates. Biological evolution produces such adjustments in a varied population by better-suited forms replicating more frequently. Adaptive characteristics might be structural, physiological, or behavioral. According to the author, animals can be classified according to different physical characteristics, such as body covering, and defensive mechanisms such as claws and teeth. Inherited behavior chains and the capacity to study make up behavioral adaptations: Inherited behaviors can be transmitted in detail (instincts), or a penchant for learning can be shared, for example, through food hunting, mating, and vocalization. Finally, metabolic changes may allow the organism to execute specific functions, such as producing venom or secreting slime.

As a result, this section delves into the subject of swarm intelligence, which is driven by the qualities of self-organization and adaptability discussed previously. It also provides examples of swarm intelligence algorithms and discusses the characteristics of swarm process automation.

A swarm is defined as "vast groups of tiny creatures in which each individual performs a primary job, but the action creates complicated behavior as a whole." It consists of many simple organizations that communicate locally, including from the atmosphere, leading to the establishment of complex or macroscopic behaviors and the ability to achieve significant results as a team due to the combination of simple, or microscopic, behaviors of each entity. Higher-order species of animals, such as ant colonies, bird flocks, and wolf packs, have similar sophisticated social systems. Even though there is usually no centralized control structure prescribing how individual people should operate, changing consumers between such agents can lead to global behavior. Ant colonies, flocks of birds, herds of animals, and schools of fish are examples of similar systems seen in nature. Multicellular organisms work together to perform activities that would be impossible for an individual to complete. Termites, for example, will be able to construct huge mounds, while ants, depending on feeding forays, will be able to transport vast amounts of food. In various ways, diverse groups exhibit swarming behavior. Wolves, for example, recognize alpha males and females as fearless warriors who communicate with the group through facial expressions. The alpha male demarcates his pack's area and keeps out non-member wolves. There are no centralized management systems in place—all levels of the system function in a resilient, flexible, and scalable way, underlying the living organisms' coordinated operation.

We define swarm intelligence as "the field that works with natural and artificial systems consisting of numerous individuals that cooperate via decentralized control and self-organization, based on the concept of the swarm." The field emphasizes the aggregate behaviors that emerge from the dynamic interaction of individuals with one another and with their environments.

This concept, as stated, contains the fundamental characteristics of a swarm system, which may be found in both naturally occurring and artificial organizations. Pattern recognition analyzes a range of platforms in the natural world, ranging from ant colonies to flocks of birds; but from an engineering viewpoint, exploring swarm intelligence spans complex material from multi-cyborg systems to optimization [55].

Swarm intelligence is a vast topic that can be divided into two categories: natural vs. artificial (the study of living organisms or human-engineered artifacts); and science vs. engineering. This is seen in Table 6.1, which compares the scientific vs. engineering classifications for clustering algorithms and artificial immune systems (AIS), respectively. As has been argued, there is a natural link between the aims of the two disciplines, which explains how, despite their differences, the two fields may complement one other.

Several technology fields have embraced the concept that swarming can solve complicated problems, a few of which are discussed below.

Table 6.1 Classification of the role of swarm intelligence and artificial immune systems in science and engineering.

	Swarm intelligence	**Artificial immune systems**
Science	Behaviors	Use models to explain phenomena and guide experimental work
Engineering	Exploit the understanding of natural swarms in designing problem-solving systems	Apply systems inspired by immune functions, principles, and models to problem solving

Combinatorial optimization, routing telecommunications networks and solving cyborgics applications are only a few of the examples mentioned. According to the two best known swarm intelligence algorithms are: Particle Swarm Optimisation (PSO) and Ant Colony Optimisation (ACO). The swarming behaviors witnessed in flocks of birds, a swarm of bees, and schools of fish inspired PSO's ideas. Individuals in PSO connect either actively or passively. As an algorithm, PSO may be used to address a variety of function optimization issues because of its quick completion. However, it is recommended that one of the main challenges in successfully implementing PSO is to develop a means of translating the difficulties in PSO particles, which has a direct impact on its practicality and performance. Ant colony optimization (ACO) is a model of ant collective foraging behavior that depicts the path chosen by ants to reach a food source. The fundamental concept behind this algorithm is that ants communicate indirectly through pheromones to determine the quickest way between their colony and food. This is also in line with the word "stigmergy," which describes the communications promoted by ants in the surroundings and seen in ant colonies. When other ants in the surroundings detect the presence of the scent, they tend to follow the pathways where the secretion levels are higher. Ants use this technique to transfer food to their nest in a surprisingly efficiently direct, non-symbolic medium of technology controlled by the surroundings, according to the basic features of stigmergy that distinguish it from other mediums of expression.

- Stigmergic knowledge is local; it can only be retrieved by insects that visit the locus where it was emitted or by larvae that live nearby.

Various ACO algorithms have been used and suggested to tackle different problems. The first ACO algorithm, dubbed "Ant System," was proposed in the early 1990s. Since then, various additional ACO algorithms have been developed and used for assignments, scheduling, and other applications. All of these algorithms are based on the notion of identifying a route utilizing pheromones with highly concentrated values. Even though ACO has been experimentally verified in a wide range of construction problems, the authors make the argument that more improvement is given to apply ACO to more complex issues involving dynamic data adjustment or the nonlinear dynamics of the objective's restrictions, as well as broadening ACO's functionality from discrete to prolonged combinatorial optimization [56].

6.2   Swarm Cyborg Taxis Algorithms

Swarm aggregation necessitates physical consistency among cyborgs in the system when completing a job. Cyborgs are put in a setting at random and must interact. This is relatively simple when using a centralized control approach but extremely difficult when using a distributed architecture.

Swarm cyborgs is a method for coordinating multicyborg systems made up of the vast majority of basic physical cyborgs that evolved from biological studies of insects, ants, and other natural systems that exhibit swarm behavior. The intended aggregated behavior comes from the connections between the cyborgs and the surroundings in swarm cyborgs. Foraging, monitoring, and aggregating are possible applications for swarms of cyborgs mentioned.

We developed a class of aggregation algorithms, namely an automated algorithm system, and a computer program that uses only local wireless connectivity information to achieve swarm aggregation. These algorithms, sometimes known as the swarm beacon-taxis algorithms, are based on a minimalist design framework that focuses on highly restricted cyborgs that can interact regionally but lack awareness of the issue of the surroundings. Aside from the fundamental obstacle-avoiding infrared (IR) sensors, the beacon and radio communication are the only sensor data accessible. It's believed that the communications gear has a limited range, is omnidirectional, and the distribution performance isn't excellent. The goal is to keep the cyborg as basic as possible, as stabilization is thought to be only achievable with short-range radio equipment and motion detectors for avoidance.

The cyborgs do not require absolute or relative location knowledge, as indicated in the advantages of this method. Even in unbounded space, the swarm can continue agglomeration (remain together).

Because the methodology requires and generates connectivity, the swarm forms an ad-hoc communication system, which is highly beneficial in many swarm cyborgics application areas, such as disseminated detecting, discovery, or cartography, because it follows conclusions to be tried to communicate among any two cyborgs and enhances data collection from the entire swarm via a wired device with only one cyborg.

This enables the swarm to travel collectively (taxis) towards an IR beacon via swarm beacon taxis methods for the cyborgs to reach a beacon. Only cyborgs directly connected to the IR beacon are captivated and light up a beacon sensor. Swarming taxis towards the beacon is an emerging characteristic of this arrangement. Figure 6.1 depicts a collection of cyborgs who must keep together while simultaneously moving toward a beacon, generally a beam of light. On the other hand, the cyborgs lack the requisite sensory capabilities to discern the beacon's direction. To make progress in the correct order, the cyborgs must work together. There must be three separate systems in place to do this task. Also, to keep the swarm from dissolving, if a cyborg travels too far, it must circle it and return to others. Finally, to prevent a collision, the cyborgs must keep a minimum space between them.

Once these requirements are met, a dispersion relation technique must be implemented to guarantee the swarm travels in the correct direction.

The swarming supports agglomeration in swarm taxi techniques by using the following methods:

Figure 6.1 The setup of swarm beacon taxis. A swarm of cyborgs (left) with limited sensors must move to a beacon (on the right).

- Coherence behavior: The coherence behavior works as follows – Each cyborg has range-limited communications technology and occasionally transmits an "I am here" message while traveling. Of course, only those cyborgs within the communication network will read the signals. Cyborgs do not convey any knowledge about their internal condition or identify their direction about the transmitting cyborg. If a cyborg loses a link and the number of active neighbors is fewer than or equivalent to the threshold, the cybernetic is considered dead. Then it believes it's leaving the swarm and does a 180-degree spin. The cyborg picks a new route at random as the number of interconnections increases (i.e., when the swarming is re-established). If any interruption in the swarm's overall connection lasts less than a specified time constant, we call it consistent.

- Avoidance behavior: Each cyborg's avoidance behavior is controlled by short-range avoidance sensor and a long-range beacon sensor. The short-range collision warning sensor is employed to prevent colliding with other cyborgs or objects in the surroundings. This sensor informs cyborgs about the obstacle's gravitational field, while the long-range beacon sensor detects if the beacon source shines onto the cyborg.

- Symmetry breaching behavior: In swarm beacon taxis techniques, asymmetric breaking implies that the humanoid robots in the swarming must somehow collect the knowledge about the beacon's orientation. Figure 6.2 depicts an example of the technique for symmetry breaking. In a swarm of cyborgs in the proximity of a beacon, some cyborgs will be immediately exposed to the beacon. In contrast, others may be obscured depending on their positioning in the

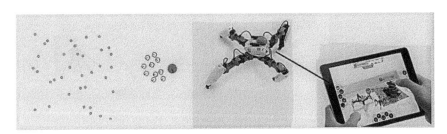

Figure 6.2 The illuminated (light-colored circle) and the occluded (dark-colored) cyborgs in swarm beacon taxis.

swarming. It shows that lighted cyborg D attempts to avoid cyborg C because C is within D's avoiding radius (a range set in the algorithms). However, because C's avoiding radius is lower, C will not notice D. Therefore, C will not detect D. The symmetrical breaking behavior in swarming beacon taxis algorithms is most likely due to the variation in avoiding radius.

The following sections go through the suggested algorithms in specifics. The updated variation of the method, dubbed the way, is explained using both techniques [57].

6.2.1   Cyborg Alpha Algorithm

The lowest point of swarm behavior in the α-algorithm is consistency. It states that the swarming is consistent if any breakdown in its general connection lasts less than a specified time characteristic. Swarm aggregation and linked ad-hoc wireless connectivity are two key emergence behaviors caused by coherence. In the α-algorithm, cyborgs exist in five distinct acquired states. There are eight transitional rules in the α-algorithm that define migrations among stages, as shown in Figure 6.1. A forward condition is a baseline in this technique. Other states can be activated depending on the cyborg's surroundings, but the cyborg resumes the forward state after the associated behavior is completed. Conversely, cyborgs in forward state keep track of the number of cyborgs or neighbors within transmission range and avoid variety and beacon detectors. The cyborg will enter the coherence state if the quantity of that of a neighbor falls beyond a certain threshold. In this stage, the cyborg will rotate 180 degrees. Suppose a cyborg loses contact with the swarm due to steering away from it. In that case, a 180-degree rotation will guarantee that the cyborg reconnects with the swarming, helping to sustain swarm agglomeration. The cyborg returns to its normal forward posture when the 180-degree rotations are completed. When the cyborg senses a rise in the number of cyborgs within the transmission range, the randomized state is activated. Because this number continues to grow, the cybernetic may be getting closer to the swarm's center. The cyborg will then revert from the forward position after making a random turn in a new direction. There are two avoiding states: one where the cybernetic is lit by the beacon and another where the beacon obscures the cyborg. When an item is identified in the α-algorithm, the cyborg rotates in the opposite direction of the object and then returns to a forward phase. The range is the sole distinction between the two avoidance states. When a cyborg is lit, the avoidance range is higher than when the cyborg is hidden. It describes the pseudocode for the α-algorithm. This algorithm limits itself to just using knowledge on cyborg interconnections, such as whether one cyborg is getting a signal from another. Because the radio is omnidirectional, there is no topographical indicator of where to go in the event of a separation. It is assumed that cyborgs can move forward as well as turn on-spot with sufficient accuracy, that they have thermal avoidance sensors, that they have limited-range communication transmitters, and that they have an omnidirectional light sensor which is used to sense whether a cyborg is lit. The algorithm is limited to using just information about cyborg relationships. When the cyborg detects a connection, it believes it travels incorrectly and changes position time to time.

As previously stated, extending the technique to a more significant number of cyborgs by making each one respond to each loss of connectivity results in an overly sensitive swarm that clusters together. Reacting to every link is akin to creating an entire network in which every vertex is attached to every other vertex, which is not the technique's goal. Attempting to make the cyborgs less responsive results in an extreme scenario that must be avoided if the swarm's cohesiveness is to be maintained. When a cyborg(s) is woven into the fabric of the swarming by solitary data transmission, there is a risk that the cyborg may not react to the loss of that connection, which is necessary for interconnected devices. One of its flaws is the algorithm's inability to prevent the swarm from breaking into separate hives. For example, when two subnets are connected by only one link, the method cannot prohibit the multitude from separating into two. The more advanced "shared neighbor algorithm," often known as the α-algorithm, has entirely solved this issue [58].

6.2.2   Cyborg Beta Algorithm

To overcome the algorithm's limitations, the graph theory notion of grouping was added to the α-algorithm. Instead of taking into consideration its degree of association to activate a response, the cyborg will start receiving from its neighbors their eigenvector table, which contains a list of their neighbors, to confirm how well others share a general neighbor; that is, whether a term of direction neighbor is the neighbor of other cyborgs' neighbors and friends.

Like the α-algorithm, the β-algorithm relies on radio connection to keep the group aggregating. It also includes five stages, as shown in Figure 6.3, with eight transitional rules that determine how movements between them happen. However, the default mode forward is the α-algorithm, which

Figure 6.3 The shared neighbor in β-algorithm.

utilizes the number of combined capacities as a deciding factor, while the β-algorithm uses the number of humanoid robots within transmission range as a defining factor. The cyborgs send out communication with their serial number and, more crucially, a list of the IDs of all the other humanoid robots within their transmission range as they move about. When a cyborg establishes a relationship with another cyborg, it can review the availability acquired from all other humanoid robots to determine if they'd have a link with the one who was lost. In other words, they can all construct a list of their common relationships thanks to the increasing volume of information transmitted by cyborgs. If a cyborg's sensors is restored and the quantity of combined capacity falls below a certain threshold, the contraption will rotate. The pseudocode for the α-algorithm is as follows [59]:

- After each lost connection, a cyborg checks how many of its surviving neighbors still have the lost cyborg in the neighborhood;
- If the number of extra cyborgs in the neighborhood is smaller than the number of the defined threshold, the cyborg turns around and returns;
- As the number of links grows, the cyborg selects a random direction.

For example, cyborg A loses contact with cyborg B, checks its relationships with other neighbors, and discovers that cyborg C and cyborg D share B as a neighbor, as illustrated in Figure 6.3. As a result, cyborg A will respond and turn around (only if the number of lost cyborgs in the neighbor is less or equal to a fixed threshold).

Simulation has shown that the β-algorithm improves swarm coherence. The cyborgs in the α-algorithm require more communications overhead and computing power than those in the β-algorithm. However, as previously stated, the increase in capacity does not influence the algorithm's sustainability because the algorithm is solely interested in transmitting knowledge between neighboring cyborgs.

6.2.3 Cyborg Gamma Algorithm

As compared with α and β algorithms, in the ω-algorithm the wireless communication channel is removed and replaced with simple sensors and a timing mechanism. The algorithm has two swarm behaviors; flocking and swarm taxis toward a beacon. The swarming keeps itself as a cohesive group while traveling towards an IR beacon due to this combination. A mixture of attractive and repulsive processes is used to create flocking. The cyborgs' IR sensors and a basic collision avoidance behavior are used to repel one other. A rudimentary scheduling device is used to produce magnetism. Each cyborg calculates the time since its previous avoidance behavior. If it reaches a specific benchmark, it turns towards its estimation of the swarm's center and travels in those directions for a set period. Figure 6.4 shows how a cyborg's movement increases the aggregation timer's timer. When a cyborg must perform an avoidance movement, the aggregation is reset to zero. The cyborg is most apparently going away from the swarming and needs to turn around if the agglomeration exceeds a particular predetermined threshold level. However, it does not rotate 180 degrees like the α-algorithm and β-algorithm but rather moves towards the swarm's apparent center. As a result, cyborgs utilizing the γ-algorithm must have detectors that allow them to estimate their direction to the swarm's prominent center of the other cyborgs. This is accomplished by combining the cyborg's directional microphones with communication systems to enhance the predicted range of the cyborg [60].

Compared to the results provided for the β-algorithm, the ω-algorithm performs considerably more consistently. According to sources, the algorithm successfully sustained cyborg accumulation for more than a few seconds, at

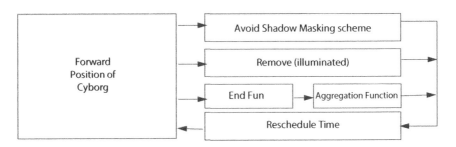

Figure 6.4 The state diagram for the ω-algorithm.

worst for swarm aggregating without beacon taxis. The β-algorithm sustained aggregating for more than 15 minutes for each trial in the original group of tests. The method has been tested on swarming five to twenty cyborgs, with five increases for each investigation. The ω-algorithm has always contacted the beacon satisfactorily in all of these studies, with no cyborgs lost. While the primary purpose for developing the β-algorithm was to investigate fault-tolerance and scalability in actual cyborg swarms, the method also has the added benefit of entirely freeing up modern communications bandwidth for usage in surveillance applications. However, because cyborgs can only estimate the swarm's center when conducting a coherence move, there's a chance that individual cyborgs will get detached, necessitating a greater swarm density (determined by the w parameter) to reduce the danger. Compared to the β-algorithm, this results in less transmission range, limiting its use in sensor node activities that need overall effect.

6.3   Swarm Intelligence Approaches to Swarm Cyborg

Global optimization methods are used as a source of motivation in various existing research topics in the domain of swarming cyborgs. Swarming cyborgs have sparked a lot of interest, as seen by these initiatives. The Swarm-bots, Pheromone Cyborgics, and I-Swarm projects are counted among these. In addition to this, the Symbrion and Replicator projects in swarm cyborgics focus on creating symbiotic evolving cyborg creatures based on bio-inspired methods and current computer paradigms [61].

The Swarm-bots project, which ended in March 2005, was designed to investigate novel techniques. Each cyborg calculates the time ever since previous avoidance behavior. If it reaches a specific benchmark, it turns toward its estimation of the swarm's center and travels in those directions for a set period. It shows how a cyborg's movement increases the aggregation timer's timer. When a cyborg must perform an avoidance maneuver, the aggregation is reset to zero. The cyborg is most apparently moving apart from the swarming and needs to be brought around if the agglomeration exceeds a particular predetermined threshold level. The research proved that a swarm of s-bots may be utilized for cooperative transportation or to reach difficult locations accessed by a single cyborg unit.

The Swarmanoid project intends to expand on Swarm-bots' past research by designing, developing, and controlling innovative, networked cyborg systems that operate entirely in a three-dimensional context. A swarm of cyborgs that can find heavy things and join together to lift and move the complex items to a new site has been spotted from the study. Recently, this research has produced heterogeneous swarms in which different forms of cyborgs execute various jobs, such as monitoring and giving depth perception in a three-dimensional environment.

The Pheromone Cyborgics project seeks to develop a scalable method for coordinating the activities of several tiny cyborgs to accomplish large-scale monitoring, exploitation, and danger detection outcomes. The chemical markers (pheromones) employed by insects (particularly ants) for communication and coordination inspired this study. The findings of the study revealed that cyborgs could perform specific tasks. Arduous duties include finding crucial entry points in the surroundings and directing the way through a structure to a hidden invader. This idea may be used for search and recovery missions too risky for humans to conduct. For instance, a team of cyborgs may be dispatched to a hazardous location to evaluate surrounding environmental conditions, look for survivors, and discover sources of dangers such as petrochemical or gas spills, toxic pollutants, pipe breaches, radiation, and so on.

The I-Swarm project aims to create genuine micro-cyborg swarms, drawing inspiration from ants in both distributed and critical technologies and self-organizing biological swarming structures. The project aims to develop many heterogeneous humanoid robots with varying sensors, opportunists, and processing capacities. The swarm's cyborgs are intended to perform a range of tasks. Precision, biological, medicinal, and cleaning activities are all included.

The Symbian and Power source projects are two of the most current swarm cyborgics initiatives influenced by swarm intelligence methods. The project's primary goal is to inspire biological techniques to create innovative concepts of evolution by natural selection for multi-cyborg creatures. They combine biologically inspired energy management systems (EMS) with cyborg technology. In swarm cyborgs, incorporation and clustering occurrences may allow cyborg creatures to operate their hardware and software systems independently. Artificial cyborg creatures become self-configuring, self-healing, self-optimizing, and self-protecting in this fashion, resulting in highly adaptable, evolvable, and adaptable cyborg systems that may be utilized to accomplish civil engineering. The cyborg creatures may also reprogram themselves without human involvement or supervision, allowing for the emergence of hitherto unimagined capabilities.

6.4   Swarm Cyborg Applications

Swarm cyborg applications is a novel approach to the cooperation of many cyborgs inspired by observations of massive numbers of social insects such as ants, earthworms, wasps, and bees, compelling examples of individual conversations. Artificial intelligence researchers have defined swarm cyborgs as "an implementation of global optimization techniques in a large number of cyborgs." Unlike effective systems, which use centrally controlled or hierarchical sensing and control systems to manage cybernetic behavior, swarm cyborgics takes a decentralized approach. The desired observable behaviors emerge from a local interaction process between cyborgs and their environment. Three desirable properties of swarm cyborg systems are:

- Reliability, which is a system's ability to continue to function in the face of partial breakdowns or other aberrant situations.
- Adaptability, which is the capacity to adapt to new, diversified, or changing environmental needs.
- Flexibility, which is the capacity to scale a self-organizing system to support bigger or fewer groups of individuals without significantly affecting functionality.

Cyborg devices have huge appeal because they contain lightweight materials contrasted with conventional approaches intended for the same job. Thus, cyborg units may theoretically be modularized, made of fabric, replaceable, and possibly discarded, because of the swarm's dependability, which allows them to be built to withstand a variety of disturbances.

In addition to redundancies, the swarming would proactively adapt to the work situation, another requirement for high dependability. It was also conceivable to imagine the swarm operating as a massively parallel computer program, allowing it to do tasks that were previously impossible for other forms of cyborg systems, such as sophisticated single cyborgs or centralized groups of cyborgs.

Swarms feature qualities such as self-organization and collaboration that are currently beyond the grasp of existing multi-cyborg systems, in addition to the characteristics mentioned above that are relevant to cyborg systems. According to a new study, the primary benefit of the swarming cyborg's method is resilience, which shows itself in various ways. For starters, a swarm of cyborgs can self-organize or continuously reconstruct how particular cyborgs are organized since they are made up of several very basic and generally homogeneous cyborgs that are not preassigned to an explicit function or task within the swarm. Second, the swarm method is highly forgiving of solitary cyborg failures. The failure of a single cyborg has little effect on the overall aim of the programs. Finally, there is no dominant failure point or vulnerability in a swarm with decentralized control.

Indeed, the increased degree of resilience seen in cyborg hives is essentially free in the sense that it is inherent to the swarm cyborgics approach, as opposed to the significant engineering cost of fault tolerance in traditional cyborg systems.

Some parameters have been put up that indicated separating the study of swarm cyborgics from other cyborgs research. However, the author emphasizes that the description and list of conditions are based on their interpretation and that these parameters should not be used as a checklist to determine if research is a swarm cyborgics study or not. The following are the criteria that were extracted directly from:

- Individuals that are autonomously extraterrestrial: They should have an inversion layer in the world, be located, and properly engage with the environment.
- A vast number of cyborgs: The research should help coordinate a swarm of humanoid robots. Swarm cyborgics excludes study that is only appropriate to control a limited number of cyborgs and does not strive for universality.
- A few homogeneous groupings of cyborgs: The cyborg system under investigation should consist of a small number of homogeneous groups of cyborgs, with a large number of humanoid robots in each set. That is, research involving highly diverse cyborg groupings, regardless of their size, are deemed to be fewer swarming cyborgs.
- Somewhat inept or inefficient cyborgs: The cyborgs utilized in the study should be comparatively inept or inefficient in their own right when it comes to the task at hand. That is, either 1) the cyborgs should struggle to complete the work on their own, necessitating the collaboration of a group of cyborgs, or 2) the deployment of a group of cyborgs should increase the task's handling performance.
- Cyborgs with restricted processing and computing aptitudes: The cyborgs utilized in the study should only have restricted processing and communication skills. This restriction guarantees that cyborg coordination is dispersed. The cyborg group's usage of worldwide media platforms is likely to result in unsalvageable products. As a result, it would function in opposition to the first criterion indicated above.
- Swarms of mutants: These can be beneficial when one cyborg is incapable of completing the work or several simultaneous tasks are required to complete the assignment. Some

concepts in the realm of application that can be used in a swarm of humanoid robots have been proposed. We highlight several task areas below, along with real-world challenges as examples, to underline the characteristics of the tasks that make them appropriate for swarm cyborg devices.

- Studies that span a geographic area: Swarm cyborg technologies are distributed systems that are well-suited for activities involving the state of a space. Swarm cyborg systems' widespread sensing capability can monitor the prompt identification of dangerous occurrences, such as a chemical spill. A swarm cyborg system would have two key benefits over sensor networks in coping with this.

  - A swarm cyborg technology can concentrate on the location of a problem by deploying its membership towards the root of the problem, allowing the swarming to be better localized and determine the current problems nature;
  - A swarm cyborg system may also self-assemble and produce a patch to stop the leaking.

- Dangerous tasks: Persons who build a swarm cyborg system aren't required to make the scheme acceptable for sectors with hazardous jobs, clearing a place on the market today.
- Tasks that lead to different results in time: A swarm cyborg system may scale up or down in response to the job at hand. For example, when the ship's tanks decompose, the size of an engine problem from a wrecked ship might proliferate. As a result, a swarming cyborg system may be expanded by dumping more humanoid robots into the buried ship's vicinity.
- Redundancy-required tasks: The durability of swarming cyborg systems derives from the swarm's inherent redundancies, which allows the system to decline peacefully, making it less vulnerable to malfunctions. For example, swarm cyborg systems can generate dynamic communications infrastructure on the battlefield. When some of the numbers required are struck by enemy fire, these networks can benefit from the resilience gained by reconfiguring the communications node.

Swarms of humanoid robots are also helpful when numerous items are necessary for transferring an object from a distant place or creating an object from nearby dimensions, in addition to the activities listed above. This is because these activities may be accomplished more quickly when performed by many cyborgs. Other activities might include foraging, monitoring, investigation, modeling, and aggregating, as well as any other job that requires several cyborgs to perform it faster.

According to Winfield [68], "foraging is a complex task involving the coordination of several tasks including efficient exploration (searching) for objects, food, or prey; physical collection or harvesting of objects; homing or navigation whilst transporting those objects to collection point(s); and deposition of the objects before returning to foraging.". As Winfield points out, there are just a few varieties of foraging cyborgs used in application areas, including emergency response, grass mowing, room cleaning, resource gathering, and hazardous materials cleanup among other potential uses. Surveillance systems are frequently required in locations where human presence and action are harmful. They can take various forms, such as following a target or monitoring the surroundings. Many sensors will be set at fixed places around an area in similar approaches. On the other hand, a swarm of cyborgs can organize themselves to cover the region in question and dynamically adjust as the technology evolves. Moreover, numerous tiny, low-cost cybernetic organisms with a limited number of diverse communications capacities can be manipulated to cooperatively search and engage in activities in an unknown large-scale hostile region that is dangerous for a human presence.

Decomposition is one of the most basic swarm behaviors in nature, and it has been seen in a wide range of organisms, from bacteria to social insects and humans. Aggregate organisms can evade and leave the area, withstand harsh environmental circumstances, and locate mates. The use of cyborgs in aggregate is illustrated in one of the early cyborg implementations. The cyborgs must create a set-size cluster around an infrared beacon in this scenario. In this approach, cyborgs must continuously generate a sound comparable to the sound made by birds known as a "chorus." However, the results obtained were only relevant in a noise-free setting. Another investigation into the accumulation of cyborgs was conducted by swarming techniques. The methods devised mainly rely solely on local wireless connection knowledge to accomplish swarm consolidation. These algorithms have been proposed on a minimalistic framework, which focuses on highly restricted cyborgs that can converse regionally but lack global environmental information.

6.4.1 Challenges and Issues

Swarm cyborgs are still in their early stages of development, despite drawing much interest from the scientific community and receiving a lot of funding. Many critical issues still exist, including obtaining an explicit knowledge of rampaging behavior and trying to translate this into workable technology, which is perhaps the most difficult challenge; the advancement of affiliated cyborgs, which has to be comparatively cheap and task-specific; the rise of appropriately low and miniaturized sensors and devices; and decrease energy consumption, with the potential of reducing power consumption by as much as 80%; and combining all of these technological innovations into stable and dependable systems.

It is claimed that one of the significant advantages of swarm cyborgs is their resilience to failure. Recent research, however, has revealed that swarm cyborg systems are not as resilient as previously assumed. A simple yet effective technique for emergent swarm taxis (swarm motion towards a beacon) highlights the difficulties. The study found that motor failures might cause the partially-failed cyborg(s) to "anchor" the swarm, preventing it from moving towards the beacon. High levels of resilience in swarm cyborgs are usually not substantiated by empirical or theoretical analysis, as claimed in this chapter, which also highlighted several concerns, including what is meant by the resilience and how to evaluate the durability or high availability of a swarm cyborg system. To answer these concerns, researchers used failure mode and effect analysis (FMEA) to investigate automatic failure in cyborg swarms, using a case study of a wirelessly linked cyborg swarm in both simulated and experimental trials. According to the FMEA case study, a cyborg swarm is impressively tolerant of complete cyborg loss but is less tolerant of slightly failed cyborgs. A cyborg with failing motors but all other subsystems working, for example, might anchor the swarm and make it difficult or impossible for it to move. The authors, therefore, came to the following conclusions: (1) fault tolerance in swarms must take into account the impact of partial cybernetic failures, and (2) future safety-critical swarming will require built-in mechanisms to mitigate the impact of such partial failures. Therefore, the authors proposed a novel cyborg behavior that detects neighbors with system failures and then separates them from the remainder of the swarm: a type of built-in immune system to damaged cyborgs. Various sorts of failure mechanisms and the impact of particular cyborg failures on swarming have been studied in swarm cyborg systems. The reasons for failure and consequences for swarm beacon taxis are as follows:

- Case 1: Complete failures of particular cyborgs (entirely failed cybernetic organisms due to, say, a power outage) may cause the swarm taxis approaching the beacon to slow down. These are generally benign, in the sense that "dead" cyborgs merely become obstacles in the surroundings that other nanobots in the swarm must avoid. Given that they are obstacles, there will inevitably be a decrease in the number of cyborgs accessible for collaboration. However, if the number of failed cyborgs grows, one of them may "anchor" the swarm, hindering its taxis toward the beacon.
- Case 2: A cyborg's infrared sensors fail. The cyborg may leave the swarm and get lost due to this. The cyborg that leaves the swarm will become a moving obstacle for the remaining cyborgs. When some cyborgs lose and become a moving obstacle, the number of cyborgs necessary for teamwork may be reduced because some have now been lost and moved away from the swarm.
- Case 3: Only a cyborg's motors fail. The partially failed cyborg will possibly "anchor" the swarm, hindering its progress toward the beacon if only the engine fails, keeping all other capabilities working, including IR detection and signaling.

6.5   Conclusion

Most of the discussions in this chapter were based on the biological inspiration of ants, bees, and birds. Implicit transmission in the swarm cyborg real-time application seems to offer more robustness. Due to the distributed design, a distributed operating structure was selected to prevent the failure of a single point. About mapping and locating, An effort is currently being made to tweak the difficulties in this field concerning mapping and locating. Caging is preferable to current techniques for object transit and modification because the restrictions of the domain may be lowered and maintained easily. Research on programmable cyborgs has progressed significantly in the previous two decades. However, this domain is still in its infancy. Circulating trajectories and training are critical areas where the authors have garnered much attention. Several novel heuristics and algorithms have been proposed to tackle the difficulty in this field. Academicians have shown great interest in strengthening reinforcement learning (RL). Multicultural and uniform systems are frequently explored in the area of work allocation.

Abstract

Swarm cyborg systems focus on decentralized coordination amongst many cyborgs with limited ability to communicate and cooperate. Although failure intolerance and robustness to particular cyborg failure have often been presented as evidence of the usage of swarming autonomous vehicles, new research has demonstrated that swarm cyborg systems are prone to specific failure types. In this chapter, the technique of cyborg self-healing swarms is proposed and inspired by the granulation confinement and repair seen in the immune system. A case study by a swarm team shows that partly failing cyborgs have the most damaging influence on swarm behaviors, as proven in earlier reports. To this end, we have devised an immune-inspired method that allows recovery from specific fatigue failure during the swarm operation and overcoming issues associated with partly unsuccessful cyborg swarming behavior.

Keywords: Simulation constraint, cyborg actuators, bio-inspired algorithm, artificial immune system, unified modeling language centroid, numerical simulation, cytokines

7.1 Introduction

This chapter discusses the chartered financial analyst (CFA) method. It presents a technique for developing innovative immune-inspired algorithms based on a set of principles. In the first section we will examine the work provided in terms of the CFA method, taking into account Hart and Davoudani's information technology modeling approach presented in 2011, which describes our research into the problem area of swarm cybernetic systems, especially the "anchoring" difficulty that arises in swarm beacon taxis, which is probably largely owing to cyborgs(s), before discussing our work in using CFA to create an immune-inspired algorithm in response to the swarming beacons taxis "alignment" difficulty [62].

Kuldeep Singh Kaswan, Jagjit Singh Dhatterwal and Avadhesh Kumar. *Swarm Intelligence: An Approach from Natural to Artificial*, (149–184) © 2023 Scrivener Publishing LLC

7.1.1 Understanding the Problem Domain in Swarm Cybernetic Systems

The limitations of a designed challenge must be considered throughout the model creation and verification phases. This allows for constructing AIS compatible with the application's limitation and verified in the individual user's prerequisites specification rather than physiological considerations. We investigate the topic of swarm cybernetic systems to better comprehend the simulation environment and constraints [63]. This section focuses on the problems and difficulties of swarm cybernetic implants, particularly preserving the resilience of swarm cybernetic structures. Swarm beacon taxis, an aggregating job in swarm cybernetic systems where the swarm cooperatively travels towards a beacon, is the primary application addressed in this section. An aggregation method was created in swarm beacons taxis that achieves swarm aggregation using local wireless connection information. Algorithm, automated system, and computer program are the three terms α algorithm, β algorithm and ω algorithm. This presentation employs this application as an empirical test case [64].

Various sorts of failure mechanisms and the impact of specific cyborg errors on the swarm have been studied in swarm cybernetic systems. The failure types and implications for swarm beacon taxis are as follows: 1) complete failure of particular cyborgs (entirely failed cyborgs due to, say, a power outage) may delay the swarm moving towards the beacons, 2) failure of a cyborg's IR sensors, and 3) failure of a cyborg's actuators only. These failure types might cause the failing cyborg to "anchor" the swarm, preventing taxis from reaching the beacon. The influence of a least in part cyborg to "anchor" the swarm, inhibiting its movement toward the beacon implicit in the ω-algorithm, was the subject of our case study.

We applied the algorithm in the swarming cybernetics numerical simulation, the Player/Stage, to investigate the "anchoring" issue. These tests are primarily designed to replicate the effect of malfunctioning humanoid cyborgs in swarm signal taxis or the alleged "anchoring" problem. While there are five failed cyborgs in the simulations, we track the movement of the swarm's centroid towards the beacon during these trials. These tests served as a benchmark against which we measured our immune-inspired strategy. And during studies, the proposed methodology is evaluated to demonstrate the impact of the failed cyborg(s) on the structures: When no faults are encountered, the ω-algorithm (M1) for swarming beacon taxis allows the swarm to attain a centroid separation of less than 0.5 cm from the beacon [65].

With a failed cyborg in the surroundings, the implementation of the ω-algorithm (M1) for swarm beacon taxis enables all cyborgs in the swarm to attain a distance of less than 0.5 cm from the beacon.

The results of the tests in Chapter 6 indicate that even with two partially failed cyborgs, the swarm would always reach the beacons, and the time delay is relatively modest. However, because the simulations included three defective cyborgs, the swarm began to undergo the anticipated "anchoring" effect. The defective cyborgs have become an anchor, and the swarming will travel around them, avoiding the signal. These studies back up Bjerknes' claim that there is a problem with "anchoring" (2009).

These studies helped us better comprehend the applicability and issues that swarming cybernetic systems, especially pack beacon taxis, face. Based on our findings, we investigated biological systems and presented an immune-inspired approach adapted to the consequence of primarily failed humanoid cyborgs. While there are cyborgs with resource system failures, this results in a high energy drain in swarming cybernetic systems, which can manage certain types of faults and begin repair methods to allow information exchange amongst cyborgs.

After describing how we investigated the issue environment in swarm cybernetic systems, we will now represent our research in Section 7.1.2 on applying the CFA principle to designing electromechanical swarm systems. This is in line with our objective of developing an immune-inspired strategy for use in swarm cybernetic systems, especially for the swarming beacon taxis' "anchoring" problem [66].

7.1.2 Applying Conceptual Framework in Developing Immune-Inspired Swarm Cybernetic Systems Solutions

The CFA proposal emphasized the necessity for bio-inspired technologies, such as AIS, to be constructed methodically. We show the stages of CFA in Figure 7.1 depending on our characterization of CFA.

The CFA method is based on the following procedures, as shown in Figure 7.1:

1) Probes, observations, and experiments are the first three;
2) An abstract description of biological processes based on a model;
3) Computation framework for analysis; and
4) Algorithms based on biomimicry.

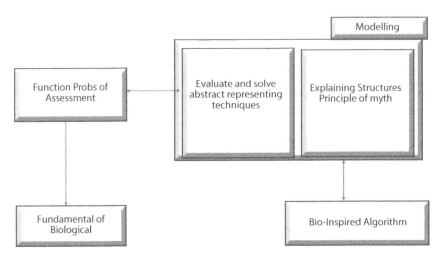

Figure 7.1 Conceptual framework of AIS.

The objective of this work was to propose a new AIS for self-healing swarm cybernetic systems, designed specifically for the influence of probably largely humanoid cyborgs, results from a vast energy drain in swarm artificially intelligent systems that can encompass specified types of error and introduce repair techniques that allow power generation information exchange among humanoid cyborgs. For your convenience, we've summarized each step of CFA as follows [67]:

- Immunology and probes: Confined to research material published in books, periodicals, and publications, we look at critical parts of immunology in the scientific literature to see whether they may be used as inspiration for self-healing mechanisms in swarm cybernetic systems.
- Simplifying the computer model: We constructed a computer program and simulated granuloma development, which is described in the recent literature. The concept and simulations are streamlined following the restriction we discovered when investigating the problem area of swarm cybernetic systems, especially the "attaching" issue in swarming beacon taxis mentioned.
- Algorithm framework/principle: We provided a design approach and an algorithmic methodology derived from creating models and simulations computationally.
- Artificial immune systems (AIS): A new AIS for self-healing swarm cybernetic systems, defined and demonstrated in

Chapter 6. We detail each effort given in this work in modifying the CFA to build an immune-inspired approach for a self-healing swarming cybernetic system that significantly contributes to energy exchanging amongst cyborgs in the system, based on the steps of CFA summarized above. We start with microbiology and probes, then move on to mathematical methods, conceptual algorithm prototypes, and the algorithms themselves.

The initial probes were provided in the published research on immunology to discover immune processes and features that might be used to inspire our immune-inspired solutions. We concentrated our discussions on the granuloma development mechanism. The relevance of the granuloma is that it forms a "wall" of activated macrophages around infected cells so that when the contaminated cells die, the neighboring macrophage tries to prevent infection from spreading. Bacteria can be discharged without these issues from the malignant cells, allowing microbial reproduction to spread to other cells in the system. According to our study of the immunological research on granuloma formation, the etiology or appearance of invasive carcinoma is complicated, involving several processes working together to produce an inflammatory lesion capable of containing and destroying infectious diseases. The majority of the material is customized to specific illnesses and requires additional clarification by immunologists. We aim to comprehend the general process of neoplastic transformation based on our investigations into the immunological research, which we have discussed since our work focuses more on observing the mechanisms of cell proliferation, which is not unique to any illnesses. We also argued that creating a granuloma and eliminating pathogenic bacteria from cells are apparent analogies between the possible repair of a swarm of cyborgs, as in the case of swarm beacon taxis [68].

The analogy in Table 7.1 characterized the features of both swarm cybernetic implants and granuloma development. We then argued that granuloma formation might be a source of motivation for creating immune-inspired algorithms based on this comparison.

We previously discussed how granuloma development is essential in immune systems because it serves as a communication exchange, preventing bacterial infections from spreading to other cells and containing diseases by drawing other cells such as monocytes and T-cells to the vascular endothelium. We recommended that this be used to address the aforementioned "anchoring" problem, allowing cyborgs to control certain types of faults and begin repair methods to allow energy exchange across cyborgs in

Table 7.1 Properties of swarm cybernetics and granuloma formation.

Properties of swarm cybernetics	Properties of granuloma formation
A large number of cyborgs	A large number of cells
Few homogeneous groups of cyborgs	Few homogeneous cells
Relatively incapable or inefficient cyborgs	Each cell needs to perform the desired task
Cyborgs with local sensing and communication capabilities	Chemokines and cytokines

the ecosystem. The concept is that a swarm of several cyborgs functioning together may continue to work even if some of the cybernetic organisms fail, as mentioned earlier. To aid comprehension of the interconnections of cells throughout the evolution of neoplastic transformation, we built a computer model consisting of a unified modeling language (UML) model and a simplified agent-based simulator. We constructed a model and simulation of the overall development and evolution of granuloma formation, rather than a specific illness, using the CoSMoS process [69].

We didn't want to simulate the building to get a biological understanding but rather to understand the complexities of a generic effect to condense a series of architectural options. We can utilize these concepts to develop a new AIS algorithm. This follows the recommendation, which emphasized the conceptual framework and simulations customized to the engineering domain and constraints for constructing an AIS engineering solution. This necessitated more investigation of biology to build the model and simulation. We initially created the software architecture by writing down the system's behaviors in which we are engaged, separating the granuloma development behavior into critical phases, and describing each stage using our probing and immunology publications.

This follows the argument that the simulation must be adequately defined since there are so many different factors in the biological system that it is difficult to replicate them all. Before constructing the agent-based simulations, we utilized UML diagrams to create our model. We built the memory consolidation after completing the domain model, which focuses on how the processes would be implemented and conducted in the simulator. Finally, we used NetLogo to create a simulation of granuloma development. We constructed a simulator closer to the analogy of granuloma development by using an agent-based simulation that preserved the inter-connections of cells during the granuloma formation process.

We described our work on the final two phases of the conceptualization approach (CFA). One is to prepare the conceptual model and instantiate framework/principle for creating a novel AIS in Chapter 5 based on the modeling and simulation work given in Chapter 4. Section 5.1 presented four fundamental design concepts derived from the models and simula-tions and a granuloma creation method for self-healing swarm cybernetic systems. We eventually constructed the algorithms for swarm homeostatic systems using the sensor-based simulation toolset, Player/Stage, after developing the granuloma creation method in Chapter 5.

This is primarily to address the "anchoring" issue with swarm beacon taxis and the development of swarm biomimetic systems capable of containing certain types of errors and initiating repair techniques that allow energy sharing between cyborgs in the event of cyborg electric power failure. The results were compared to the trophallaxis work's specific treatments charge mechanism and the shared nearest charger method. We demonstrated that the granuloma formation method could address the "anchoring" issue in swarm beacons taxis. Based on the findings, the swarm can accomplish the beacon even when more than three failed cyborgs are in the environment.

Section 7.2 will address our views on creating immune-inspired solu-tions for swarm biomechanical systems, especially to begin repair methods to allow energy sharing amongst cyborgs due to energy failure, based on the characterization of our work in the following section.

7.2   Reflections on the Development of Immune-Inspired Solution for Swarm Cybernetic Systems

In this section, we describe designing AIS algorithms for self-healing swarming cybernetics systems that may exchange energy among defective and non-faulty humanoid cyborgs in the ecosystem by following the basic methods presented here. In Section 7.2.1, we provide comments on the development of the AIS algorithm according to CFA phases, and in Section 7.2.2, we discuss the advancements in swarming cybernetic systems.

7.2.1   Reflections on the Cyborg Conceptual Framework

We have discovered a particular engineering challenge that we would like to address during the early stages of this project. We'd want to see a unique immune-inspired approach for self-healing swarming cybernetic devices that can solve the swarming signal taxis' "framing" issue caused by failed cyborg(s) that suffer high energy drain in the ecosystem. This is in line with those who recommended that an application's challenge and constraint be considered before moving forward with modeling and simulations created using the CFA technique. Having a good understanding of the issue domain early in the project aided us in creating the immune-inspired algorithm using the CFA method. Second, using an implementation perspective to the CFA, the program or algorithm type drove our judgments throughout, following the CFA (in our case, the swarm beacon taxis). The benefit of using this technique is that we could customize our probes to the pathophysiology of the subject we were working on. Rather than researching broad immunology, we looked at microbiology, which may be an excellent inspiration for tackling the problems we wanted to tackle. Our studies looked into potential immunological solutions after identifying the "anchoring" issue caused by the least in part cybernetic that suffered a highly energetic drain in the system, resulting in its motor failure. We discovered the process of cell proliferation using our immunology probes, which is a process in which immune system cells strive to prevent viral infections from infecting cells of the immune system. It's also a reaction to an intruder that necessitates the mobilization of the immune system to identify and, if feasible, resolve the issue. We didn't thoroughly examine immunological processes either; instead, we looked for a viable method the AIS consulting firm had local experience in. We also believed that additional immune mechanisms might likely inspire our issues, notwithstanding the granuloma phase transformation. We discovered a parallel between the creation of granulomas and swarming cybernetics programs that rely on probes, which is summarized. Rather than trying to cover every fundamental and function in a sufficient period by looking into a wide variety of physiological inspirations, which is impossible to do, we mainly looked at and addressed the concepts that might serve as a source of inspiration for the specific situation at hand. Finally, we realized that granuloma development involves a diverse set of cells and connections. We discovered that covering every phase in granuloma development would be highly challenging. We can choose what to incorporate and exclude from our model and simulations even though we already understood the type of incident we were concerned about and the information we wanted to utilize in the ultimate application of our work. In general, while endeavoring to create an immune-inspired algorithm to address an engineering challenge, we may offer the accompanying recommendations to others:

- Determine the application or issue domain that you want to address.
- Investigate the problem by creating a series of tests that demonstrate the problem's impact.
- Using the CFA method, identify probable immunological concepts that might motivate solving the challenge.

After the issue domain is defined, we develop an AIS algorithm based on the CFA method. Even though our explanation is based on our own experience with the CFA, we feel that by adopting a principle approach like CFA, one may obtain some context for the construction of immune-inspired algorithms [70].

7.2.2   Immunology and Probes

The initial step of CFA is to investigate immunology, as mentioned in section 7.5, and here is where we get our ideas. During this phase, we must determine which forms of physiology should be utilized as inspirations to construct immune-inspired techniques with many biological materials to investigate. The steps of CFA suggested do not describe how to determine which biological systems would be ideal for providing motivation or how to identify the features of the methods that may be an excellent template for an algorithmic. As Andrews argues, determining the bio-inspired topic of interest is very simple; for example, because our bio-inspired area of focus is AIS, our neural network is the defense mechanism in this study. However, determining which parts of the immune system may serve as a valuable source of motivation required additional research.

The procedure of tumor progression was chosen as an intriguing immunological feature to examine in this degree based on our software program and the challenges. It also believes that before modeling and simulating immune systems, one must first grasp the domain and constraints. After determining that we wanted to learn more about granuloma development, the next step was to determine how it works. However, while researching immunology to understand it better, we discovered that the majority of the literature explains granuloma development in the context of certain illnesses. We wanted to define the significant cells and connections that occur to comprehend the overall characteristics of granuloma development. This was accomplished using CFA's modeling stage, which enabled us to identify biological markers of granuloma production and construct models and simulations.

In general, we discovered that because our main goal was to establish an immune-inspired technique, specifically for the "attaching" problem in swarm cybernetic structures, rather than trying to investigate the immune system's many properties and behaviors, we only focused on those that could be a source of motivation for the significant issue behavior working with [71].

7.2.3   Simplifying Computational Model and Algorithm Framework/Principle

The goal of the modeling phases in the CFA is to reduce abstract representations to improve comprehension of fundamental biology, leading to the construction of an observational for the invention of bio-inspired algorithms. This step will aid in extracting essential biological characteristics, culminating in the construction of a bio-inspired algorithm. On the other hand, CFA does not fully explain the modeling stages but instead emphasizes the demands and advantages obtained from this step. As a result, we use the CoSMoS method to create our model and simulations systematically. We used unified modeling language (UML) diagrams and agent-based simulations to describe the model. We thought both approaches were appropriate for our genetic features' structure and the model's intended output in simulations.

We were able to pinpoint the key, thanks to our modeling efforts. We were able to identify the critical cells and signaling pathways involved in granuloma development formation features that we wanted to incorporate in the experiment. This is because granuloma development involves many cells and connections, and we cannot mimic all of them because most of them are not well known by immunologists. We only illustrated the interactions between the significant cells and the signaling pathways in the agent-based simulation we discussed in Chapter 4; thus, it was a reduced version of the initial granuloma formation. As a result, it was mostly an exploratory simulation to develop some basic notions and concerns about the granuloma development process. The simulation was created primarily using UML diagrams from written explanations of biological. We examined the mechanism and features of granuloma development that might be transferred to our software application by streamlining the model and simulations. Implementing the CFA may not finish here, even though we created the simulation depending on our needs. For example, we might revisit the model and simulation from Chapter 4 in the future to see how we can improve it. After that, we might pose questions about the more particular features of granuloma development, such as introducing more cells and interconnections to the simulation. This would allow us to probe back into the biological and enhance the theory and the simulations. We feel these simulations and computations may be refined and evolved further into a tool that could give biological insights. To do so, we must recalibrate the microbial community's modeling using real-world data to begin creating insights that physical specialists can confirm.

In conclusion, we think that the modeling steps in CFA have aided us in:

- understanding the biological characteristics of granuloma development based on the modeling domain that we would want to address,
- building a model and simulations, and
- developing a model and virtual world.

Putting the design concepts into the algorithm: We would not have created the concepts without the model and simulations since they are based on our comprehension of the granuloma formation process, as shown in the model and simulations. It may be time-consuming to lengthen the time spent developing the model and simulations. We may, however, shorten the time required to create the design features and immune-inspired algorithms once the modeling and simulations have been constructed.

7.2.4   Reflections on Swarm Cybernetic Systems

We learned that there are many features in immune systems that may be investigated and implemented for addressing many sorts of engineering problems based on our experiences building immune-inspired solutions for swarming cybernetic systems. The majority of modeling and simulation modeling in the case of granuloma development is done to monitor better the mechanisms of cells and the characteristics of granuloma formation. There is no more work to be done based on the outcomes of the simulation methods after they have been comprehended. However, in our instance, the models and simulations we used helped us understand the characteristics of granuloma formation and helped us understand the qualities of neoplastic transformation in general. However, it can serve as a source of motivation for swarming cybernetic systems' "stabilizing" problems. As a result, we think that other immune system features may be described and investigated, and used as a source of motivation for engineering issues.

When we did a comparison our work in this study for swarm cybernetic systems to other remedies, such as those that can conduct repair techniques that allow electricity sharing among both cyborgs whenever there is a failure of cyborgs' energy in the systems, we felt that providing a CFA as a principal approach to develop immune-inspired remedies has aided in discovery. Since the creation of the model and simulations is designed especially with the problems that we have in consideration, it will help the immune systems better. The better design concepts we discovered are beneficial during the algorithmic creation process. These design concepts can also solve other issues in swarm cybernetic systems since they can be expanded to and changed as needed.

We only tested our method in swarm beacons taxis to solve the "anchoring" problem, but we believe it will benefit other swarm cybernetic systems problems. One of the primary difficulties with swarm cybernetic systems is energy connected to the program's cyborgs' high energy drain. Enabling the cyborgs to exchange power among themselves will aid the system's primary goal. It was discovered that our immune-inspired program could repair and distribute up to five defective cyborgs in the system. However, as the number of failing cyborgs in the system grows, it becomes increasingly impossible for the non-faulty cyborgs to restore and exchange their energies with the defective cyborgs. This is mainly because we only tested with ten cyborgs in the network in our investigation. This work may be expanded in the future by adding additional cyborgs to the networks. We also discovered that the percentage of failed cyborgs is essential to the system due to our research. Consider the following scenario:

- In a system with ten cyborgs, the non-faulty cyborgs could repair and share their energies with the defective cyborgs.
- In a system with twenty cyborgs, the non-faulty cyborgs might well be able to restore and share their energies with the defective cyborgs if there are ten defective cyborgs.
- If a system has fifteen defective cyborgs, the no-fault cyborgs may restore and share their energies with the defective cyborgs.

To summarize our work, we look forward to developing immune-inspired self-healing swarm cyborg systems in a preferred stock to aid us in solving the "anchoring" issues, particularly enabling cyborgs to encompass certain types of error and introduce repair techniques that allow electricity sharing among both cyborgs when the processor architectures' energy fails.

7.3   Cyborg Static Environment

This section introduces the basic concepts and analysis methods used throughout this study and defines the information-cost-reward (ICR) framework. The ICR framework explains how a swarm gains and utilizes information related to its ability to obtain the reward, given the particular structure and environment of the swarm's task. The framework is used to form hypotheses and analyze the swarms' performance with various control strategies. It also provides a context and terminology for describing design patterns for cyborgs swarms.

There are two cyborg tasks explored in this study: the consumption task and the collection task. In the consumption task, cyborgs search for worksites in the environment and obtain rewards by staying close to them while gradually depleting them. In the collection task, cyborgs extract small resource packets from worksites and deliver them to the base. Thus, they have to make several foraging trips to deplete a worksite. In both tasks, the locations of the worksites are initially unknown and must be discovered by searching the environment.

This section considers data obtained from the consumption task in static environments. Because the settings explored here are fixed, i.e., worksite locations are determined at the beginning of an experimental run and remain constant during the run, performance of the swarms is only affected by the behavior of cyborgs, rather than by changes in the environment external to the swarms. The collection task in static environments is investigated.

In the first part of the next section, the performance of the three types of the swarm (solitary, local broadcasters, and bee swarms is evaluated. Following the performance analysis, information flow, i.e., how cyborgs gain and share information, is analyzed. The term "information flow" describes how the number of informed cyborgs that know where worksites are located changes over time. It is shown that there is a discrepancy between the amount of information about worksites that a swarm has and the amount of reward that it is receiving at a given point in time. This discrepancy can be expressed as a sum of various costs that the swarm must pay to transform information into a reward. The fees described here are unitless and related to the amount of compensation the swarm is losing by not utilizing information efficiently. The nature and the volume of the incurred costs depend on the structure of the swarm's environment and how cyborgs obtain and share information. The ICR framework ties together various environmental and swarm characteristics by portraying a swarm as a single cognitive entity that searches for information, utilizes it, and changes the environment, given space and time constraints.

7.4   Cyborg Swarm Performance

In this section, the performance of swarms is evaluated in terms of the time it takes each swarm to discover and consume all rewards from the environment. A total of 20 domains are explored: four scenario types, each with worksite distance D $\in\{5,9,13,17,21\}$m from the base.

7.4.1   Solitary Cyborg Swarms

The performance of solitary swarms in the consumption task depended on the number of worksites, NW, the worksite distance from the base, D, and the number of cyborgs, NR. The performance was better when there were more worksites in the environment, as it was more probable for a cyborg to find resources. Recall that the total amount of resources in the atmosphere was held constant when NW was varied by scaling the static consumption task completion time of solitary swarms. The task completion time was shorter when worksites were numerous or close to the base. In reference to the number of resources per worksite, the increased performance in scenarios with a higher NW was a result of the better ability of cyborgs to find and exploit worksites and not a development of more abundant resources in the environment. This trend was stronger when swarms were enormous since cyborgs and worksites were more densely populated; the work arena was thus discovered faster. For example, when D = 5m, the task completion time in the Scatter25, compared to the Heap1 scenario, was faster by 20% when the number of cyborgs NR = 10, by 42% when NR = 25, and by 56% when NR = 50.

7.4.2   Local Cyborg Broadcasters

Similar to the solitary swarms, the performance of local hosts was generally better when the number of worksites was more significant. However, two conditions caused an exception to this rule: a lack of recruitment in small swarms and congestion in large swarms.

When the swarms were small (NR = 10), the cyborgs found all scenario types with the same D similarly tricky. Because cyborgs became more dispersed in the environment over time, recruitment probability decreased as an experimental run progressed. When the number of cyborgs was small, one or two worksites were depleted by utilizing recruitment at the beginning of an experimental run. The remaining worksites were discovered much later and processed in a more solitary fashion. In contrast, recruitment was more probable when swarms were more enormous, meaning that different subgroups of the swarm exploited worksites in parallel. Therefore, they consumed them faster in the Heap4 and Scatter25 scenarios than in the Heap1 or Heap2 scenarios.

On the other hand, when the swarms were large (NR = 50) but worksites were close together (D ≤ 9m), recruitment occurred very frequently and caused congestion around worksites. Such physical interference between cyborgs prevented them from accessing resources and, more importantly, finding other, non-congested worksites.

In reference to the static consumption task completion time of local broadcasters, the task completion time was shorter when worksites were numerous, as long as the worksites were far away from the base and the number of cyborgs NR ≥ 25.

7.4.3 Cyborg Bee Swarms

Contrary to the solitary swarms and local broadcasters, bee swarms generally found it harder to complete the consumption task when the number of worksites was large. This was mainly when the swarms were small (NR = 10) or when worksites were far away from the base. Unlike cyborgs from the other swarms, bee cyborgs returned to the ground to recruit when they discovered a worksite, meaning that they had to spend additional time exploiting it. Moreover, bee swarms were likely to suffer from exploitation interference between cyborgs, where other members depleted a worksite of the swarm while the cyborgs were recruiting in the base. Exploitation interference caused the recruiter and its recruits to travel to and search for a worksite that was no longer there, thus wasting time that could have been spent exploring the environment or working. The interference was more substantial in settings with more worksites, as there was a higher probability of them being discovered and depleted by another cyborg.

7.4.4 The Performance of Swarm Cyborgs

The performance of the explored control strategies relative to each other depended on the type of the experimental environment. Solitary swarms completed the consumption task faster than the other swarms in the Scatter scenarios when worksites were close to the base. In these environments, recruitment, utilized by both local broadcasters and bee swarms, led to physical interference between cyborgs since the probability of discovering worksites and recruiting to them was high. Additionally, bee swarms also experienced exploitation interference, where cyborgs were recruiting to worksites that were meanwhile depleted by others. The disadvantage of local broadcasters and bee swarms was more substantial when there were more cyborgs in the swarm, i.e., when the interference between cyborgs was more substantial.

On the other hand, Heap1 scenarios represented the most challenging environments, where only a single worksite existed, and a resource was thus difficult to find. Local broadcasters and bee swarms thus outperformed the solitary swarms in most Heap1 environments. Finally, in the intermediate Heap2 and Heap4 scenarios, bee swarms generally could not perform as well as the other swarms, both due to exploitation interference and because they had to spend additional time traveling to the base to recruit. In these environments, solitary swarms and local broadcasters did similarly well when D was small, while more challenging environments with large D favored local hosts.

It is also notable that the number of scenarios where multiple strategies did similarly well was higher when the swarms were small. The probability of cyborgs meeting each other was lower when there were fewer cyborgs, causing communication between local broadcasters and the bee swarm to be less common. Therefore, the positive effects of recruitment, which could help the cyborgs exploit worksites that were hard to find, and the adverse effects of interference, which could prevent cyborgs from working effectively, were less pronounced when swarms were smaller.

Moreover, large swarm sizes affected the swarms differently in different environments. For both solitary swarms and local broadcasters, a more significant number of cyborgs usually improved performance more significantly in the Scatter compared to the Heap1 settings. In contrast, more enormous bee swarms enjoyed a similar advantage across different scenarios, given the same D. For example, swarms of 50 solitary cyborgs enjoyed a 55% to 62% reduction in task completion time compared to 10-cyborg swarms in the Heap1 scenario. In reference to the effect of swarm size on the static consumption task completion time, the numbers above the box plots indicate how much the completion time was reduced for each swarm when using 50 compared to 10 cyborgs. All swarms completed the task faster when there were more cyborgs used. Solitary swarms and local broadcasters benefited more from a large swarm when more worksites were in the environment. Bee swarms benefited from a large swarm size similarly regardless of the number of worksites. There was 73% to 76% reduction in the Scatter25 scenario. Similarly, swarms of 50 local broadcasters completed the task 54 to 63% faster than 10 cyborgs in the Heap1 system and 67% to 77% faster in the Scatter25 scenario. However, 50-cyborg bee swarms completed around 62 to 72% faster than 10 cyborgs in Heap1 and Scatter25 scenarios. This result suggests that the performance of swarms that utilize recruitment in a designated location, i.e., the base, is less affected by the structure of the environment.

Other authors have investigated cyborg swarms performing tasks similar to the consumption task explored here. For example, cyborgs had to find resource patches to "consume" and complete "jobs" on a manufacturing floor or respond to discovered intruders. In line with the results presented here, it has been shown that communication between cyborgs can improve performance when worksites are challenging to find. Swarm performance increases sublinearly with swarm size due to interference between cyborgs.

7.5 Information Flow Analysis in Cyborgs

Analyzing when and how a swarm acquires information and how it spreads between cyborgs is the first step towards understanding why some control strategies are more suitable than others in a given environment. This section introduces two characteristics of a swarm related to its information flow: scouting efficiency and information gain rate. Scouting efficiency refers to the ability of a swarm to discover new information in the environment. Information gain relates to scouting efficiency and a swarm's recruitment strategy and characterizes cyborgs' ability to acquire and spread knowledge. The rate of change in ΔI over time is described as the information gain rate, i.

7.5.1 Cyborg Scouting Behavior

Each cyborg's control strategy is associated with a specific scouting behavior. All processes explored here use the Levy movement to search the environment. However, scouts in the bee swarm periodically return to the base to check whether cyborgs are recruiting to a worksite. This limits the amount of time they spend scouting.

A swarm's scouting efficiency can be approximated by measuring the time of the first worksite discovery in a given experimental run. The longer it takes a swarm to discover its first worksite, the worse its scouting efficiency. Rather than the last or average worksite discovery, the first is evaluated to prevent interference between cyborgs from affecting the measured ability of a swarm to scout.

While all swarms were less efficient at scouting in environments where worksites were far away from the base, the scouting efficiency of bee swarms was affected more significantly than that of other swarms. This trend was the strongest in Heap1 environments, where it was tough to discover a worksite, and it was weaker in different Heap environments. The scouting efficiency of the bee swarms differed from that of other swarms more strongly when swarms were small, i.e., when NR = 10. On the other hand, in Scatter25 environments, where worksites were numerous and thus easy to find, the bee swarm's scouting efficiency was affected similarly to that of other swarms.

7.5.2 Information Gaining by Cyborg

The amount of information that the swarm has at a given point in time is defined as:

$$I(t) = \sum_{W}^{N_A} S_W(t) \tag{7.1}$$

where N_A is the number of active (i.e., not depleted) worksites in the environment and $SW(t)$ is the number of cyborgs that know about a worksite W at time t. Note that this definition of "information" differs from that traditionally used in engineering, where information is measured in the context of transmission of symbols drawn from a finite pool of possibilities. Since a piece of data about a swarm's environment can have an infinite number of possible values, for example, real-value coordinates that represent a worksite location, the information here is defined in terms of the number of cyborgs that have acquired a piece of data, i.e., the number of data pieces that the swarm possesses.

A swarm's information gain represents the change in the amount of information a swarm has. It is defined as:

$$\Delta I(t) = I(t) - I(t-1)$$
$$= \sum_{W}^{N_A} [S_W(t) - [S_W(t-1)] \tag{7.2}$$

We can obtain a normalized information gain, $\Delta I(t)'$, by dividing ΔI by the number of cyborgs, N_R:

$$k^{\Delta I(t)'} = \frac{\Delta I(t)}{N_R} \tag{7.3}$$

We can identify when scouts find new worksites or when cyborgs are recruited by measuring information gain. A swarm gains further information in these cases, and using ΔI. Similarly, when cyborgs abandon active worksites and are assumed to no longer "know" about them, they negatively gain information. When no data is acquired or lost, $\Delta I = 0$.

Other information metrics for multi-agent systems exist, such as transfer entropy (TE) and local information storage (LIS). Inspired by Shannon's understanding of information, TE and LIS measure how communication affects the state of an agent based on the conditions of other agents that it receives information from. They can thus predict the following form of agents in tightly coupled multi-agent systems, such as a group of cyborgs performing flocking. The "state" can represent its current discretized velocity or orientation. The discretization is necessary since the representation of information in Shannon's sense requires a finite number of possible values that a variable can take. This approach has a few problems when measuring information flow in swarms. Firstly, because it measures the coupling between "states" of two agents at two different time steps, transfer entropy is, to some extent, a proxy measure of information flow.

On the other hand, information gain, ΔI, is calculated as a change in the number of informed cyborgs, and it thus directly captures the amount of knowledge that the swarm gains or loses at a given point in time. Secondly, based on the number of informed cyborgs, we do not need to define what a cyborg's "state" is about having information. Informed cyborgs may perform several different operations, such as gathering resources, traveling to the base, etc. Thirdly, as will be demonstrated below, information gain can be directly related to the amount of uncertainty cost that the swarm pays and thus to the ability of the swarm to turn information into a reward. This allows us to not only characterize information flow but also to relate it to swarm performance. To the author's best knowledge, no study has demonstrated how and whether entropy can be directly associated with swarm performance in missions where the resulting collective behavior depends on factors other than the ability of cyborgs to observe each other's actions and coordinate their behavior.

The information gain time series looks very different for different swarms and environments. In Scatter25, where it is relatively easy to discover worksites as they are numerous, all swarms generate a significant information gain, especially at the beginning of experimental runs, when scouting is the most successful. Solitary cyborgs maintain $\Delta I' > 0$ until all worksites are depleted. The cyborgs are relatively evenly spread across the work arena and usually do not get in each other's way while exploring and exploiting the environment. The graph region during which $\Delta I' > 0$ is referred to as a positive information gain region. Solitary swarms have a single positive information gain region. Local broadcasters, on the other hand, start recruitment immediately after initial worksite discoveries are made, which leads to physical and exploitation interference between cyborgs and a significant decrease in information gain after a few minutes, while the cyborgs are avoiding each other and searching for depleted worksites that they were recruited to. There are two positive information gain regions, the larger one appearing at the beginning of the simulations. Finally, bee cyborgs learn about worksites in a solitary fashion at the beginning of each run and recruit each other in the base later. Bee swarms show two positive information gain regions in this scenario as local broadcasters. Still, the regions are further apart than local hosts since bee swarm cyborgs need additional time to travel to the base and recruit.

In the Heap1 scenario, where there is only a single worksite to discover, $\Delta I'$ of all swarms is significantly smaller than in the Scatter25 method. Solitary swarms find it the most difficult to obtain information about the worksite. Many I' outliers correspond to isolated events when cyborgs find the worksite. Still, the only positive region, which indicates a clear trend of worksite discovery, appears at the beginning of the experimental runs, and it is tiny. Local broadcasters show an improved ability to discover the worksite, with several positive $\Delta I'$ regions spread across the simulation run. The time series also indicates that most of the information gained from local broadcasters is due to recruitment. A small number of cyborgs usually discover the worksite at the beginning of an experimental run and broadcast it to other cyborgs nearby. Finally, bee swarms show the most vital ability to gain information in this scenario. A small $\Delta I'$ region at the beginning of the time series represents an initial worksite discovery by scouts, followed by a more significant positive part, representing the recruitment of more workers in the base. After some time, a small negative region appears, indicating that some recruits abandon the worksite due to their inability to access it due to congestion.

7.5.3   Information Gain Rate of Cyborgs

The investigated control strategies differ in how quickly their positive information gain regions can grow, especially in environments such as Heap1, where worksites are challenging to discover. To characterize this growth, information gain rate, i, is calculated based on the total information gain $\Delta I'$ of positive regions and the length.

To calculate i, the information gain time series is first down-sampled into time intervals Ti seconds long by summing the information gain of all cyborgs in each interval. Down-sampling $\Delta I'$ in this way makes it possible to identify and measure trends in $\Delta I'$ since individual information gain events, such as cyborgs finding a worksite or cyborgs being recruited, usually occur a few seconds apart in discrete time intervals. Positive regions are then distinguished from the rest of the down-sampled time series by considering intervals during which the down-sampled information gain remains positive. Information gain rate i_p in each positive region is defined as:

$$i_P = \frac{\sum_{T=0}^{T_P} \Delta I * (t)}{T_P} \tag{7.4}$$

where T_p is the length of a positive region in seconds, and $\Delta I(T)*$ is the total down-sampled information gain in a given time interval.

The information gain rate of a swarm i is the maximum value of iP measured in an experimental run:

$$i = \max(iP) \tag{7.5}$$

The maximum, rather than the median or average iP, is used because it is less likely to be affected by physical and exploitation interference that results from recruitment.

The time interval Ti, used for down-sampling the information gain time series, is a parameter to the information gain rate calculation, set to $Ti = 60s$. Appendix C shows that while this particular value distinguishes between the information gain rate of various swarms, the strongest, using a different value does not affect the order of the swarms based on i.

In solitary swarms, worksite discoveries are more probable when worksites are abundant or the work arena is small. Consequently, the information gain rate of solitary swarms increases with the number of worksites, NW, and decreases with worksite distance, D. A similar trend can be observed for local broadcasters. On the other hand, the information gain rate of bee swarms varies less across scenarios and generally does not increase with NW unless the worksites are far away from the base (D = 21m) or when swarms are small. Since bee swarms use a designated location to spread information, they can achieve a relatively high information gain rate under challenging environments like Heap1. The probability of cyborgs discovering a worksite is low. However, their information gain rate usually cannot increase further in more accessible environments, such as Scatter25, due to interference between cyborgs that prevents them from working and thus from recruiting.

Consequently, the information gain rate of bee swarms is usually the highest in the Heap environments, followed by local broadcasters and solitary swarms. On the contrary, local hosts reach the highest information gain rate in the Scatter25 settings, recruiting near worksites. The probability of such recruitment is high when worksites are numerous, especially when they are also close together (D <= 9m). As D increases, information becomes more difficult to obtain and spread, and the information gain rate of all three swarms becomes more similar.

7.5.4   Evaluation of Information Flow in Cyborgs

It is essential to point out that the ability of cyborgs to find and spread information quickly does not always result in the swarm's ability to perform a task efficiently. There are notable differences between which swarm achieves the highest information gain rate and which swarm completes the quickest job. For example, even though bee swarms reach the highest i in the Heap environments, they do not outperform local broadcasters in explored territories. On the other hand, solitary swarms, which achieve the lowest information gain rate in all environments, can complete the consumption task faster than any other swarm when worksites are easy to find.

To better understand the discrepancy between information flow and swarm performance, it is essential to investigate what happens to information once it reaches cyborgs and how they utilize it.

7.6   Cost Analysis of Cyborgs

It is apparent from the comparison between information flow and task completion time of swarms that there is a certain pressure from the environment that prevents the cyborgs from converting the information they have about worksites into a reward from those worksites. Moreover, this pressure acts differently on swarms with different control strategies. It can be said that alien swarms pay additional costs for utilizing information. In this section, the work cycle of cyborgs is first described, and the fees paid at each stage of the work cycle are defined. It is then demonstrated that the costs, when added together, explain the difference between the reward that a swarm receives at a given point in time and the expected reward that a swarm should receive based on the information that it carries. Note that a god-like observer calculates these costs to evaluate the system—they are not intended to be calculated on the fly by individual cyborgs. The nature of its information flow and the tendency of a control strategy to incur costs define a set of swarm characteristics that determine whether a control strategy is suitable for a given task and environment.

7.6.1   The Cyborg Work Cycle

In both the consumption and the collection task, a cyborg needs to find information about a worksite and utilize that information to obtain the reward. The reward can be obtained directly from the worksite in the consumption task while a cyborg remains close. In the collection task, a cyborg receives compensation when it drops off resources in the base.

A cyborgs' work cycle can be generalized for both task types. A cyborg starts by being unemployed (U) and searching the environment for information. When it discovers a worksite, either by itself or as a result of being recruited, it subscribes (S) to that worksite. It then travels to it and becomes laden (L) with resources. It starts earning (E) reward when it reaches a rewarding generator. In the consumption task, the reward generator is the worksite itself, and laden cyborgs immediately become making tactical cyborgs. The reward generator is the base in the collection task, and laden cyborgs need to travel there to earn rewards. Note that the total number of cyborgs in a swarm is $NR = U + S$ and that $S \geq L \geq E$.

During each stage of the work cycle, cyborgs can incur certain costs. There are three types of cost: uncertainty cost, CU, incurred by unemployed cyborgs that do not know where work is located, misplacement cost, CM, that all subscribed cyborgs pay until they reach a rewarding generator and start earning rewards, and opportunity cost, CO, incurred by cyborgs that are subscribed to depleted worksites and are thus unable to find or perform work.

The cyborg starts out being unemployed (U). It becomes subscribed (S) once it learns about a worksite, decreasing the uncertainty cost, CU, of the swarm. It then travels to the worksite while incurring misplacement cost, CM, after which it becomes laden (L) with resources. When close to a rewarding generator, the cyborgs earn (E) rewards and decrease the swarm's misplacement cost. During the consumption task, the reward generator is the worksite itself, and a cyborg thus becomes laden and starts earning rewards simultaneously, incurring no further CM. During a collection task, a cyborg contributes to the total CM of the swarm until it reaches the base. Additionally, a cyborg may incur opportunity cost, CO, if it travels to a worksite that has been depleted. When the cyborgs abandon the depleted worksite and become unemployed again, the total CO of the swarm decreases.

Following is an example of how costs are incurred by cyborgs that utilize recruitment. At the beginning of a run, all cyborgs are unemployed, paying the maximum uncertainty cost. The CU decreases when cyborgs learn about a worksite, while CM increases as some cyborgs are recruits not yet located at the worksite. The total uncertainty cost decreases when one worksite gets depleted since there is one less active worksite that the swarm needs to know about. However, cyborgs still subscribed to the depleted worksite incur an opportunity cost until they determine that it is depleted and abandon it. When all worksites are finished, the task is completed, rendering all prices 0.

Quantifying these costs first requires calculating the amount of reward, r, available per worksite and cyborgs:

$$r = \frac{R_T}{N_R \times N_W'} \tag{7.6}$$

where R_T is the total amount of reward available in the environment, N_R is the total number of cyborgs, and N_W' is the number of worksites at the beginning of an experiment. During experiments with static environments, $R_T = 100$. The task would be completed if all cyborgs could simultaneously obtain reward r from all worksites.

7.6.2 Uncertainty Cost of Cyborgs

At the beginning of a run, all cyborgs are unemployed, and the swarm has no information about where the reward is located. Therefore, the hive is paying uncertainty cost C_U, equal to the total compensation from all worksites (all worksites are active at this point). When a cyborg finds out about a worksite, the swarm's C_U decreases by r. At any given time, the amount of uncertainty cost a swarm pay is thus:

$$C_U = \sum_{W=1}^{N_A}(N_R \times r) - \sum_{W=1}^{N_A}(S_W \times r)$$

$$= \sum_{W=1}^{N_A}[(N_R - S_W) \times r] \qquad (7.7)$$

where N_A is the number of active worksites and S_W is the number of cyborgs subscribed to a worksite W.

The change in uncertainty cost, ΔC_U, relates to the swarm's information gain, ΔI (Eq. 7.2), in the following way:

$$C_U = C_U(t) - C_U(t-1)$$

$$= [\sum_{W=1}^{N_A(t)}(N_R \times r) - \sum_{W=1}^{N_A(t)}(S_W(t) \times r)]$$

$$-[\sum_{W=1}^{N_A(t-1)}(N_R \times r) - \sum_{W=1}^{N_A(t-1)}(S_W(t-1) \times r)]$$

$$= [\sum_{W=1}^{N_A(t)}(N_R \times r) - \sum_{W=1}^{N_A(t-1)}(N_R \times r)] - I \times r \qquad (7.8)$$

Or:

$$\Delta I \times r = -\Delta C_U + [\sum_{W=1}^{N_A(t)}(N_R \times r) - \sum_{W=1}^{N_A(t-1)}(N_R \times r)] \qquad (7.9)$$

In other words, the swarm's information gain between time steps t and $(t-1)$ is directly proportional to the sum of the decrease in the swarm's uncertainty cost and the change in the total available reward from all active worksites. If the number of active worksites at time step t remains the same as in time step $(t-1)$, i.e., when no worksites are depleted or added to the environment, then $\sum_{W=1}^{N_A(t)}(N_R \times r) - \sum_{W=1}^{N_A(t-1)}(N_R \times r) = 0 \Delta I \times r = -\Delta C U$.

As mentioned in the cyborg's work cycle description above, cyborgs might need to travel to a work site or to a rewarding generator to obtain the reward. During the period between when the cyborgs subscribe to a worksite and when it starts earning a bonus from it, the cyborgs are mis-placed from the reward generator and pay a misplacement cost, C_M:

$$C_M = \sum_{W=1}^{N_A}[(S_W - E_W) \times r] + \sum_{W=1}^{N_D}[(L_W - E_W) \times r] \qquad (7.10)$$

where E_W is the number of cyborgs making a reward from a worksite W, N_D is the number of depleted worksites, and L_W is the number of cyborgs laden with resources from a worksite W. The first term on the right-hand side of Eq. (7.10) represents the misplacement cost that subscribed cyborgs pay from active worksites, either during traveling to worksites or, in the case of the collection task, during traveling to the base to unload resources. The second term represents cases when cyborgs laden with aid from depleted worksites travel to the ground during the collection task.

The relationship between a reduction in uncertainty cost and an increase in misplacement cost determines what portion of cyborgs that learn about a worksite can obtain a reward from it. In an ideal case, no misplacement cost is paid, and a reduction in uncertainty immediately increases the pre-mium. We can characterize this relationship in terms of the misplacement cost coefficient, m, as:

$$m - \frac{C_M}{\sum_{W=1}^{N_A}(S_W \times r)} \qquad (7.11)$$

When $m = 0$, a decrease in uncertainty cost is fully turned into reward, i.e., $C_M = 0$. When $m = 1$, all cyborgs that know about worksites are misplaced from a reword generator, and no reward is obtained, i.e., $C_M = \sum_{W=1}^{N_A}(S_W \times r)$. Intermediate values of $0 < m < 1$ indicates that some cyborgs are misplaced, and some are rewarded. The misplacement cost coefficient is affected by how a cyborg's control strategy utilizes informa-tion and where information is shared in the work arena.

Solitary cyborgs do not pay CM during the consumption task since they do not recruit and since scouts are already present at a worksite when they learn about it. In swarms that do communicate, CM is incurred by recruited cyborgs until they reach a worksite advertised. In the bee swarms, scouts incur CM as they travel to the base and back to draft.

In 25-cyborg swarms, the misplacement cost coefficient m is generally the highest in bee swarms, and it is always 0 in solitary swarms. However, when the number of worksites is small, most notably the Heap1 scenarios, or when worksites are very close to the base (D = 5m in all Heap scenarios), local broadcasters experience congestion near worksites, and their m is higher or similar as that of bee swarms. The congestion that a local broadcaster worker causes local hosts to share recruits the whole time while depleting a worksite. In environments where worksites have large volumes and are close to each other, such a worker has a high probability of recruiting too many cyborgs, preventing some of them from accessing the worksite and causing them to incur misplacement costs for an extended period. On the other hand, bee cyborgs recruit in the base and therefore access worksites in a less congested fashion.

7.6.3   Cyborg Opportunity Cost

On some occasions, unladen cyborgs become subscribed to a worksite that has been depleted. This can happen either to recruits or cyborgs during the collection task while traveling from the base back to a depleted worksite. During this time, a cyborg is missing an opportunity to explore the environment, and it is thus incurring an opportunity cost, CO:

$$C_O = \sum_{W=1}^{N_D} [(S_W - L_W) \times r] \qquad (7.12)$$

Note that cyborgs laden with resources from a depleted worksite pay misplacement cost instead.

Opportunity cost measures the negative impact of exploitation interference, i.e., the tendency of a swarm to commit to worksites that become depleted while cyborgs are away from them. The more a swarm owner reserves a worksite by having too many cyborgs subscribed to it, the higher opportunity cost it can potentially pay when that worksite becomes depleted. The price is related to the number of cyborgs that a single piece of discovered information can affect, i.e., information gain rate and how cyborgs recruit.

When comparing the opportunity cost incurred by different swarms, it is crucial to consider the price while active worksites are available in the environment. When the last worksite is depleted, cyborgs still subscribed to it are not missing an opportunity to do more work since the environment is empty. Consequently, when the CO of different swarms is compared, it is always shown as 0 in Heap1 scenarios. It depicts CO paid by 25-cyborg swarms. In a systems with ten cyborgs, the non-facility cyborgs could be able to repair and share their energies with the defective cyborgs.

Solitary cyborgs do not incur CO during the consumption task because they do not recruit, meaning that when a worksite is depleted, all cyborgs that are subscribed to it immediately become aware of that fact and abandon the worksite. On the other hand, local broadcasters, who recruit near worksites continuously until depleted, pay the highest CO in the Heap environments. Their CO is usually more elevated in the Heap4 settings when D is large. The number of cyborgs is small (NR = 10), i.e., when recruitment is less probable and when a smaller number of cyborgs usually process a single worksite. Because worksite processing takes longer in these cases and because more potential recruits are exploring the environment, there is a higher chance that cyborgs will be recruited to a worksite that is about to be depleted. On the other hand, in Scatter25, worksites have small volumes and are thus depleted quickly, which decreases the probability of new workers being recruited to an almost empty worksite. Finally, bee swarm cyborgs incur CO that is similar across the different environments. Since they recruit in the base, cyborgs' arrival times to worksites are more identical than when local broadcasters recruit.

7.6.4   Costs and Rewards Obtained by Cyborgs

In this section, the relationship between how a swarm's information, the costs that it incurs, and the reward that it obtains is formalized. First, the amount of actual reward ΔR that a swarm is earning at a given point in time needs to be calculated:

$$\Delta R = \sum_{W=1}^{N_W} (\rho \times E_W) \tag{7.13}$$

where $N_W = N_A + N_D$ is the total number of worksites (active and depleted), and ρ is the reward intake rate, i.e., the amount of reward gained per second by an earning cyborgs E. In the consumption task, $\rho = 1/400s$. In the collection task, $\rho = 1s$.

If cyborgs could immediately turn information into reward, i.e., if they did not have to travel to worksites and did not suffer from contention for the same resource, the swarm could earn the expected reward R':

$$R' = \sum_{W=1}^{N_W} (S_W \times r) \tag{7.14}$$

Eq. (7.15) shows that the sum of the displacement and opportunity costs equals the difference between the expected and actual rewards, multiplied by. The term refers to the real per-cyborgs reward that the swarm will receive in $1/\rho$ seconds. The equation signifies that a swarm cannot unutilized information about worksites for free—it has to pay costs associated with its control strategy and the environment's structure.

$$
\begin{aligned}
C_M + C_O &= [\sum_{W=1}^{N_A} (S_W \times r) - \sum_{W=1}^{N_A} (E_W \times r) + \sum_{W=1}^{N_D} (L_W \times r) - \sum_{W=1}^{N_D} (E_W \times r)] \\
&\quad + [\sum_{W=1}^{N_D} (S_W \times r) - \sum_{W=1}^{N_D} (L_W \times r)] \\
&= [\sum_{W=1}^{N_A} (S_W \times r) + \sum_{W=1}^{N_D} (S_W \times r)] - [\sum_{W=1}^{N_A} (E_W \times r) \\
&\quad + \sum_{W=1}^{N_D} (E_W \times r)] \\
&= \sum_{W=1}^{N_W} (S_W \times r) - \sum_{W=1}^{N_W} (E_W \times r) \\
&= R' - \frac{r}{\rho} \times \Delta R \tag{7.15}
\end{aligned}
$$

The potential reward, $R*$, is defined as a sum of the expected reward and a reward that could be received by all unemployed (i.e., non-subscribed) cyborgs from all active worksites if the unemployed cyborgs knew where the worksites were located.

$$R^* = \sum_{W=1} [S_W \times r] + \sum_{W=1} [(N_R - S_W) \times r] \tag{7.16}$$

Since $N_W = N_A + N_D$, the potential reward can also be expressed as:

$$R^* = [\sum_{W=1}^{N_A}(S_W \times r)] + \sum_{W=1}^{N_D}(S_W \times r)] + [\sum_{W=1}^{N_A}(N_R \times r) - \sum_{W=1}^{N_A}(S_W \times r)]$$

$$= \sum_{W=1}^{N_A}(N_R \times r) + \sum_{W=1}^{N_D}(S_W \times r) \tag{7.17}$$

The sum of all three costs—uncertainty, displacement and opportunity—is equal to the difference between the potential and actual rewards, multiplied by $\frac{r}{\rho}$ (Eq. 7.18); this equation formalizes the relationship between the swarm's information flow, which affects the amount of uncertainty cost paid, the swarm's tendency to incur the misplacement and opportunity costs while utilizing the information, and the reward that the hive can extract from the environment at a given time.

$$C_U + C_M + C_O = [\sum_{W=1}^{N_A}(N_R \times r) - \sum_{W=1}^{N_A}(S_W \times r)] + [\sum_{W=1}^{N_A}(S_W \times r)$$

$$- \sum_{W=1}^{N_A}(E_W \times r)$$

$$+ \sum_{W=1}^{N_D}(L_W \times r) - \sum_{W=1}^{N_D}(E_W \times r)] + [\sum_{W=1}^{N_D}(S_W \times r)$$

$$- \sum_{W=1}^{N_D}(L_W \times r)]$$

$$= [\sum_{W=1}^{N_A}(N_R \times r) + \sum_{W=1}^{N_D}(S_W \times r)] - [\sum_{W=1}^{N_A}(E_W \times r)$$

$$+ \sum_{W=1}^{N_D}(E_W \times r)]$$

$$= R^* - \frac{r}{\rho} \times \Delta R \tag{7.18}$$

In an ideal world, where cyborgs could locate themselves at worksites immediately upon learning about them and where there would be no physical or exploitation interference between cyborgs, the misplacement and opportunity cost would not exist. However, because swarms operate in the real world, where time and space play a role, we need to consider these costs to account for the discrepancy between the information a swarm possesses and the reward that it can receive at a given point in time. Furthermore, since cyborgs do not know where worksites are and need to explore the environment, decreasing their uncertainty is also essential. The information-cost-reward framework, introduced in the next section, explains how the information flow and the tendency of cyborgs to incur costs fit together and how they affect the performance of a swarm with a particular cyborgs control strategy in a given environment.

7.7   Cyborg Swarm Environment

Swarms employing different control strategies perform differently in each environment. The control strategies also differ in how information is acquired from and shared between cyborgs and the costs incurred when turning data into a reward. A cyborgs control strategy has four characteristics that affect the swarm's performance: scouting efficiency, information gain rate, and tendency to incur misplacement and opportunity costs. While the scouting efficiency and information gain rate affect how the uncertainty of a swarm about its environment decreases, the misplacement and opportunity costs characterize how effective a swarm is in turning information into a reward. This section explains the relationship between these characteristics and the swarm's performance.

7.7.1   Cyborg Scouting Efficiency

Scouting efficiency is related to the ability of a swarm to discover new information about worksites in the environment. The scouting efficiency of all three swarms is smaller when there are few worksites in the background or when worksites are far away from the base. While solitary swarms and local broadcasters are similarly affected by worksite distance, bee swarms suffer a much higher decrease in performance when worksite distance is significant. The poor scouting efficiency of bee swarms is caused by the fact that bee swarm scouts periodically return to the base to check whether informed cyborgs could recruit them. As a result, bee swarms perform poorly compared to the other swarms when the number of cyborgs is small or when worksites are far from the base.

7.7.2 Cyborg Information Gain Rate

Information gain rate, i, characterizes how quickly a swarm can acquire new information and how quickly the data can spread through the swarm. It is related to the swarm's scout ability and recruitment strategy. Because they use a designated area to exchange information, bee swarms enjoy the highest information gain rate in most environments, followed by local broadcasters and solitary cyborgs. Additionally, the i value of bee swarms is more stable across different settings than other swarms.

A high information gain rate is advantageous in environments where it is challenging to discover worksites, most significantly in the Heap1 scenarios or when worksites are far from the base. In these environments, local broadcasters and bee swarms achieve the best performance. On the other hand, in environments where worksite discoveries are more probable, fast information gain rate leads to physical and exploitation interference that prevents cyborgs from working effectively. In other words, the potential of cyborgs to incur misplacement and opportunity costs increases with i. For example, in most scenarios, local broadcasters that enjoy a performance advantage over solitary swarms cannot outperform them in Scatter25 when worksites are close to the base. The effect of information gain rate on swarm performance is more evident when hives are more significant since interactions between cyborgs are more probable.

7.7.3 Swarm Cyborg Costs

Misplacement cost, CM, is incurred by cyborgs that know about a worksite but cannot obtain rewards from it because they are located elsewhere. The relationship between CM and a decrease in uncertainty cost, CU, is expressed by the displacement cost coefficient m. When m = 0, the swarm turns information into a reward immediately. On the other hand, when m = 1, none of the informed cyborgs is located at the relevant worksite, and no compensation is gained without travel. In the consumption task, m of solitary swarms is always 0 since they do not use recruitment, and all informed cyborgs are thus always located at their worksites. In contrast, bee recruiters that recruit from worksites have the highest m in most environments.

Heap1 scenarios with an enormous worksite distance favor both local broadcasters and bee swarm, even though bee swarms have the highest m in these environments. Similarly, Heap2 and Heap4 environments tend local hosts over solitary swarms, even though solitary swarms do not pay misplacement costs. On the other hand, in the least challenging environments, where worksites are numerous or where the work arena is small, solitary swarms can perform well enough, while swarms that use recruitment are punished for not turning information into reward as effectively as unattended cyborgs.

7.7.4   Solitary Swarm Cyborg Costs

Opportunity cost, CO, results from a tendency of a swarm to overcommit to worksites, and it is paid by cyborgs that are subscribed to worksites the other cyborgs have depleted. Solitary swarms do not pay CO in the consumption task, as cyborgs never leave worksites until exhausted. Bee recruiters pay an intermediate amount of CO since the cyborgs recruit in the base, and thus to a certain extent, synchronize the time they arrive and deplete worksites. Local broadcasters, who recruit the whole time while depleting a worksite, incur the highest CO in most environments.

Similarly, as is the case with misplacement cost, a strategy that can achieve a higher information gain rate and incurs a higher opportunity cost outperforms another approach with a slower information gain rate and a lower opportunity cost under challenging environments. In the Heap1 settings, opportunity cost is irrelevant, causing both the bee swarm and local broadcasters to outperform solitary swarms. In Heap2 and Heap4 scenarios, local hosts pay the highest CO, but they also produce a more minor misplacement cost than bee swarms. This leads to better work performance, as the opportunity cost only has to be paid for a small number of worksites. However, when worksites are numerous, as in Scatter25 scenarios, cyborgs need to spread their working effort evenly across the environment. In these cases, strategies that incur the highest CO have a low performance.

7.7.5   Information-Cost-Reward Framework

The relationship between characteristics of a cyborg's control strategy and properties of the environment is complex. By measuring the ability of swarms to acquire and spread new information, and their tendency to incur costs when utilizing that information, we can understand why specific control strategies do well in certain tasks. Environments where it is more difficult for a single cyborg to discover worksites favor strategy with a high information gain rate while allowing for a certain amount of costs to be paid. On the other hand, less complex environments do not require the information gain rate to be high, and they punish swarms that pay high costs.

These relationships form the basis for the information-cost-reward (ICR) framework. The ICR framework extends the cyborgs work cycle to describe the work cycle of the whole swarm and its relationship to the structure of the environment.

Under this framework, a swarm is understood as a single entity that acts on its environment to obtain the reward. Reward, situated in worksites, is dispersed in the environment in a certain way. A certain probability, p(W), is associated with a worksite being located at a given point in space. Scouts play the role of a swarm's sensors. They gain information about where worksites are, decreasing the swarm's uncertainty about the environment, i.e., the amount of uncertainty cost, CU, (Eq. 7.7) that the swarm pays. Since the swarm has new worksites, its expected reward, R′ (Eq. 7.14), increases. Scouting success affects the swarm's information gain rate, i (Eq. 7.5). It is dependent on the difficulty of the environment, characterized by the number of worksites and the worksite distance from the base, as well as on the swarm's scouting efficiency.

Scouts can become workers upon acquiring new information, but they can also pass the information to other swarm members to recruit more workers. Their ability to disperse information within the swarm depends on the swarm's communication strategy and, like scouting success, it affects the swarm's information gain rate, i. Workers act as actuators of the swarm. They turn the information they have into reward, R. However, there is a potential, unique to each control strategy, that the workers will need to incur misplacement cost, CM, to obtain the reward. Furthermore, workers eventually cause worksites to deplete by acting on the environment. This can result in opportunity cost, CO, incurred by workers who cannot update their information quickly enough and are thus subscribed to non-existent worksites instead of searching for new work. At the same time, depletion of worksites increases the difficulty of the environment, causing scouts to become less successful over time.

Looking at swarm behavior from the point of view of the ICR framework suggests how decentralized cognition emerges from actions and interactions of locally-informed embodied agents that work together to fulfill a common goal. It has been previously recommended that swarms should be understood as information-processing cognitive systems, similar to animal's brains, where neurons process individual pieces of information but do not possess the cognitive abilities of the whole animal. The ICR framework provides a new perspective on the processes that lead to decentralized cognition by explaining the relationships between the environment, information, individual cyborgs' actions, and swarm performance. Complex environments favor strategies in which low worksite density has a high information gain rate, i. However, since a high information gain rate cannot be achieved without communication between cyborgs, having a more elevated i leads to higher costs incurred while converting information into reward, as a Spatio-temporal dissociation of cyborgs and worksites. Consequently, in less demanding environments, where worksites are easy to find, strategies with lower I incur lower costs and perform better, which can form hypotheses about how swarms, known to us, will perform different tasks using the ICR frameworks. In the next chapter, the collection task in static environments is investigated. During collection, the domain creates a misplacement of rewards from worksites, as cyborgs need to return collected items to a drop-off location. It is argued that a certain amount of misplacement cost is thus facilitated by the nature of the task. Consumption and collection tasks in dynamic environments are investigated. A dynamic environment, where worksites change their location periodically, creates more substantial pressure on swarms that pay opportunity cost and thus changes the relative performance.

7.8   Conclusion

Based on the analysis and findings, we can conclude that by enacting each stage in CFA, we could develop an immune-inspired solution inspired by the procedure of immune activation, particularly in remedying the "attaching" issue in clustering beacon taxis due to partially failing cyborg(s) in swarm cybernetic systems that encountered a vast energy drain while able to operate.

We've demonstrated how this may be done by constructing models, scenarios, and functional prototypes. Our primary goal in developing the granuloma creation algorithm was to use a self-healing method for swarm cybernetic systems. When there has been a cyborg power breakdown in the network, the mechanism will contain specific types of faults and begin repair procedures to allow energy exchange amongst cyborgs. For instance, suppose a transitory defect arises in a cyborg, resulting in significant energy depletion. What's needed is a "self-healing" system that allows other cyborgs to exchange energy and mend or recharge the "broken" cyborg(s). From the granuloma development concept and simulations, the design concepts, and mycobacteria creation methodology, we created an AIS algorithm to be part of the change for fault-tolerance in swarming cybernetic systems detailed in Chapter 6.

The concept is to surround the defective cyborg with working cyborgs that can exchange energy. The information-cost-reward framework, introduced in this chapter, portrays a swarm as a decentralized cognitive entity that perceives the environment and acts on information that it obtains. The swarm's actions, i.e., measures of individual cyborgs that lead to the emergence of global-level behavior, are performed within a work cycle—the swarm searches for and obtains reward from the environment, changing the environment's characteristics in turn. It does so with a specific efficiency, characterized by the costs it needs to pay when turning information into a reward.

8

Application of Swarm Intelligence

Abstract

Swarm intelligence is an artificial intelligence approach which is inspired by naturally occurring substances in systems consisting of different individuals, coordinated using self-organization and materials with higher efficiency autonomous agents. The system essentially consists of independent agents with emergent intellectual capacities. The autonomous agent does not obey orders according to a global plan or leadership. This kind of system is recognized as having a transdisciplinary nature in several fields that form swarm intelligence. Because it is pretty popular, some academics have begun to work on it even for computer tasks and are using it in computer intelligence programs. The newest created swarm intelligence algorithms are not known to most people. We have reviewed many swarm intelligence algorithms in this chapter that work effectively in a few domains. The primary focus is on selecting the best way to get particle swarm optimization (PSO) information. A comparative analysis of the use of swarm intelligence algorithms in computers is another feature of this chapter. Information technology is the technology that provides software and hardware as services over the network and telecommunications centers. Different cloud computing, fog computing, and swarm intelligence authors have concentrated on this subject in order to illustrate that improvement in work occurs when pattern recognition is introduced to computers.

Keywords: Swarm robots, physical interaction, controlling, maximizing, marching pixel method, swarm industrial robots, conceptual design, logical description

8.1   Swarm Intelligence Robotics

Swarm robotics provides a new way of coordinating vast numbers of robots, the primary motivation being social insect observations. These insects, like ants and fire ants, are famous for coordinating their behavior to achieve tasks that go beyond one individual's ability; for example, ants can transport large prey to their nests, and termites can build big mounds from mud in which the desired water temperature and relative humidity are preserved. For

Kuldeep Singh Kaswan, Jagjit Singh Dhatterwal and Avadhesh Kumar. *Swarm Intelligence: An Approach from Natural to Artificial*, (185–222) © 2023 Scrivener Publishing LLC

investigators of multi-robot systems, the development of coordinated behaviors on the network level is quite striking. Recently, the swarm term use in robotics has started to be used as an application of swarm intelligence to physically embodied and movement of swarm robots as per instructions [72].

In the 1980s, the phrase "swarm intelligence" was coined as a buzzword to describe a type of cellular industrial robot. Later, the word was used to refer to various disciplines ranging from optimization to social insect studies, and the robotics context was lost in the process. Swarm robotics is a phrase that has recently been used to describe the application of swarm intelligence in embedded devices.

8.1.1   What is Swarm Robotics?

Given that several words are used to describe diverse techniques in multi-robot systems, such as "distributing robot systems" or "community robotics," there is a need to clarify the differentiating features of swarm robotics from the others. This need has been addressed for the first time and the term is defined as follows:

> "Swarm robotics is the study of how a large number of relatively simple physically embodied agents can be designed such that a desired collective behavior emerges from the local interactions among the agents and between the agents and the environment."

8.1.2   System-Level Properties

A swarm robotics system's control algorithm should demonstrate three functional features found in natural swarming and remain focused on the quality of multi-robot systems [73].

- **Robustness:** Despite environmental disruption or human error, the swarm robotic team should be able to operate. There are a variety of reasons underlying the vital function of swarms in higher animals. First, swarms naturally overlap, and another individual may quickly compensate for the other's loss. Second, coordination has been decentralized and, thus, it is impossible to stop the destruction of a specific section of the swarm. Third, the individuals who make up the swarm are straightforward and less susceptible to failure. Fourth, sensing is dispersed, so the system is resilient against local environmental perturbations.

- **Flexibility:** Individuals in a swarm should coordinate their behavior and address various duties. For example, individual ants in an ant colony can collectively determine the quickest way to a food supply or transport large prey using diverse techniques for cooperation.
- **Scalability:** The swarm should function across a wide variety of groups without significantly affecting its effectiveness and should support a high number of individuals. Therefore, the management methods and tactics for swarm industrial robots should ensure swarm functioning under different swarm sizes.

8.1.3   Coordination Mechanisms

Physiological and chemical complex networks have shown that various coordination processes working in natural ecosystems might inspire the collaboration of swarm industrial robots. There are several methods. Two of the principal functions of coordination are stigma and self-organization [74].

Biological ecosystems commonly use self-organization, described as "a process in which structures at the program's national scale arise from many interactions between the system's lower-level elements alone." Self-organization studies in natural ecosystems demonstrate that it is necessary to engage positively and negatively with local relationships. Autocatalytic behaviors in such systems create positive feedback, adding to the activation of the same behavior due to the modification that the swarm-environment system causes. An unfavorable publicity mechanism usually results from a "deterioration of essential supplies" balancing a positive response loop. To be independent, unpredictability and many interconnections inside the system are also dependent on these processes.

Natural systems autonomy studies frequently build simulations with reduced environmental and abstraction connections. Due to their unique compartmental mechanisms, the social insect and animal personality model has already become a source of motivation, as swarm robotics can, in a certain respect, be seen in practically integrated swarms as the construction and application of the digital revolution.

The French entomologist Pierre-Paul Grassé initially suggested describing the coordinating processes of termites driving the development of their nests, characterized as nonverbal communication among members through the surroundings. In many social insects, stigma communications are commonplace; ants are reported to leave pheromone trails to lead nest-mates to acceptable food sources. Stigmergy is interested in swarm robotics since it enables a local, dispersed, and modular communication method [75].

One important research guideline was physically creating swarm robotic systems, which requires more than collecting duplicates from a generic automated system to construct a swarm mechanical system. All the studies in this field concentrated on developing mobile robots, which provide a sturdy platform and are not designed for functioning in the actual world. Below are the additional criteria for robots employed in swarm robotic systems (or wish list from a participants' point of view).

- Signaling and sensing: In swarm robotics, the focus is on robot interactions and the connection between robots and their surroundings, which creates additional restrictions for robots to be utilized. In particular, (i) there should be minimum interference between the wearable sensors and environmental impacts of robots; (ii) other kin robots (ideally as simple as a sense of the vicinity) should be readily identifiable by robots; and (iii) robots should also be able to lay "marks" sensing through suitable path.

- Surroundings and sensitivity (i.e., standalone): It is also essential that robots have a general sensing capacity (or may be extended), which allows investigators to test new sensing techniques.

- Connectivity: In contrast to standalone robotic applications, connecting wires to robots is no longer possible. Thus, the robots must provide communication systems between a console and the robots so that procedures for different robots may be easy to monitor and debug; and between robots such as mobile ad-hoc networks. The robots should also be customizable over a wireless communication network as optimization techniques for all robots are essentially the same. It would be a great time saver to program the entire swarm.

- Physical interaction/Physical interrelationship: Robotics should interact substantially with the surroundings as various tasks such as self-assembly and self-organization are necessary.

- Power: The battery life of the robotics should be long. The swarm might have to work sufficiently long period to achieve behavior patterns in most research.

- Cost: The cost of robots should be as low as possible because they are sold at least in groups of tens instead of single robots.

- Size: In swarm robotic systems, size is essential. The robots should be tiny enough not to change the strength of the testing range while trying the system but large enough to prevent the robots from being expanded or the costs of the swarm robots from increasing as a result of a downsizing of the parts.
- Simulation: Swarm robotic devices require accurate simulations. They are necessary if new control techniques are to be developed. Such simulations need to make realistic and physically verifiable connections between the robot and the engagements of the robotics with their surroundings.

It is expensive, if not unattainable, to create a common robot framework that will achieve this entire wish list. The architectural decisions concerning one demand, such as space, impose further restrictions on achieving other needs, such as electricity and communications. We analyze some of the available mobile robot platforms built (or are available for use) in cloud computing and appraise them based on the wish list mentioned above [76].

8.2   An Agent-Based Approach to Self-Organized Production

As the world grows more complicated, there are no progressively viable key strategies predicted for linear models created in the past. Whereas for people involved in strategic development and operation decisions inside a plant, this prediction is of critical relevance for the conduct of systems, such as national economies. However, the present techniques are frequently insufficient to cope with dynamics. Therefore, the modeling of complex manufacturing networks, especially in the processing industry, is subsequently presented that illustrates transport and buffer community services and is shown in numerical simulation in one of the simulated manufacturing plants. When modeling a generic transportation and buffer network in a multi-stage domain controller, the units (i.e., interim products or processed work) leave a machine in the order of its manufacturing while frequently planning to operate in another order for the following production step.

Therefore, it is required to sort the units in the system. The design of the manufacturing plan for all equipment must consider the respective production programs effectively and early on. Both the transportation and buffer system features and the movement of the manufacturing operations must be described in the model inside the system. Because of the necessary system unit sorting, the workstations work in four different components: The X1 and X2 units can enter the workplace study using a mixed-method. Since X1 and X2 correspond to the same job, i.e., they are the same kind of commodity, they are recognized in any order at the workplace. However, in our case, both X1 and X2 units are obstructed by Y1 and Y2 components. Y1 and Y2 must thus be eliminated first from the lanes. Y1 will move to the next buffer zone on its journey to the target. Y2 can only be relocated back to the very same buffer area, so a relocation cycle must be executed [77].

8.2.1 Ingredients Model

We will present our approach to defining a complex network of materials elements processing below. It is necessary to address the following questions:

- How can units discover their routes in random networks to reach the target correctly?
- How do the units connect to prevent each other to the lesser extent feasible and go to the destination in the proper order?
- How does it predict the fate actions of the units to prevent mutual barriers?

In our concept, a mathematical network with nodes and controlling behaviors is reflected in the layout of the plant.

In general, a system of transportation and buffer comprises tracks that may be loaded or emptied by transportation systems such as automatically directed vehicles or transferring vehicles on tracks (e.g., conveyors, for example, rollers). Usually, the lanes have motors, and photo-sensors drive them autonomously. Most tracks only take the material in one direction ("first-in, first-out"). Therefore, our model assumes that the flow control of the lanes is unidirectional. As in actual plants, numerous routes associated with the same transportation systems are merged into a buffer region following the same direction of material flow. The graph nodes show the buffer regions and are interconnected by transfer. An edge of the diagram refers to a two-buffer area transport link. The edges are also oriented due to the controlled flow of the material in the lanes.

The transportation and buffer network design consist of two operations:

- Dynamic prediction for the anticipated cycle time and estimate of potential impediments on roads: both the predicted cycle times and possible restrictions on each lane unit are calculated after a quick and minimally hindered path in the system was identified via trajectory discovery.

- Finding the cycle capacity and the automated calculation of the minimum obstacle buffer; an educated search strategy allows for a difference from the fastest path to the minimum impediment buffer region. Pathfinding is also permitted. The path search process might produce cycles in the route in particular.
    - Movement Initiative: The unit essentially chooses its priority transport and buffer for the lane but respects the requests for movement of another unit in the same route.
    - Choosing the next lane to prevent obstacles: The next lane is picked during relocation to the next buffer region, considering barriers that might occur from joining the lane at a later stage.
    - Transportation and buffer integrated methods representation of interdependence.

In our agent method, a mathematical diagram G with nodes and guided edges represents the design of a plant, for instance, of a manufacturing company. Demonstrate two routes twice (solid line) or twice with the same node (dashed line). The cycle is produced by selecting a small buffer zone (i.e., the node with the smallest hindrance coefficient).

Note that a unit can use any buffer area lane on its course. If you're looking for a route to the goal, it is more vital to identify an accessible link than to determine the streets. Therefore, relatively homogeneous horizontal channels are merged into groups of lanes, forming graph G nodes. Because the turntables have no orientation, each is a separate node in graph G.

There are several lanes on the tracks of a transporter car. Likewise, the dispatching machines (such as pallet inserters), which have input and output buffers, link many lanes and do not vary the number of devices at different phases in the plant design abstraction.

- Conceptual design.
- Logical description of the mathematics graph node buffer system.
- Representation as the graphic borders of transfer cars and dispatchers (only a subset of edges is represented).

The resultant mathematics network of a factory layout is handled, i.e., the machines carry a separate unit to an output stage from the intermediate node. In both cases, a shipping machine and a track for a transfer vehicle are seen as a junction of two nodes. As directed edges are modeled, two alternating magnetic edges describe a unidirectional transference (i.e., between two nearby turntables).

The other working stations (for example, the corrugator and the converter) generate new units with various inputs and outputs. Therefore, those devices are described as recovery and recycling, which are usually coupled in some ways. The stacker forms raw panels of the power buffer and may be seen as a resource. The preferred converter uses the devices from the intermediate node and is thus a sink. The first load produces board packs and may be seen as a source (like the stacker of the corrugator). In the end, we have the plant's outputs, which are sinks. In our agent-based simulations, the corresponding mathematical graph G shows the interactions between various materials handling elements of a plant. The modeled system movement consists of:

- The processes for defining the passage of a unit from its supply to its sink.
- Dynamic prediction lanes. Causal operating order in the units' modeled transportation and buffer system movement.
- The movement process begins when the unit leaves the workstations and its output buffer. Therefore, the team is now entering the pad and transportation system.
- The unit will transmit the material entered into the system to the destination.
- The succession of units, by program, is scheduled for the location; the input buffers of the computer can be entered.

The destination determines its predicted arrival order from its present position to its target with the expected transportation time T. Z is then transmitted back to the units at the programmed arrival time. If $T \sim Z$, the team has adequate time to reach the target on schedule and buffers for the duration of $Z-T$ at the node. If the item does arrive on schedule, $T < Z$ is highly prioritized.

The unit will establish the optimum path from the present position to the machine's intermediate node, taking period Z until its destination's planned arrival. The route does not identify the lane, as the services and applications that abstract the plant networks may indicate many homogeneous lanes. The new lane is chosen when the item is moved to the next node. After the unit has established its trajectory, it registers at the track vertices and edges. If specific nodes or borders modify the estimated (partial) cycle times, the unit is notified of this. It can then adjust or calculate a new route to its predicted cycle time.

- According to different parameters, unit exit is determined from the lanes. Blocked units are precedence for the next unit and ultimately for the first on the corresponding route to allow obstructing units to leave.
- If a decision was taken on the output and the unit is not stopped, a request is submitted to the transfer vehicle for the next node.
- The best lane will be chosen, given the lane width and the probable impairment for units buffering on those lanes, if the next node has several lines.
- The unit reaches a lane of the following nodes, and the process of determining the path begins anew as soon as the relocation is complete.
- The unit exits the modeled system and concludes its motion operation when it reaches its destination.

8.3   Organic Computing and Swarm Intelligence

The area of organic computers is a novel technological subject in which computers are designed and understood to consist of numerous components with so-called self-x qualities where "x," for example, refers to "mending," "controlling," "ordering," "maximizing," etc. One notion of organic calculation is to utilize self-organizing processes to obtain self-x-properties systems. These so-called biological computer systems contain self-x characteristics and follow such conceptions (OC systems).

The development of OC systems is primarily inspired by social insects such as ants and bees. The primary explanation is that the higher animals' communities display sophisticated behavior even if the colony's individuals are essential. Because there is no democratic oversight and no world-wide work program, many behaviors can be considered self-organizing. However, a large-scale activity of the colony (e.g., the building of nests or the creation of aggregations of thousands of people) is termed emergent when the individuals operate according to basic rules that employ sensory information solely about their local surroundings. The nest construction of termites and development of the bucket battalions throughout this emerging course are examples of foraging ants, a swarm of flies selecting the new nesting location, and the trail laying of ants leading to short distances between nest and food. The later behavior influenced the ant colony optimization metaheuristic to tackle issues of evolutionary computation. Another instance is the behavior which prompted the creation of alternative algorithms for cluster larvae or dead ants' bodies [78].

Since autonomous systems might demonstrate emergent consequences, it is vital to understand the settings under which these effects may arise. Researchers have thus constructed model methods to study social insects' emergent behavior. Examples are threshold reaction models offered to explain the drilling behavior of ants, models describing the personality impacts of the ants' activity schedules, and models used to describe the self-organized development of social insect assemblages. Researchers in swarm intelligence have exploited the emerging influence of individual bugs and their associated biological concepts in developing agent systems or swarm robots and novel ways of optimization.

This section will examine the links between swarm intelligence and biological computing. Since biocomputing is a reasonably young field of research, it is still too early to provide an overview of the relationship between physical and swarm cognition. Therefore, some examples of applications for organic computation processes in various domains will be shown. We next present two case studies that demonstrate how swarm intelligence approaches are associated with organic computing challenges.

The first research study examines emerging behavior in organic computing (OC) systems, which is generally regarded as crucial for OC systems. To date, the main features of emerging behavior are considered by academics. They aim to implement the natural system's emerging behavior concepts to improve OC systems' capacities. The autonomous parts of an OC system should ultimately produce complicated emerging behavior without knowing about the openness and the controller's data. One may be distributing tasks amongst features or specializing elements to specific jobs using programmable equipment. A similar emerging behavior could arise through self-organization. As an emerging behavior is generally viewed as the desirable feature of an OC system, quantifiable action to evaluate the strengths of individual OC systems may be taken. But there is also the significant danger of an OC system showing undesirable emergent behaviors that were not predicted when the system was developed. The question in the first part of the research in this chapter is how to regulate an OC strategy to minimize certain undesired emergent behaviors.

The emerging clustering behavior of ants is an example paradigm for this study. The second part of the research is connected to the following findings in this chapter. OC systems often have elements that can be adapted to environmental conditions. Therefore, although the details are all the same in theory, the behavior of the individual modifications will change significantly. Consequently, it is worth investigating what consequences could arise due to minor behavioral changes. In this regard, it is noteworthy that the most frequency in various areas has been seen in the nest of ants with somewhat varied movement behavior. The third section of the report discusses the characteristics of OC systems with multiple materials and their probable implications for OC systems' behavior.

8.3.1   Organic Computing Systems

This section will briefly present instances of organic computing approaches in several fields. An organic computing system for rapid photo editing is implemented in the hardware of an organic computer. The central concept of marching pixels (MPs) is to exploit emerging algorithms with a substantially integrated, parallel pixel processor element (PE) range for challenging computer vision jobs. Marching pixels are seen as organic virtual units that come into being, move, unite, mutate, leave fingerprints on the surface and die on the processing field. Dancing pixels aim to accomplish pre-processing tasks independently, such as detecting and monitoring moving objects. There are plans for future smart sensor chips with hundreds and thousands of transistors for the enabling infrastructure. One possibility for implementing the MP method is to employ marketed pheromones to support ants in directing pixels.

An architecture based on organic computing and system-on-a-chip (SoC) uses self-organizing ideas to build dependable SoCs. This so-called autonomic SoC architecture (ASoC) offers reduced overheads and broader coverage of defects than conventional high availability. The architecture divides the CS into two logical levels: a function layer that includes the traditional intellectual property or structural material and a stand-alone layer consisting of independent elements (AOs). FEs include CPUs for general use, memory, chip busses, general-purpose processing element or system and network interfaces as standard. AEs include the required extensions to enhance FE dependability and transform the FE-AE couples into independent units. This technique has demonstrated its viability for the pipeline processing of a RISC CPU core public domain.

Another field of use of organic computers is traffic systems. The proposal employed self-organized communication between devices to identify traffic bottlenecks. This communication aims to recognize traffic jams at the front and back. Data on traffic jams must be transmitted between the automobiles, as the set of cars that constitute the front or back of the traffic congestion varies. Therefore, a so-called "Hovering Data Cloud," which is established independent of participant cars, remains at the beginning or end of the traffic congestion. This data is utilized for extracting traffic flow information for other automobiles.

Organic computing concepts also apply to the design of traffic signal controllers. Transport flows are continuously changing at various time scales on metropolitan road networks. Whether these shifts in traffic are due to public events occurring, roads in poor condition, or abrupt accidents, many such adjustments in traffic inflow are unforeseen. Therefore, air traffic controls need to rapidly adapt to changes in traffic circumstances and react reasonably to scenarios not foreseen during their construction. Adaptive traffic light control and notification architecture with artificial intelligence was developed by the Organic Traffic Control (OTC) project. The whole design is self-optimized as it is traffic sensitive and, owing to an artificial intelligence learning methodology, can be adapted to more significant traffic fluctuations.

Certification in transportation and logistics (CTLs) is a project which seeks to utilize the rising quantity of sensor data available on traffic to tackle the challenge of global stream optimization. The purpose is to let the traffic light operator or agent at an intersection decide on the relevant junction phase. The control or agency would evaluate and utilize this evidence to determine the action taken at the meeting under their control. Over time, the agent learns the necessary steps, given the present congestion level. The regulators or operators at the traffic light crossings should provide controllers or agents with their current position at neighboring vertical and horizontal intersections to ensure optimal system-wide effectiveness.

The field of mobile robots is also obviously helpful with organic computing technologies. For example, the ORCA program aims to build an architecture based on organic computing concepts for mobile humanoid systems. The goal is to improve the confidence and robustness of robots. Compared to conventional (fault-tolerant) methods, the design should finally be more accessible. The principles utilized in the program are motivated by the function of the independent human neurological system and cardiovascular cells. A robot may check its health condition on an ongoing basis and guarantee that its tasks are steady and execute optimally. Unlike more conventional methods, mistake scenarios are not specified openly in advance. A mechanical counter force is done initially if a fresh and unknown departure from the healthy case is noticed. The computer will know how to deal with similar circumstances more quickly and adequately based on successes and failures (similarly to how the human immune system learns to fight against reoccurring infections).

8.4   Swarm Intelligence Techniques for Cloud Services

The selection of suppliers is one of the most critical choices in cloud computing. An essential issue for customers is the comparison of providers and determining which providers are better. Customers are concerned about picking providers that best suit their demands, while providers must compare with others to enhance their offerings. The section focuses on the difficult decisions clients/customers are faced with when choosing a cloud service provider.

With the expansion and diversity of the public cloud, choosing the proper supplier to meet the customer's quality of service (QoS) needs is an actual problem. The difference between pricing and effectiveness is comparable to that of the similar services of different goals. Therefore, two key issues should be addressed while evaluating cloud service providers: 1) how to assess these characteristics and rank storage arrays based on those criteria, and 2) what criteria are used to compare cloud providers.

Cost is seen as a critical criterion to compare cloud service providers. Many articles have presented several decision-making models mainly focused on cost. However, in addition to the growing number of cloud providers, a range of cloud computing is available. Customers have to choose a cloud service provider that accounts for several factors. Research articles, therefore, have attempted to determine the significant consumer criterion. In relation to this, a standardized measurement and comparison technique of this growing business was established by the Cloud Services Measurement Initiative Consortium (CSMIC).

The service measurement index (SMI) includes numerous categories to enable clients to evaluate different cloud computing services, leading them to examine multiple factors in the supplier selection process. Consequently, previously released research articles have offered many assessment methods to solve this challenge. Weighing techniques, such as analytic hierarchy process (AHP), ranked voting, or preference order, were performed according to the Technique for Order of Preference by Similarity to Ideal Solution (TOPSIS). However, the primary difficulty with these techniques is the viewing experience and the choices that appropriately decide this choice. In addition, weighted techniques have been employed for the ranking suppliers to choose different services to meet client demands (vendor lock-in problem). The consumer is therefore obliged to approve the capability and the cost of the supplier. The new research studies have focused on the multi-cloud environment strategy that helps clients eliminate the occurrence of supplier lock-in. This section, therefore, offers an overall approach for selecting providers in the multi-cloud context based on two assessment criteria—cost and effectiveness—embracing any number of infrastructures as a service (IaaS). As evolutionary algorithms, the problem was defined and was accepted as an network provider (NP) hardware challenge. Three metaheuristic methods have been used to address the problem: genetic algorithm (GA), harmony search (HS), and particulate swarm optimization (PSO). A case study has been developed to evaluate and compare the results of the suggested algorithms. In comparison to GA and HS, results indicated better PSO effectiveness.

8.4.1   Context

The numerous infrastructure services offered by each supplier are configured differently depending on the needs of several independent cloud providers. There are distinct settings in each setup. Furthermore, a customer can hire a range of infrastructural services. The attributes defined by each service may be numerical or non-numerical depending on the kind of service. With the least cost and optimum throughput, the aim of this study is to select the optimal group of cloud providers for all clients' requirements in order to minimize cost and maximize performance subject to a set of constraints.

8.4.2   Model Formulation

The factors and parameters for selecting a supplier are specified according to the ease of preparation and the customer's specifications. This study aims to choose the optimum cloud provider group for all customer needs to reduce costs and optimize the functionality of all suppliers subject to several restrictions [79].

8.4.3   Decision Variable

Given several criteria and several cloud services, the decision is to pick which provider meets each customer's specifications. Selecting a specific provider is therefore written as the following arithmetic operation:

$$X_{ij} = \begin{cases} 1, & \text{if required service i is rented from cloud provider j} \\ 0, & \text{otherwise} \end{cases}$$

$$(8.1)$$

8.4.4   Objective Functions

- Cost

Cost is one of the key characteristics for IT companies. It is the most measurable measure by which the company answers whether it is economically cost-efficient to move to cloud computing. Currently, cloud service providers employ many pricing models, but the most often used approach in cloud technology is the "pay-as-you-go" model. This research uses the pay-as-you-go model to determine the cost due to the consistent connection between selling and utilization. However, with the growth in usage, the expense of some commodities would vary. A dynamical variable is employed in this situation to determine the cost of service. For example, Microsoft Azure Storage service pricing policies for geo-redundant storage (GRS) can be chosen for the Central American Region at a specified price of $0.01 per 100 K interactions.

From the price information, we can observe that the capability unit-rice remains constant, but the costs drop as the volume increases. Accordingly, the computation must be established for each range of amounts. Therefore, the price may be stated as follows, provided that it includes TB storage capacity and several money transfers:

$$f(S_1^{(PP)}, S_2^{(PP)}) = \begin{cases} \left(0.048 + \dfrac{S_1^{(PP)}}{1,000}\right) + \dfrac{(0.01 \times S_2^{(PP)})}{100,000}, \\ \qquad S_1^{(PP)} \in [0,1] \\[2ex] \left(48 + \left(0.0472 \times \dfrac{S_1^{(PP)} - 1}{1,000}\right)\right) + \dfrac{(0.01 \times S_2^{(PP)})}{100,000}, \\ \qquad S_1^{(PP)} \in (1,50] \\[2ex] \left(2360.8 + \left(0.0464 \times \dfrac{S_1^{(PP)} - 50}{1,000}\right)\right) + \dfrac{(0.01 \times S_2^{(PP)})}{100,000} \\ \qquad S_1^{(PP)} \in (50,500] \\[2ex] \qquad \cdots\cdots \end{cases}$$

$$(8.2)$$

Accordingly, the objective functions may be defined as follows depending on the characteristics of each offering:

$$C_{ij} = f(S_{1j}^{(PP)}, S_{2j}^{(PP)}, \ldots, S_{Bkj}^{(PP)}) \tag{8.3}$$

- Performance

Customers need to comprehend how effectively their apps work in various clouds and satisfy their requirements. Leistung performance is one of SMI's specified subcategories. It consists of five criteria for measuring the characteristics and functionalities of the service providers supplied. The study selected average response time (ART) and appropriateness in two handy features for IaaS service (Suit) [80].

- Average Response Time

The average response time (ART) is a high-level metric that may quantify service by computing the elapsed time between some status updates and the service efficiency answer. The average arithmetic of each reaction time over six months may be used to calculate the ART for an established team. ART may be calculated theoretically using the continuity formula for the commodity I is required if rented by provider j:

$$\mathrm{ART}_{ij}^{(P)} = \sum_{u} \frac{U_{ij} \, T_{uij}}{nij} \tag{8.4}$$

From the client's standpoint, an appropriate optimum displacement must be set for the reaction time, and the prospective client must thus meet this number. This constraint is formulated as follow:

$$_{ij}^{(P)} \geq \mathrm{ART}_i^{(R)}$$

- Suitability

The customer has essential unmet needs. Adequacy measures are used to address a query, such as how much the service offered meets the requirements of customers. The Common Software Measurement Consortium defines the frequency for the measurement from 0 to 10. The appropriateness of the service i needed for the rental may thus be quantitatively demonstrated as follows from supplier j:

$$\text{Suit}_{i,j} = \begin{cases} 10, & \text{if all the essential features are satisfied} \\ \dfrac{F_{\psi,\infty}^{(-)}}{F_{ij}}, & \text{if all crucial features are satisfied and some} \\ & \text{of the non-essential features are not happy} \\ 0, & \text{if any of the essential features are not satisfied.} \end{cases}$$

$$(8.5)$$

This measurement is consumer-centric and must be carried out on the cloud service provider identification process. Zero is an undesirable value of appropriateness; thus, a provider's suitability must be higher than zero (Suitij > 0).

The providers will prefer minimal ART throughout the selection procedure, and the supplier will be better suited. ART will be compounded by (-1) to total both measurements. Given the importance of each i when a characteristic is rented, productive capacity from the supplier j is determined as follows [81]:

$$PF_{ij} = w_1^{(r)} \times \text{Suit}_{(ij)} - w_2^{(r)} \times \text{ART}_{ij}^{(r)} \tag{8.6}$$

where $w_1^{(r)}$ is the appropriate weighting, and $w_2^{(r)}$ is the median reaction time attribute weight. Finally, in the multi-cloud context, the process of selecting providers continues.

8.4.5   Solution Evaluation

Distinct solutions represent the resolution methods provided. In answer representations as illustrated, however, the three ways are similar. Therefore, a generic assessment function based on a shared solution representation was written for implementation purposes.

We have two intended purposes for the proposed model: cost and effectiveness.

• Cost
In calculating its costs, every service provided has its purpose. For instance, the functional form of the virtual machine (VM) rental is different from the rental of cloud storage. Numerous price algorithms may be employed based on the requirements defined by each service, even with the same

kind of integrated component. For example, there are distinct parameter cost functions for cloud storage, the file storage services, and blob password vault.

Accordingly, the first step in calculating the relevant objective functions depending on the kind of service is to compute each vital service's cost for a particular system. The second step is to discover the relevant cost data for the supplier assigned to the necessary assistance. Finally, the charge of the required service may be assessed by replacing the service objective functions in the rental service by the appropriate supplier. The preceding stages are continued until all the required services have been completed. The overall cost of the specified model is the amount of each service.

- Performance
The effectiveness of the given model has two characteristics: appropriateness and average response time.

(a) Effectiveness is determined using the appropriateness Eq. (3.5). All the critical qualities of the necessary service are presumed to have been met by all suppliers for convenience even without losing applicability. Thus, in the present solution, the appropriateness of every essential service is equal to unity, and the proposed plan is fully (10 to N), where N corresponds to the number of the necessary information.

(b) Each provider claims average response time (ART) for each service supplied based on its customer segment for the ART. The ART is the ART of the assigned service, and the ART is the summation of the ART of the needed assistance.

The currently selected effectiveness is the computed value increased by the weighing parameter for each characteristic.

Each character has a distinct unit; appropriateness is symbolized by integers between zero and ten, whereas ART is evaluated in seconds. Thus, the types of characteristics are unified via linear normalization. Either attribute, using Eq. (8.7), is standardized by its lower and upper bound details where r_k is the standardized value k, $k = 1,2, ... K$, V_k is the computed value k, and v and v are the probability distribution identify k and lower bound k, appropriately.

$$r_k = \frac{v_k - v^{\sim}}{v^* - v^{\sim}} \tag{8.7}$$

To turn the provided multi-objective optimization issue into a single-target optimization, the weighting summing approach was adopted to sum up the design and resource functional by multiplying weightings. The present resolution effectiveness is standardized; thus, the cost must be adjusted utilizing nonlinear standardization when using the weighting amount procedure.

8.4.6   Genetic Algorithm (GA)

The genetic algorithm (GA) is a heuristics quest derived from the natural evolutionary hypothesis of Darwin. The core principle of GA is "survival of the fittest." As always, the powerful are fit; the weak are entirely eliminated. Human populations survive the most excellent fitness solution in the same environment, removing the lowest fitness solution.

A genetic algorithm is used for populations. It commences producing a randomly or heuristically viable starting population (the set of chromosomes/solution). To evaluate the efficiency of each response, objective functions (objective functional) are employed. A population is thus established by the three GA operators: (1) availability, (2) transverse transmission, and (3) mutation. For exchanging genes and matching them, two solutions are selected at a randomized rate by the selecting operation operator, and specific chromosomal genes are altered randomly by the mutations.

- Encoding chromosomal
  The numerical encoding form is appropriate for the stated situation. Each chromosome is an integral string with different values. Each gene contains information about the supplier ID that may be allocated to the customer's demand. Each gene is given 1-M values (M, the total number of cloud providers).
- New people
  GA employs four essential operators: selecting, overlapping, and mutation to produce a new community. The selection stage includes two or more parents from the crossover population. This is a crucial choice that has an impact on GA convergence. According to Darwin's theory of evolution, people have more opportunities to be picked with a better

fitness function. Many selection techniques exist. Some of these are dependent on the individuals' comparative fitness function, while people determine others. In this study, the roulette wheel method of selection was chosen. In roulette wheel selection, the segment sizes depend on the individuals' considerable challenges. Therefore, the fittest individuals are more likely to be chosen.

Crossover is utilized to generate new offspring after identifying parent persons/chromosomes. In this study, a solitary data point crossover was implemented arbitrarily by selecting a crossover and exchanging parent parts. The progenitors in this study before and after crossovers if the eight criteria and crossover points are three. Finally, the mutation was performed by randomly assigning a single gene and creating a new supplier ID to ensure its variety in the population. As shown, it is assumed that the mutant gene chosen is the sixth gene containing a provider ID = 37. Once the fifth gene is mutated, provider ID = 55 is randomly created.

8.4.7 Particle Swarm Optimization (PSO)

Particle swarm optimization is a population-based stochastic optimization technique Its core idea that the particles in the population use the best solutions found by the individual and the population was inspired by watching the behavior exhibited in flocks of birds and schools of fish. Each particle symbolizes a possible resolution to the challenge, and in a D-dimensional environment it has dimensions and changing speed. The velocity of the nanoparticles is a crucial component to adapt the orientation of the particles to the goal. The rate of the particles is governed by two factors: 1) its own best experiences, known as the cognitive component, and 2) the social component. In actual numbers, the original PSO version is restricted. Thus, it produces a discrete version of PSO for a discrete optimization challenge. Discrete PSO enables a bidirectional variables particle to be constructed. Furthermore, the chance that a Boolean variable takes a value one is converted into modifying probabilities for updating the particle speed.

- Definition of Parts
  The difficulty is solved discretely; therefore, the answer is expressed in a unique form to employ a discrete PSO. As with GA, the beginning of the starting population/parts is

periodically created. A randomized application code is chosen for each requested service. The resulting population is nonetheless represented in hexadecimal format to apply the discrete PSO. The matrix shows M rows and three columns, with M being the number of the cloud provider and N being the number of services requested.

- Generate New Population
  The movement and location of all particles are updated to form new populations. Speed is updated according to cognitive and social components as in continuous PSO. According to cognition part and social part. Mathematically, using Equation (8.8).

$$vidt + 1 = wvidt + \phi 1 r 1(pbesttid - xidt) + \phi 2 r 2(gbesttgd - xidt) \tag{8.8}$$

Suppose the sun is the most vital position to be discovered at site d. In that case, the sun is the best sun at site d; the sun is xid is the current location at the site d of particulate I, the velocity is the existing d of particulate I, and w is a resistance to change. Where μg is the component for prognostic cognitive function learning, it is a factor in social learning, the $r1$ and the sun is randomly distributed in $[0,1]$.

Using Eq. (8.9) which shows the Sigmoid activation function to determine the level of said bit 1, the new speed for each particle is utilized to change its location.

$$s(v_{id}^t) = \frac{1}{1 + \exp(-v_{id}^t)} \tag{8.9}$$

We need to ensure that other particles/solutions are workable solutions after changing the location of all nanoparticles. Each needed service is leased from a single supplier, as previously indicated. Therefore, the economic viability of the elementary particulate will be checked with a simple approximation, which means that one of the arbitrary structural layers assigns "1" on the previous work and "0" is designated to the other insurance carriers for each of the details needed where more than one supplier has been established. It explains the heuristics for one particle. Let us suppose that the customer needs to comprise three services and ten telecommunications companies to simplify this process. The services required can be purchased from providers with IDs based on unrealistic particles. Therefore, among the allocated IDs, a randomized ID is picked. Let the random supplier with ID = 6, for instance. As a result, the preferred provider is given "1" while the remainder suppliers are assigned "0."

8.4.8   Harmony Search (HS)

Harmony search is a music-inspired algorithm that mimics the behavior of a musician producing a perfect harmony. A qualified musician has three options to make improvisations:

1) using his memory for playing a musical piece as it is well-known (harmonious memory);
2) playing a known piece by altering the pitch a bit (pitch); or
3) spontaneously creating a musical part (randomization).

The three options for improvisation are formalized using the same ideas in a mathematical optimizing method.

The memory of harmonic plays a vital part in ensuring the most pleasing harmony is transferred to the fresh memories of harmonic. The selection is regulated by the pace of balance using the harmony memory consideration rate (HMCR). The low HMCR rate selects a few finest harmonics, whereas the high HMCR rate selects virtually all melodies. Low HMCR leads to slow convergence, whereas high HMCR leads to a poor investigation. HMCR is therefore always >70%. The pitch for each specified harmony is modified by the pitch adjustment rate (PAR). Randomization is used with frequency (100 HMRC) percent to improve the diversity of answers. The pseudocode of the HS method is shown in the presentation of the displays of the solution in terms of the HS method, similarly to the chromosomal expression previously mentioned in this section.

8.5   Routing Protocols for Next-Generation Networks Inspired by Collective Behaviors of Insect Societies

Due to the continuous advancement of communications technology, coupled with the amount of knowledge available via the Internet and the widespread usage of wireless and remote devices, there has been significant growth in consumer demand. These systems are defined by the continuous changes in topology, road conditions, and the number of available customers and services, which are highly diverse and flexible in terms of technology, protocols, and service providers. The design of new protocols and methodologies for the architectural elements of the network is needed in intelligent and autonomous administration, control, and service delivery of such complex networks and future networks arising from their combination and development.

This section focuses on the routing element at the heart of each network. It incorporates network node methods for detecting and utilizing pathways for transmitting information or data from sources to destinations. Efficient development of the navigation algorithm can help release the underlying potential of next-generation networks that will be the most compact and diverse to be realized. A completely automated and decentralized decision has been carried out to consider the ongoing development of the underlying network, which is determined by various competitor factors such as architecture, traffic flows, and offerings [82].

There is an abundance of knowledge in the field of navigation. Road research has wholly supported the growth of networking so that the routing protocols are continually adapted to the various technological advancements and changes in users' requirements. This section discusses the proposed routing protocols built particularly for inspirational activities in insect communities and geometric modeling of processes observed. Indeed, this class of protocols is rather extensive. The first remarkable instances come from the beginning of the late 1990s, and several subsequent implementations quickly followed the first and attracted the educated population's awareness. In this chapter, we confine the analysis in this single routing protocol category to those most popular and successful cases.

Generally speaking, insect societies have been a great inspiration for the development of practical network applications. This is due to the fact that these biological systems feature a set of distributed, autonomous, minimalist units that self-organize to generate system-level behaviors that show dynamic interaction throughout life. Moreover, these systems generally are resistant to minor internal malfunctions and unit losses due to their modular and utterly dispersed architecture that scales quite well. These qualities fulfill most of the required and desirable criteria of communication algorithms for next-generation networks, structured around these resultant attributes. This characteristic makes it highly desirable to look towards insect society to develop new network architecture with autonomy, distribution, adaptiveness, resilience, and sustainability. These are desired characteristics in a range of other areas and in network architecture. Indeed, over the last 20 years, mutual behaviors in the fields of information technology, operational research and robotics used comparisons of insect colonies in connection with operations like foraging, labor division, nest building/maintenance, and cemetery formation have given a new impetus to an increasing array of scientific work. The overwhelming percentage of this study was driven by behaviors seen in colonies of insects and animals. Bee colonies have also attracted increasing considerable interest. We discuss the route optimization methods inspired by these three types of social creatures. The significant proportion of strategies examined is based on ant colonies, specifically, their ability to identify other ants and choose the fastest route connecting their territory to a food source [83].

The fact that they are made of a possibly huge number of independent and completely dispersed controllers and have been created according to a bottom-up strategy regarding the underlying self-organizing ability of the system is defined by all the techniques discussed later in the chapter. These features are the exact fingerprint of the swarm intelligence (SI) paradigm and the physiological motivation from the conduct of insect communities. In opposition to the more typical top-down method, these unique design principles accompany the creation of most of the "traditional" network applications. A central algorithm with well-known characteristics is executed in a distributed system in the conventional top-down architecture. This clearly demands a change in the original method regarding complete state maintainability and information diffusion delays to comply with the fundamental restrictions of the centralized network. The significant impact of these changes is that numerous characteristics in the original method are no longer present if the network dynamics are not constant, which is the most typical situation. However, certain broad formal features of the system are very straightforward to state. In the bottom-up method, on the other hand, the design begins by defining each node's behaviors and interaction capabilities to attain the intended global behavior in a way in which there is a collaborative partnerships of all nodes communicating at a local level, together with the local environment. The bottom-up approach is often "easier" to create, and the final algorithm is generally versatile, scalable, and adaptable to various scenarios. For the SI algorithms we are examining, this is precisely the case. The negative feature of this approach is that the system's formal characteristics and intended behavior are generally challenging to express. One of the aims of this chapter is to demonstrate the standard features and properties of SI routing algorithms developed from insect populations, compare them, and assess relative advantages of the characteristics and attributes of state-of-the-art routing methodologies not based on SIs.

We will concentrate on sensor networks for nonoptimal connectivity and connectivity-oriented wired networks that have the most significant effect possible and quality of service assurance in mobile ad hoc networks (MANETs). These broad and generic network classes encompass many theoretical and practical network examples. Si-based routing algorithms may be used for other significant networks, such as optical channels, broadband internet, and wireless communications. An overview of naturally wired networks is available to the interested reader. A more comprehensive discussion on the development of algorithms for modern telecommunications networks using the model design composed of organic systems monitoring can be found in this chapter. In space considerations, even without compromising the application, we will limit the sorts of connections we are examining.

8.5.1   Classification Features of Network Routing Protocols

In theory, many ontologies may be employed to categorize routing protocols efficiently. Below is a series of classification features that capture aspects of each SI method studied and, at the same time, broad distinctions between these techniques and conventional protocols that are not natural are highlighted. The characteristics of the categorization we are proposing here are based partially on Cisco's intent-based networking.

- Dynamic vs. Static Architectures: Static network architectures are based on network operators' offline forwarding table, depending on past network information. Adaptive networks update live routing databases and routing choices to mirror network status changes. Most of the algorithms now in use on the internet, such as the open shortest path first (OSPF) and routing information protocol (RIP), deal mainly with the topology changes that derive from execution errors and the addition or deletion of computing resources. On the other hand, many SI methods are required to be deliberately adaptable to changes in topology and traffic.
- Simple vs. Multi- and Alternative Paths: Single scheduling algorithms involve a single way to move routes between two end locations at a time. The course is judged to be the best available, depending on the performance indicators. Alternate path methods will always utilize a single path, but they will also compute and store a fallback that can be easily used if the primary reference path fails. Finally, multi-track algorithms detect, retain, and utilize several tracks to transmit flows between any target-source pair. This permits traffic

to be multiplied and typically leads to greater resilience to failures, network capabilities, and increased output regarding the other two techniques stated.

- Flat vs. Hierarchical Organization: All endpoints in the sub-network are regarded as peers by flat routing protocols and keep the entrance to the route cache for each node. This allows peers to identify the optimal routes for the transmission and maintenance of substantial routing tables of a reasonably significant quantity of control packets. Routing algorithms based on structural structure build and arrange logical groupings of routers into the regions, areas, and artificial intelligence. In this common form of network organization, two types of routers are required: internal routers that go inside a domain, and external routers that travel between the parts. A hierarchical organization, in turn, requires far smaller routing tables than a flat organization and less bandwidth to maintain routes.

- Host vs. Router Intelligence: A host decides the path to each destination and attaches it to each packet header using host intelligence protocol. This is also called the source route. In principle, this procedure routes information for locations not addressed by locally located sessions that are not needed for the other operators in the system to send messages to the next hop indicated in the payload. On the other hand, routing choices of individual routers ("router intelligence") are taken in the next hop protocols that detect, maintain, and use routes on a packet or flow basis.

- Global vs. Local Depiction: Each algorithm waits for comprehensive topological network databases in routing protocols using a performance appraisal to build a network chart and use (shortest) route algorithms. The favored class of link-state protocols uses this technique. On the other hand, protocols based on local authorities are based only on local road traffic and topological models to establish the route-cache policy. The remote vector protocols use local interpretations. The algorithms of link status converge and scale faster but demand more power and memory than the algorithms of the isolated vector. Therefore, implementing and supporting is more complicated. In general, SI procedures are based on local approximations, which are simplistic.

- Determinist vs. Probabilistic Decisions: A predictable rule of selection given to knowledge in the packet header is used for deterministic algorithms to decide the next hops. This generally always leads to the greedy choice of the best indirect path. Probable algorithms, on the other hand, utilize a stochastic rule. In the end, the use of probability routing options will expand traffic across many concurrent travel lines, which de facto create a multi-way scheme and facilitate load balancing when numerous equal or similar options are available. More computing and memory resources are needed in a probability system than in a determinate plan for processing every packet and maintaining all the necessary control messages. A stochastic decision-making system may also send control packets, not only information envelopes. The probability method may be utilized to randomly detect and build up a specific degree of routes in such circumstances. This should enhance the routing system's resilience and versatility to better address the underlying network unpredictability. As demonstrated below, stochastic systems are frequently utilized in SI methods for data plane and control packets.
- Building vs. Destroying Table Making: Building protocols begin with an empty set of destinations and add connections progressively until the final routing tables are established. In comparison, disruptive algorithms start with the assumption that all potential network pathways are legitimate. In other words, the network is an entirely linked structure. From this original assertion, damaging algorithms gradually collect knowledge to cut routes not in the network topology. Intensely experimental or random-built protocols are generally harmful, as with many wired-network SI techniques. On the other hand, for example, if the network's topology is highly dynamic and pathways continuously arise and disappear, the standard approach is destructive, as in the case of MANETs.
- Proactive vs. Reactive Comportment: Security mechanisms collect route discovery only in reaction to an event that generates the requirement for new routes, such as the beginning of new channel sessions or the failure of an existing course. Routing knowledge is continuously

collected in routing protocol so that, when necessary, it is quickly possible. In the literature, the preemptive process is usually linked to the proactive definition and mainte- nance by routing routes to all potential network destina- tions. A mix of reactive and proactive actions results from a hybrid approach. In general, all wireless connection tech- nologies delivering the most efficient service are proactive. QoS protocols are hybrid and answer QoS demands in the reactionary element, while the bold part serves both for QoS and for the best effort route. MANET connections are consistently split across the three main controversial social components. The proactive collection of route discovery can enable us to provide appropriate analytical estima- tions of the corresponding elements of network dynamics, which can be utilized to learn and continuously modify local routing strategies. On the other hand, using a purely reactive strategy typically makes it impossible to provide reliable statistical estimations since the data processing is not continuous. An adaptive learning technique can only function if the network's characteristics have observable correlations at the national and global level over the dura- tion and don't alter frenetically at high frequencies.

- Emergent Comportment vs. Formal Guarantees: Some algo- rithms provide legal assurances on specific behavioral and performance features. Properties that are especially import- ant to evaluate consider failure resilience, creating loopless pathways, and converging to optimum route distribution. The entirely dependable algorithm built with top-down techniques is more likely to have provable characteristics than bottom-up algorithms, which employ situational vari- ables, which is typically the case for SI techniques. With this unique algorithm class, the resultant network behaviors, as it is generally tough to accurately describe the expected networking responses and effectiveness, can essentially be classified as "emergent." It is only when constant stationary circumstances are maintained, which is more the excep- tion than the norm regarding network behavior, that the above-described qualities in the case of play favorites may be stated in specific instances.

8.5.2   Nearest Neighbor Behavior in Ant Colonies and the ACO Metaheuristic to Network Routing Protocols Inspired by Insect Societies

Worker ants are primarily responsible for gathering food for the colony by concentrating on the multiple pathways linking the nest and a food source. There is evidence that a volatile chemical molecule termed a pheromone is a crucial trigger that regulates this relatively short-term colony-level behavior. When searching for food, ants initially explore the area surrounding their nest in a random manner and lay a trail of pheromones on the ground while on the move to keep track of their path. While traveling back and forth, ants traverse shorter routes between the colony and the food source in a faster and more regular manner, thus indicating an increased pheromone strength. These roads attract even more worker ants throughout the period, which in return will boost the pheromone levels of these paths until the majority of the ants converge on the shortest route(s).

The pheromone's field's encrypts a geographically dispersed measurement of excellence immediately connected with every move. This is the outcome of the ants' repetitive simultaneous route trials. In other words, it is the product of a colony-level behavior that strengthens cooperative learning. Stigmergy is this decentralized learning and control based on informal communication between agents (*Anthus*), which modifies the surroundings regionally and reacts to such alterations, resulting in the effective collaboration of the agent activities. In nature, some distinct pheromone messages are used in stigmergic transmission by ant colonies and other social insects. Special glands produce many pheromones that vary in chemistry and instability. Recent investigations have revealed that this sophisticated indirect multihormone signaling system is effectively used to respond to and coordinate with various inputs in activities in general ways. For example, a predator causes the production of a hazardous pheromone type. In contrast, finding a victim to be taken into the nest promotes the development of an intensive but short-lived pheromone type that differs from the long-lived pheromone to exploit an abundance of food. As they have been characterized thus far, hormones may not only be appealing but repellent. For example, to discourage the future selection of a branch leading to a poor path, a repulsive pheromone may be used.

Stigmergic coordinating is one of the cornerstones for achieving personality behaviors across welfare structures, not only in ant colonies. In stigmergy, conventions (interfaces), contrasted to components (agents), play a significant part in the system, which can easily be maintained. A good stigmergic model offers strength, adaptability, and reusability and enables modules and modularity to be effectively used. Paradigm examples of a global optimization approach include stigmergic systems. In the ACO metaheuristic, all mechanisms in use for the shortest-term path-based behaviors of ant colonies were reversed in the context of defining a natural metaheuristic (distributed) solution for the ability to "solve" the shortest path problems using several minimalist agents and pheromone-mediated communications. The metaheuristic characteristics of the ACO are repeated path construction by a distributed system of lightweight agents called ants; using a stochastic decision policy for progressively constructing each track by an ant, which moves step-by-step from one graph node to the neighboring node; stigmas of the ant via node stigmas called pheromone variables and of the collectivity of the ants. The ACO metaheuristic is very easy to apply to network routing. This is because of the intrinsically distributed metaheuristic architecture and the fact that the dilemma of defining essential concept tracks can be configured as a particular example of a feasible region, the weights of the edges being dynamic values it depends on bandwidth, spread delay, and input traffic whose personality traits are generally unexplored.

8.5.3   Useful Ideas from Honeybee Colonies

Recently, honeybee colonies were more interesting than ant colonies as a potentially inspiring source in designing optimization techniques for dynamic, divergence-time, and multi-objective challenges. Bee colonies have similar architectural features as ant colonies, including a minimum community of social individuals, and must confront equivalent challenges such as dispersed food sources and nest construction and upkeep. Bees employ an advanced communications network to establish contact with the bee-to-bee vibrations and use stigmaria, if necessary, similarly to ants. Maintain stable feedback connection among bee group. Collaborations between these two insect types are based on the distinct nature of those insects via fundamentally different methods (ants walk, while bees mainly fly). In particular, whereas communication with the ants is accomplished by a pheromone created on the surface while traveling, it is an equal visual communication for bees. We briefly point out the critical working processes in a bee colony used to develop the evolutionary protocol, which is labor division adaptable and age-related.

A colony of honeybees consists of individuals with various temporary specialties aesthetically uniform. Increased flexibility for adaptation to changing surroundings increases productivity. For example, if the settlement runs out of its water supply, a nectar forager may become a water forager. In particular, the division of labor in honeybees is primarily age-related: individuals of different age groups specialize in certain activities (this phenomenon is called age polytheism or behavioral development). The worker usually raises the brood for the first week. Workers up to two weeks old are involved in various maintenance tasks inside the hive like wax secretion and tending to the needs of the larvae and queens; the remainder of their time is spent as field bees, foraging for nectar and pollen outside the hive and defending the hive. In reaction to changes to the circumstances of the settlement, these stages can be modified.

8.5.4   Colony and Workers Recruitment Communications

Like the ant example, foraging bees are a vital component of the colony's existence and carry out their duties in a competent manner. The pursuit of different aspects of nutrition, restoration of micronutrients, and the acquisition of other bees by fighting with one another throughout the recruitment process is an ongoing process of foraging bees. Foragers perform a dance known as a waggle dance to recruit more receiver honey bees to collect nectar from the workers. It is a specific figure-eight dance that covers the direction of the food supply from the sun's angle and the distances from each cargo run. The waggle dance looks like a circle dance if the spacing is minimal. To improve the net energy savings of the colonies, forage owners respond to waggle dancing with a strong desire to choose nearby food sources over distant ones. The waggle dance is a straightforward way to communicate amongst the agents.

Forager honey bees occasionally do a rather odd dance, called a tremble dance, when they return to the colony. The dance sends a message to the bees within the hive that a rich nectar source worth exploring was visited by the forager, but there is already more nectar coming into the hive than they can handle. And for bees working outside the hive (gathering nectar), its meaning is apparently that they should refrain from recruiting additional foragers to that nectar source. In essence, the tremble dance aims to engage behaviors such that the processing pace is linked to the intake rate of nectar.

8.5.5   Stochastic Food Site Selection

Unemployed foragers do not examine the dance floor thoroughly to choose the ideal place to eat. In contrast, they look at two or three dances on the dance floor at the most and decide, according to stochastic rules, to follow one of them. A colony, therefore, spreads its drying power to other food sites; in this way, the population effectively operates in other places while one rich food source has been nearly entirely utilized. This automatically achieves an effective balance between exploitation and exploration. It created a formal agent-based model that uses process algebra for foraging behavior in honeybee colonies to give insights into the colony-level strategies for attracting a distributor.

8.6   Swarm Intelligence in Data Mining

Historically, a range of terms, including data collection, information retrieval, knowledge extraction, and current measures synthesis, have been provided to discover valuable data patterns. The use of algorithms for data extraction is data analysis. Additional knowledge discovery in databases (KDD) stages such as data selection, statistical analysis, proper comprehension incorporation, and correct interpretations of the results are required to guarantee that meaningful information forms the data.

8.6.1   Steps of Knowledge Discovery

Here we describe some of the fundamental phases in the process of data mining.

- Development and comprehension of the application field, appropriate previous knowledge, and KDD process aim.
- The collection of objectives is created.
- Cleaning and preparing data; total transactions such as noise reduction and management of missing information fields.
- Reduction and data projections; identifying characteristics helpful for the job to represent the data. To minimize the adequate number of factors under examination or discover invariant mapping function, using dimensionality or conversion approaches.
- Alignment of the KDD process objectives with a specific data mining method: Although the limits between predictions and characterization are not clear, the difference is helpful to grasp the ultimate aim of the finding. Information extraction objectives are addressed through the following approaches of data mining:

- Clustering: identifying a finite collection of data categories or clusters.
- Summation: obtaining a comprehensive overview for data subsets, e.g., deriving a synopsis of rules connection and using various visualization methods.
- Modeling dependence: finding a model describing central variable relationships.
- Regression: developing a function that translates a memory location to real-value variable predictions and finding structural connections among parameters.
- Classification: to train a function classifying data in a predetermined class.
- Detection and mapping and divergence: detection from available data measured or baseline values of the most important modifications.

8.7   Swarm Intelligence and Knowledge Discovery

Optimization of data mining and particulate swarming may not seem to have many comparable features. They can, nonetheless, be utilized together to build a technique that often results in the results, even if other approaches are too costly or hard to execute. It employs optimizations of particle swarm methods to recognize patterns and analyze images. An uncontrolled categorization and picture separation technique is suggested based on a novel PSO clustering process. The PSO techniques are indicated for quantifying color images and spectrum unmixing. Optimization issues require visual data mining via augmented reality data and formal specification environments. The technology developed a hybrid method based on PSOs and conventional optimization algorithms. To comprehend the architecture of both raw and processed information, this method is used for high-dimensional data from microarray genome expression investigations. Experiments with Alzheimer's disease-related data sets demonstrate that the combination of PSO and traditional optimization approaches allows for a high-quality visual display. The behavior of some swarm development characteristics has also been investigated.

Particle swarm optimization (PSO) is utilized as a data mining technique. Empirical performance comparison of three variations of PSO is utilized for classification tasks to assess the utility of PSO for data mining with another optimization technique (Optimization Algorithm). These activities are seen as key instruments in a broad range of decision-making support systems from industry, business, militaries, and science. For laboratory investigation, the data sources utilized are frequently used and regarded as a de facto standard for the dependability rating of a rule classification algorithm. Results in these areas show that PSO algorithms compete with other technology and may be used effectively in increasingly challenging problems.

New sorts of Internet software applications are recommended systems that assist customers in making their way across today's complicated online stores and entertainment web pages. It revealed a novel recommending system that uses a PSO algorithm to learn users' specific preferences and offer tailor-made choices. Experiments are conducted to check the system's performance, and findings are compared to algorithmic genetic results (GA), the Pearson algorithm to propose the plan, and a conventional non-adaptive system.

The PSO domain of ascending classifier is another very significant application. Cascade classifiers in recent years were employed to tackle issues in information processing. The improved method and decreased complication are the principal motives for such a technique. The class-related rejection threshold is an essential topic for cascade classification systems. The research has shown that class thresholds in rejecting mistakes are better than a single world threshold. The use of the PSO to determine points improves the compromise between error and rejection resulting from class rejection thresholds. The solutions to truly valued complex optimization problems have proven highly efficient. They have been used to improve the points of a cascade classification system that identifies handwritten digits to demonstrate the advantages of such an approach. The inputs disregarded in a cascade classifier are managed using more expensive features or classification systems in the first step. A neural network training PSO technique examined how different soft computing approaches may depict the chaotic behavior of financial markets. To check and adopt techniques as like neural tree technique, neural wavelet networks, and the least-squares wavelet neural network. The PSO method optimizes the characteristics of the various learning approaches. According to experimental data, PSO can have an essential function in adjusting the characteristics for maximum efficiency.

One of the leading causes of mortality among women is breast cancer. Different approaches to artificial intelligence have been applied to enhance diagnostic processes and assist the doctor's work. Preliminary research for breast cancer was detected utilizing a mix of flexible neural tree (FNT), neural network (NN), and neural wavelet network (WNN) models. For the FNT model, an empirical approach and PSO based on a tree structure is utilized to identify an excellent FNT. The PSO optimizes free parameters for the NN and WNN. Each technique is assessed and uses the data set for heart disease. The results from the simulation demonstrate that a smaller number of the variables with a decreased input number and without substantial reduction in detection precision are available for the developed FNT model. The total accuracy may be increased via the use of an ensemble technique by voting mechanism.

In the Takagi-Sugeno fuzzy systems hierarchy or multilevel fuzzy system (TS-FS) development, a hierarchical structure is developed using special instructions utilizing probabilistic incremental program evolution (PIPE). PSO accomplishes the fine tweaking of the if-then rules inherent in the system. Both PIPE and PSO optimism are interwoven with the suggested approach. The new path leads to fewer rules and better developing skills. Some forecasting issues are used to assess the proposed hierarchic TS-FS. The recommended hybrid method shows good accuracy and a lower hierarchical design than the previous TS-FS.

A POS method was created as an alternative method for locating periodic orbits in a three-dimensional (3D) model of barred galaxies. This practical approach transforms the problem of finding periodic orbits into the challenge of detecting global minimizers of a function defined on the Poincaré surface section of the Hamiltonian system. Several routine maintenance orbits have been systematically traced by combining the PSO procedure with misdirection technologies.

Cluster analyses have become an essential strategy for analyzing explored data and patterns and artificial intelligence. The clustering tries to discover meaningful groupings and extract them from underlying data. Articulatory techniques, hierarchical methods, density-based clustering, and grid-based classification are the four basic types of clustering algorithms. Document clustering is a crucial process in arranging unmonitored documents, automatic separation of subject matter, and content recovery. The efficient navigation, summarization, and information organization are based on quick and good-quality clustering algorithms. Recent research has demonstrated that partial clustering methods are more appropriate because of their comparatively small computing demand for clustering big datasets. The K-means technique in clustering is the most commonly used algorithm for finding a partition minimizing the mean measurement of an MSE error. Although K-means is a beneficial technique for clustering, it suffers from numerous inconveniences. K-means are not convex in their optimization problem and may have local minima.

Therefore, there is a method to stay at the global minimum while reducing the optimization problem (also at local maxima and saddle point). The performance of the K-means model depends on the cluster centers initially selected. Furthermore, the Euclidean standard is noise or surface-sensitive. Therefore, noise and anomalies should impact the K-means algorithm. Apart from the K-means method, several algorithms were employed for information retrievals, such as genetic algorithm (GA) and self-organizing map (SOM). A hybrid algorithm based on the PSO was proposed for document clustering. In the whole solution space, the PSO clustering algorithm conducts global searches. Four separate document image datasets were filed with PSO, K-means, and a hybrid PSO clustering method for the tests. The findings show that the hybrid PSO algorithm can provide more consolidated results than the K-means.

For data collecting, data fusion, and management applications, swarming agents may utilize geographically dispersed processing nodes. The architectural layer is where active analytic processing of big data takes place, such as collectively processing data from diverse sources from or near the source of information by simple mobile agents. The performance standards are related to the purpose of a supervisory system to identify large-scale terrorist operations against civilians at an early stage. At the same time, many other areas are subject to the same design. The system's pattern recognition and categorization operations are derived from coordinating two population agents' actions inside the same computing environment. Significant spatio-temporal patterns of the observable data stream are drawn by sensing agents. Classification agents classify the patterns identified according to their criteria. The outcome is adaptable and resilient system-level behavior.

An evolved PSO-based learning technique was created for effectively clustering N data points in K clusters. The hybrid PSO and K-means technique, called alternative KPSO-clustering (AKPSO), has a unique alternative metric methodology. The cluster centers of geometrical structural data sets are automatically detected. The AKPSO method considers the particular alternative metric to improve the standard scheduling technique for treating different data sets in architecture. The simulation results indicate the resilience and effectiveness of the new AKPSO approach compared with various well-known clustering methods.

Some studies on co-evolutionary particle swarm optimization (Co-PSO) exist in the literature. The conventional PSO method is used by one community and the Co-PSO by the other community as their surroundings. Preliminary findings have shown that Co-PSO is a viable technique for resolving limited optimization issues. The challenge is that uniform distribution makes it difficult to fine-tune the solution.

8.8   Ant Colony Optimization and Data Mining

Deneubourg was initially introduced to cluster algorithms based on ant colonies by imitating many sorts of emerging phenomena that are natural. The ant species *Pheidole pallidula* and *Lasius niger* were observed gathering bodies of dead colony members to form cemeteries (piles of corpses of dead nest mates). This aggregation phenomenon is based on a fundamental attraction process between deaths transmitted by the ants: tiny groups of objects entice workers to dump more items. This favorable enantioselective feedback leads to the development of bigger and better clusters. The fundamental notion for clustering algorithms is to collect and deposit individual things in other places where different items of this sort exist. It suggested that a cluster's algorithm tracks genuine behavior. In this way, the system incorporates biomedical spatial maximum likelihood, eliminating randomly moving agents that urge the algorithm to investigate uninteresting areas. The approach enables ants to identify item groups flexibly. The use of permutations of distinct reaction threats has been proposed to mimic the behavior of ants linked with various activities (dropping and collecting items). The number of items in its vicinity and their resemblance are two main criteria that should impact every local activity made by an ant-like creature. It utilized an average resemblance, blending distances with their numbers and integrating them into a threshold reaction function like the algorithm. This is an exclusive unattended classification approach inspired by the behavior of a certain species of ant called *Pachycondyla apicalis*. Inspired by the self-assembling behavior observed in real ants, the performance of artificial ants by AntClass, AntTree, and AntClust were compared to those among them.

A clustering approach for ant K-means (AK) was suggested, in which the K-means is altered by the AK algorithm to locate the objects in the probability cluster that the pheromone updates, while the rule of pheromones updates the total within cluster variance (TWCV).

A new clustering strategy was suggested called ant colony optimization, which had a higher performance than the rapid self-organizing K-means approach and the K-means genetic algorithm. It meant showing the changeability of time series data, a segmentation technique based on a particle swarm optimization algorithm. The authors employed the bottom-up approach for time series classification, which yielded satisfactory results. The research results demonstrate that the segmentation of time-series data by the ACO algorithm accurately determines the number of segments and reduces the segmentation costs compared to the time series segmentation by the bottom-up approach.

The machine learning approach was created as a metaheuristic method for particle swarm optimization, termed a colony classifying system, and applied to three instances of instructional design. In line with the guidelines of example instances, the learning algorithm deals with the problem of analytical thinking by creating and maintaining the knowledge base using a streamlined process, the pheromones knowledge matrix, and the fitness function accessible. In terms of the prediction accuracy of data sets and complexity of principles, the performances of an ant colony classifier are contrasted with the well-known C4.5 Decision Tree method.

It advocated the use of adaptable, diversified ants, time-spending transport activities, and a mechanism for classifying new axes, which turns an algorithm's spatial anchoring into an explicit division. Empirical findings show the capacity to automatically aggregate and sort the number of nodes inherent in data gathering and provide high-quality solutions. However, the topographical mapping technique did not work particularly well.

Web mining tries to detect relevant information from the primary data acquired by users interacting with the Web. Web usage mining, adaptive Web sites, corporate and support services, customization, network traffic analysis, and so on, are becoming increasingly crucial for efficient site administration. To detect Web use tendencies (data clusters), a linear genetic programming technique and clustering algorithms are used to assess trends. Empirical data indicate that the clustering of ant colonies is booming compared to an organizational map (for clustering Web usage patterns).

8.9   Conclusion

In this chapter, two of SI's most influential and famous optimization approaches were introduced along with the fundamental theories and techniques of swarm intelligence—Ant Colony Optimization and Particle Swarm Optimization. The objective here was to propose the final observations on the issue in the last section and offer the complete array of public research topics. Studying and researching the subject was both challenging and intriguing. It was entirely unfamiliar to me, on the one hand, and reasonably new and multidisciplinary. It was, on the other hand, very fascinating to start learning how surprisingly intellectual the communal behavior of swarms is in nature and to begin realizing the knowledge gleaned by studying them for various subjects (for example, animal behavior, quantum mechanics, social psychology) can genuinely function in a harmonious relationship.

References

1. A. Leon-Garcia and I. Widjaja, Communication Networks: Fundamental Concepts and Key Architectures, ser. Computer Science and Electrical and Computer Engineering. New York, NY: The McGraw-Hill Companies, Inc., 2000.
2. Making the Nation Safer: The Role of Science and Technology in Countering Terrorism. Washington, D.C.: National Academy Press, 2002, ch. 5: Information Technology, pp. 135–176, a Report to the National Academies from the Committee on Science and Technology for Countering Terrorism.
3. P. Chaudhuri, D. Chowdhury, S. Nandi, and S. Chattopadhyay, Additive Cellular Automata: Theory and Applications. New York, NY: John Wiley & Sons, Inc., June 1997, vol. 1.
4. W. Poundstone, The Recursive Universe: Cosmic Complexity and the Limits of Scientific Knowledge. Chicago, Ill.: Contemporary Books, 1985.
5. I. Prigogine and I. Stengers, Order Out of Chaos: Man's New Dialog with Nature. New York, NY: Bantam Books, Inc., 1984.
6. E. Bonabeau, M. Dorigo, and G. Theraulaz, Swarm Intelligence: From Natural to Artificial Systems, ser. Santa Fe Institute Studies in the Sciences of Complexity. New York, N.Y.: Oxford University Press, 1999.
7. B. Bullnheimer, R. F. Hartl, and C. Strauss, "An improved ant system algorithm for the vehicle routing problem," University of Vienna, Vienna, Austria, Tech. Rep., POM Working Paper No. 10/97, 1997.
8. V. Maniezzo, A. Colorni, and M. Dorigo, "The ant system applied to the quadratic assignment problem," Universite Libre de Bruxelles, Belgium, Tech. Rep., Tech. Rep. IRIDIA/94-28 1994.
9. R. Schoonderwoerd, O. Holland, J. Bruten, and L. Rothkrantz, "Antbased load balancing in telecommunications networks," Adapt. Behav., vol. 5, pp. 169–207, 1996, early work on SI in networks.
10. L. Kaelbling, M. Littmand, and A. Moore, "Reinforcement learning: A survey," Journal of Artificial Intelligence Research, vol. 4, pp. 237–285, 1996.
11. M. Littman and J. Boyan, "A distributed reinforcement learning scheme for network routing," Carnegie Mellon University, School of Computer Science, Carnegie Mellon University, Pittsburgh, PA 15213, Tech. Rep., 1993.

12. G. Di Caro and M. Dorigo, "Antnet: A mobile agent's approach to adaptive routing," Universite Libre de Bruxelles, Belgium, Tech. Rep., Tech. Report IRIDIA/97-12, 1997.

13. H. V. D. Parunak, M. Purcell, and R. O'Connell, "Digital pheromones for autonomous coordination of swarming UAV's" American Institute of Aeronautics and Astronautics, Tech. Rep. AIAA 2002-3446, 2002.

14. D. Subramanian, P. Druschel, and J. Chen, "Ant and reinforcement learning: A case study in routing in dynamic networks," Rice University, Department of Computer Science, Tech. Rep.

15. M. Millonas, "Artificial life iii," ser. Sante Fe Institute Studies in the Sciences of Complexity, C. Langton, Ed., vol. XVII. New York, NY: Addison-Wesley Publishing Co., 1994, pp. 417–445.

16. N. Wiener, Cybernetics: Or Control and Communication in the Animal and the Machine, 2nd ed. Cambridge, MA.: The M.I.T. Press, Inc., 1961.

17. G. Di Caro and M. Dorigo, "Antnet: Distributed stigmergetic control for communications networks," Journal of Artificial Intelligence Research, vol. 9, pp. 317–365, 1998.

18. R. Serra and G. Zanarini, Complex Systems and Cognitive Processes. New York, NY: Springer-Verlag, 1990.

19. J. Rosen, Symmetry in Science: An Introduction to the General Theory. New York, NY: Springer-Verlag, 1995.

20. E. Aarts and J. Korst, Simulated Annealing and Boltzmann Machines: A Stochastic Approach to Combinatorial Optimization and Neural Computing. John Wiley & Sons, 1989.

21. Beni, G., Wang, J. (1993). "Swarm Intelligence in Cellular Robotic Systems". Proceed. NATO Advanced Workshop on Robots and Biological Systems, Tuscany, Italy, June 26–30 (1989). Berlin, Heidelberg: Springer. pp. 703–712. doi:10.1007/978-3-642-58069-7_38. ISBN 978-3-642-63461-1.

22. Solé R, Rodriguez-Amor D, Duran-Nebreda S, Conde-Pueyo N, Carbonell-Ballestero M, Montañez R (October 2016). "Synthetic Collective Intelligence". BioSystems. **148**: 47–61. doi:10.1016/j.biosystems.2016.01.002. PMID 26868302.

23. Reynolds, Craig (1987). Flocks, herds and schools: A distributed behavioral model. SIGGRAPH '87: Proceedings of the 14th Annual Conference on Computer Graphics and Interactive Techniques. Association for Computing Machinery. pp. 25–34. CiteSeerX 10.1.1.103.7187. doi:10.1145/37401.37406. ISBN 978-0-89791-227-3. S2CID 546350.

24. Banks, Alec; Vincent, Jonathan; Anyakoha, Chukwudi (July 2007). "A review of particle swarm optimization. Part I: background and development". Natural Computing. **6** (4): 467–484. CiteSeerX 10.1.1.605.5879. doi:10.1007/s11047-007-9049-5. S2CID 2344624.

25. Vicsek, T.; Czirok, A.; Ben-Jacob, E.; Cohen, I.; Shochet, O. (1995). "Novel type of phase transition in a system of self-driven particles". Physical Review Letters. **75** (6): 1226–1229. arXiv:cond-mat/0611743. Bibcode:1995

PhRvL   75.1226V.   doi:10.1103/PhysRevLett.75.1226.   PMID   10060237. S2CID 15918052.

26. Czirók, A.; Vicsek, T. (2006). "Collective behavior of interacting self-propelled particles". Physica A. **281** (1): 17–29. arXiv:cond-mat/0611742. Bibcode:2000PhyA.281...17C.   doi:10.1016/S0378-4371(00)00013-3. S2CID14211016.

27. Buhl, J.; Sumpter, D.J.T.; Couzin, D.; Hale, J.J.; Despland, E.; Miller, E.R.; Simpson, S.J.; *et al.* (2006). "From disorder to order in marching locusts" (PDF). Science. **312** (5778): 1402–1406. Bibcode:2006Sci...312.1402B. doi:10.1126/science.1125142. PMID 16741126. S2CID 359329.

28. Toner, J.; Tu, Y.; Ramaswamy, S. (2005). "Hydrodynamics and phases of flocks" (PDF). Annals of Physics. **318** (1): 170–244. Bibcode:2005AnPhy. 318..170T. doi:10.1016/j.aop.2005.04.011.

29. Bertin, E.; Droz, M.; Grégoire, G. (2009). "Hydrodynamic equations for self-propelled particles: microscopic derivation and stability analysis". J. Phys. A. **42** (44): 445001. arXiv:0907.4688. Bibcode:2009JPhA...42R5001B. doi:10.1088/1751-8113/42/44/445001. S2CID 17686543.

30. Li, Y.X.; Lukeman, R.; Edelstein-Keshet, L.; *et al.* (2007). "Minimal mechanisms for school formation in self-propelled particles" (PDF). Physica D: Nonlinear Phenomena. **237** (5): 699–720. Bibcode:2008PhyD.237. 699L. doi:10.1016/j.physd.2007.10.009. Archived from the original (PDF) on 2011-10-01.

31. Colorni, A., Dorigo, M., Maniezzo, V.: Distributed Optimization by Ant Colonies. In: Varela, F., Bourgine, P. (eds.) First Eur. Conference Artificial Life, pp. 134–142 (1991).

32. Dorigo, M., Maniezzo, V., Colorni, A.: Ant System: Optimization by a Colony of Cooperating Agents. IEEE Transactions on Systems, Man, and Cybernetics—Part B: Cybernetics 26, 29–41 (1996).

33. Dorigo, J.M., Gambardella, L.M.: Ant Colony System: A Cooperative Learning Approach to the Traveling Salesman Problem. IEEE Transactions on Evolutionary Computation 1, 53–66 (1997).

34. Chu, S.C., Roddick, J.F., Pan, J.S.: Ant Colony System with Communication Strategies. Information Sciences 167, 63–76 (2004).

35. Karaboga, D.: An Idea Based on Honey Bee Swarm for Numerical Optimization. Technical Report-TR06, Erciyes University, Computer Engineering Department (2005).

36. Passino, K.M.: Biomimicry of Bacterial Foraging for Distributed Optimization and Control. IEEE Control Systems Magazine 22, 52–67 (2002).

37. Chu, S.C., Tsai, P.W., Pan, J.S.: Cat Swarm Optimization. In: Yang, Q., Webb, G. (eds.) PRICAI 2006. LNCS (LNAI), vol. 4099, pp. 854–858. Springer, Heidelberg (2006).

38. Chu, S.C., Tsai, P.W.: Computational Intelligence Based on the Behavior of Cats. International Journal of Innovative Computing, Information and Control 3, 163–173 (2007).

39. Bishop, J.M.: Stochastic Searching Networks. In: Proc. 1st IEE Conf. on Artificial Neural Networks, London, pp. 329–331 (1989).

40. Chang, J.F., Chu, S.C., Roddick, J.F., Pan, J.S.: A Parallel Particle Swarm Optimization Algorithm with Communication Strategies. Journal of Information Science and Engineering 21, 809–818 (2005).

41. Tsai, P.W., Luo, R., Pan, S.T., Pan, J.S., Liao, B.Y.: Artificial Bee Colony with Forward-communication Strategy. ICIC Express Letters 4, 1–6 (2010).

42. Y. J. Zheng, "Water wave optimization: A new nature-inspired metaheuristic", Computers & Operations Research, vol. 55, pp. 1-11, 2015.

43. H. Huang, Dynamics of Surface Waves in Coastal Waters: Wave-current-bottom Interactions, ISBN-13: 978-3540888307, ISBN-10: 3540888306, Springer; 2010.

44. N. Booij, R. C. Ris and L. H. Holthuijsen, "A third-generation wave model for coastal regions: 1. Model description and validation", Journal of Geophysical Research: Oceans (1978–2012), vol. 104, no. C4, pp. 7649-7666, 1999.

45. Shi, Yuhui (2011). "Brain Storm Optimization Algorithm". In Tan, Y.; Shi, Y.; Chai, Y.; Wang, G. (eds.). Advances in Swarm Intelligence. Lecture Notes in Computer Science. **6728**. pp. 303–309. doi:10.1007/978-3-642-21515-5_36. ISBN 978-3-642-21514-8.

46. Qiu, Huaxin; Duan, Haibin (2014). "Receding horizon control for multiple UAV formation flight based on modified brain storm optimization". Nonlinear Dynamics. **78** (3): 1973–1988. doi:10.1007/s11071-014-1579-7. S2CID 120591309

47. *Cheng, Shi; Shi, Yuhui (2018). "Thematic Issue on "Brain Storm Optimization Algorithms"". Memetic Computing. **10** (4): 351–352. doi:10.1007/ s12293-018-0276-3*

48. Mirjalili, S.; Lewis, A. The Whale Optimization Algorithm. Adv. Eng. Softw. 2016, 95, 51–67.

49. Alamri, H.S.; Alsariera, Y.A.; Zamli, K.Z. Opposition-Based Whale Optimization Algorithm. J. Adv. Sci. Lett. 2018, 24, 7461–7464.

50. Trivedi, I.N.; Pradeep, J.; Narottam, J.; Arvind, K.; Dilip, L. Novel adaptive whale optimization algorithm for global optimization. Indian J. Sci. Technol. 2016, 9, 319–326.

51. Ling, Y.; Zhou, Y.; Luo, Q. Lévy flight trajectory-based whale optimization algorithm for global optimization, IEEE Access, vol. 5, pp. 6168-6186, 2017, doi: 10.1109/ACCESS.2017.2695498.

52. Tan, Y.; Zheng, Z.Y. Research Advance in Swarm Robotics. Def. Technol. 2013, 9, 18–39.

53. Nedjah, N.; Junior, L.S. Review of methodologies and tasks in swarm robotics towards standardization. Swarm Evol. Comput. 2019, 50, 100565.

54. Senanayake, M.; Senthooran, I.; Barca, J.C.; Chung, H.; Kamruzzaman, J.; Murshed, M. Search and tracking algorithms for swarms of robots: A survey. Robot. Auton. Syst. 2016, 75, 422–434.

55. Couceiro, M.S.; Rocha, R.P.; Ferreira, N.M.F. A novel multi-robot exploration approach based on Particle Swarm Optimization algorithms. In Proceedings of the 2011 IEEE International Symposium on Safety, Security, and Rescue Robotics, Kyoto, Japan, 31 October–5 November 2011; pp. 327–332.

56. Wang, Z.; Qin, L.; Yang, W. A self–organizing cooperative hunting by robotic swarm based on particle swarm optimization localization. Int. J. Bio-Inspired Computer. 2015, 7, 68–73.

57. Kumar, A.S.; Manikutty, G.; Bhavani, R.R.; Couceiro, M.S. Search and rescue operations using robotic Darwinian particle swarm optimization. In Proceedings of the 2017 International Conference on Advances in Computing, Communications and Informatics (ICACCI), Udupi, India, 13–16 September 2017; pp. 1839–1843.

58. Hereford, J.M.; Siebold, M.; Nichols, S. Using the Particle Swarm Optimization Algorithm for Robotic Search Applications. In Proceedings of the 2007 IEEE Swarm Intelligence Symposium, Honolulu, HI, USA, 1–5 April 2007; pp. 53–59.

59. Clerc, M.; Kennedy, J. The particle swarm-explosion, stability, and convergence in a multidimensional complex space. IEEE Trans. Evol. Comput. 2002, 6, 58–73.

60. Kennedy, J. Particle swarm optimization. In Encyclopedia of Machine Learning; Springer: Boston, MA, USA, 2010; pp. 760–766.

61. Shi, Y.; Eberhart, R.C. Parameter selection in particle swarm optimization. In Evolutionary Programming VII; Springer:Berlin/Heidelberg, Germany, 1998; pp. 591–600.

62. Andrews, P. S., Timmis, J., Owens, N. D. L., Aickelin, U., Hart, E., Hone, A., & Tyrrell, A. M. (Eds.) (2009). Proceedings of the 8th International Conference on Artificial Immune Systems (ICARIS 2009). Springer.

63. Arvin, F., Samsudin, K., & Ramli, A. R. (2009). Swarm robots long term autonomy using moveable charger. In Proceedings of the 2009 International Conference on Future Computer and Communication (ICFCC'09), (pp. 127–130). IEEE.

64. Auska, B. J., Grossa, T. S., & Srinivasan, S. (2006). An agent-based model for real-time signaling induced in osteocytic networks by mechanical stimuli. Journal of Biomechanics, 39(14), 2638–46.

65. Babaoglu, O., Canright, G., Deutsch, A., Di Caro, G. A., Ducatelle, F., Gambardella, L. M., Ganguly, N., Jelasity, M., Montemanni, R., Montresor, A., & Urnes, T. (2006). Design patterns from biology for distributed computing. ACM Transactions on Autonomous and Adaptive Systems, 1(1), 26–22.

66. Bayindir, L., & Sạhin, E. (2007). A review of studies in swarm robotics. Turkish Journal of Electrical Engineering and Computer Science, 15(2), 115–147.

67. Beni, G. (2005). From swarm intelligence to swarm robotics. In International Workshop of Swarm Robotics (WS 2004), vol. 3342 of LNCS, (pp. 1–9). Springer.

68. Bentley, P. J., Lee, D., & Jung, S. (Eds.) (2008). Proceedings of the 7th International Conference on Artificial Immune Systems (ICARIS 2008). Springer.

69. Bernardino, H., Barbosa, H., & Fonseca, L. (2010). A faster clonal selection algorithm for expensive optimization problems. In Proceedings of the 9th International Conference on Artificial Immune Systems (ICARIS 2010), vol. 6209 of LNCS, (pp. 130–143). Springer.

70. Bersini, H. (2006). Immune system modeling: The OO way. In Proceedings of the 5th International Conference on Artificial Immune Systems (ICARIS 2006), vol. 4163 of LNCS, (pp. 150–163). Springer.

71. Bersini, H., & Carneiro, J. (Eds.) (2006). Proceedings of the 5th International Conference on Artificial Immune Systems (ICARIS 2006). Springer.

72. Xinchao, Z. (2010). "A perturbed particle swarm algorithm for numerical optimization". Applied Soft Computing. 10 (1): 119–124. doi:10.1016/j.asoc.2009.06.010.

73. Xie, Xiao-Feng; Zhang, Wen-Jun; Yang, Zhi-Lian (2002). A dissipative particle swarm optimization. Congress on Evolutionary Computation (CEC), Honolulu, HI, USA: 1456-1461.

74. Cheung, N. J.; Ding, X.-M.; Shen, H.-B. (2013). "OptiFel: A Convergent Heterogeneous Particle Swarm Optimization Algorithm for Takagi-Sugeno Fuzzy Modeling". IEEE Transactions on Fuzzy Systems. 22 (4): 919–933. doi:10.1109/TFUZZ.2013.2278972. S2CID 27974467.

75. Nobile, M.; Besozzi, D.; Cazzaniga, P.; Mauri, G.; Pescini, D. (2012). "A GPU-Based Multi-Swarm PSO Method for Parameter Estimation in Stochastic Biological Systems Exploiting Discrete-Time Target Series". Evolutionary Computation, Machine Learning and Data Mining in Bioinformatics. Lecture Notes in Computer Science. 7264. pp. 74–85. doi:10.1007/978-3-642-29066-4_7.

76. Yang, X.S. (2008). Nature-Inspired Metaheuristic Algorithms. Luniver Press. ISBN 978-1-905986-10-1.

77. Tu, Z.; Lu, Y. (2004). "A robust stochastic genetic algorithm (StGA) for global numerical optimization". IEEE Transactions on Evolutionary Computation. 8 (5): 456–470. doi:10.1109/TEVC.2004.831258. S2CID 22382958.

78. Tu, Z.; Lu, Y. (2008). Corrections to "A Robust Stochastic Genetic Algorithm (StGA) for Global Numerical Optimization". IEEE Transactions on Evolutionary Computation. 12 (6): 781.   doi:10.1109/TEVC.2008.926734. S2CID 2864886.

79. Kennedy, James (2003). "Bare Bones Particle Swarms". Proceedings of the 2003 IEEE Swarm Intelligence Symposium: 80–87. doi:10.1109/SIS.2003.1202251. ISBN 0-7803-7914-4. S2CID 37185749.

80. X. S. Yang, S. Deb and S. Fong, Accelerated particle swarm optimization and support vector machine for business optimization and applications, NDT 2011, Springer CCIS 136, pp. 53-66 (2011).

81. Parsopoulos, K.; Vrahatis, M. (2002). "Particle swarm optimization method in multi-objective problems". Proceedings of the ACM Symposium on Applied Computing (SAC). pp. 603–607. doi:10.1145/508791.508907.

82. Coello Coello, C.; Salazar Lechuga, M. (2002). "MOPSO: A Proposal for Multiple Objective Particle Swarm Optimization". Congress on Evolutionary Computation (CEC'2002). pp. 1051–1056.

83. Mason, Karl; Duggan, Jim; Howley, Enda (2017). "Multi-objective dynamic economic emission dispatch using particle swarm optimization variants". Neurocomputing. **270**: 188–197. doi:10.1016/j.neucom.2017.03.086,

84. K. S. Kaswan, S. Choudhary and K. Sharma, "Applications of Artificial Bee Colony Optimization technique: Survey," 2015 2nd International Conference on Computing for Sustainable Global Development (INDIACom), 2015, pp. 1660-1664.

Index

Printed and bound by CPI Group (UK) Ltd, Croydon, CR0 4YY

27/10/2024

14580174-0002